\MAJOR NOAH:

AMERICAN-JEWISH PIONEER /

by ISAAC GOLDBERG

Sometime Special Lecturer on Hispano-American Literature,
Harvard University

PHILADELPHIA

THE JEWISH PUBLICATION SOCIETY OF AMERICA

1936

PRINTED IN
THE UNITED STATES OF AMERICA
PRESS OF THE JEWISH PUBLICATION SOCIETY
PHILADELPHIA, PENNA.

BY THE SAME AUTHOR

CONTENTS

CONTENTS

CONTENTS

LIST OF ILLUSTRATIONS

FOREWORD
AND ACKNOWLEDGMENTS

THE Revolution and the era that followed upon it produced a number of Jews as remarkable for their Americanism as for their Judaism. Indeed, and it is easy to understand why, their Americanism appeared as a natural phase or aspect of their Judaism. Underlying each was a passion for deliverance; in the first case this ardor was politico-economic, and in the second, religious. The Jew in Europe had suffered both economic and religious persecution. America offered him the boon of a double liberation.

Of these pioneers, America in general and Jews in particular know too little. Often that little is obscured by legend and hearsay. In preparing this biography of Mordecai Manuel Noah, one of the first United States, as distinguished from Colonial, Jews, I have in every possible instance gone back to the available documents,—his own writings, contemporary reports, official records, letters, magazines, newspapers and even consultation with descendants.

Indeed, it is through one of them, Mrs. Elmer Grandin, of Patchogue, Long Island, the widow of Walter N. Lawrence, grandson of Major Noah, that I was so fortunate as to be presented with a large collection of manuscript letters, most of them written by Noah himself, many of them by his wife, and one by his mother. A number of these letters bear upon

Noah's beginnings as a merchant and a politician, and serve, incidentally, to do away with the current notion that he had slain several opponents in duels. They throw light upon his career, upon his intense affection for his wife and children, upon his views as to the education of the young. Frequently, too, I have given Noah's story in his own words. In this way the reader is introduced to his published writings and speeches and to an important aspect of his dynamic personality.

Noah is the very prototype of the early United States Jew. From the beginning, as a native-born Philadelphian, he identifies himself with the fortunes of the infant republic. He writes himself into its politics, its diplomacy, its journalism, its oratory, its drama, its philanthropy, its Utopian projects, its civic and communal life. A man of fine physique, he is not one to hide his light under a bushel. His interests are many. His ambition runs parallel with his interests, and he is fortunately able to endure the strains of much travel, much controversy, and recurrent peaks of excitement. There is a restlessness in the man,—a nostalgia, as the French have it, for the elsewhere. He roams the cities of his nation . . . He roves across the continents . . . His versatility, which by half is opportunism, is also the symptom of his goading and goaded self.

There was lust for power in Noah, coupled with a fundamental dedication to certain first principles. He had the simple appetites of Sancho Panza; his head was a Don-Quixotic merry-go-round. His passion for power, however, was chiefly an aspect of his devotion to his people, of whom early he appointed himself the paladin. As for his psychology, I am sure that if we knew more about his parents, especially his father, we should understand better the undoubted phases of eccentricity, the restless activity, the grandiose ideas that were not the least part of his charm.

He was born at the close of one war. He came to maturity during another: the War of 1812. He died on the eve of a third: the Civil War. The destiny of a new nation rang in his thoughts, resounded in his actions, over a booming pedal note: the destiny of an ancient tribe. His native country was the chosen people of the Western world; the country of his spirit was what he considered the Chosen People of God. Apparently, but only so, it was a double allegiance that guided him. Yet here, as he saw it, was no conflict; it was his aim to achieve rather a fructifying unity.

Noah was one of the most attractive of the post-Revolutionary pioneers. He claims our interest not only as a Jew; not only as an American who, during our earliest years as an independent republic, identified himself with the major activities of the nation; but also, and not least, as an errant creature like the rest of us.

The indebtedness incurred during the preparation of this biography was as pleasant as it was many-faceted. The more the pity, then, that it must be repaid chiefly in printer's ink.

To the officials and employees of the following libraries I am especially grateful for every courteous assistance in the matter of books, transcriptions, and photostatic reproductions of documents and illustrations:

The Library of Congress, Washington; the Boston Public Library; the New York Public Library; the Harvard College Library; the library of Columbia University; the Drama collections of Harvard and Columbia Universities, respectively; the American Antiquarian Society, Worcester, Mass.; the Jewish Theological Seminary, New York; Dropsie College,

Philadelphia; Buffalo Historical Society; the New York Historical Society; American Jewish Historical Society, New York.

Without the letters presented to me by Mrs. Elmer Grandin my account would have lacked authenticity and documentation. Other individuals who were of very practical assistance are:

The Reverend D. de Sola Pool, Rabbi of the Spanish and Portuguese Synagogue (K. K. Shearith Israel), New York; the Reverend Israel Goldstein, Rabbi of the Congregation B'Nai Jeshurun, New York; Rabbi Abraham A. Neuman, Congregation Mikveh Israel, Philadelphia; Dr. Henry Cohen, Rabbi of the Congregation B'Nai Israel, Galveston, Texas; Leon Hühner, Curator of the American Jewish Historical Society; the late Max J. Kohler; the late George Alexander Kohut; Nathan Isaacs, Professor of Business Law, Harvard University; Professor Harry A. Wolfson, of the Semitics division, Harvard; Dr. H. A. Savitz of Boston; Rabbi Louis M. Epstein of Brookline, Massachusetts.

For records of the Noah genealogy I acknowledge especially the help of Dr. de Sola Pool, who furnished me with a complete transcription of the synagogal entries; no less valuable were the data in the possession of Marian Florence Nathan and Walter Kraus, M.D., of New York.

Robert L. Noah, grandson of my subject, drew upon his family memories. Albert Mordell, the Philadelphia lawyer and author, was generous with bibliographical and documentary investigations in libraries of his city. Lee M. Friedman, the well-known Boston attorney and collector of Judaica, opened his many resources to me. Harry Friedenwald of Baltimore, Jacob Heller of Boston, Dr. Isidor H. Coriat of Boston, Edward D. Coleman, of New York and Dr. Albert Ehrenfried of Boston, were equally obliging with references.

In conclusion, for expert research assistance I find myself, as so often before, thanking my old friend, John McCauley of New York; and, for the Index (this too, has become an old refrain), my wife . . . The imperfections of the task I must claim for myself alone. The data about the Jews in the early history of our country, and about Mordecai Manuel Noah in particular, are not invariably in the best of order. For suggestions, corrections, and correspondence in general upon how to make later editions of the biography more exact, I may be addressed in care of the publishers.

ISAAC GOLDBERG.

Brookline, Massachusetts.

1936.

I

FROM INQUISITION TO REVOLUTION

1. Prologue on the Tagus

SOMETIME in the first third of the eighteenth century, Samuel Nunez Ribeiro had risen in Lisbon to the eminence of Physician to the Court. A native of the Portuguese capital, and descendant of the wandering Jews, he had, outwardly at least, embraced the Christian faith and was living the secret life of the marrano.

A day was sure to come when some hound of the Inquisition would scent out the uncorrupted Judaism at the core of his apostasy, and denounce him to the authorities. It had been noticed that Jewish families never left their homes on Friday nights, the opening of the Hebrew Sabbath. Their attendance at mass was seen to be perfunctory. One Sabbath in 1732, as part of its religious duties the Inquisition burst into the Nunez home. There was no time for the family to conceal their Hebrew prayer books in the hollow seats of chairs worked by springs. The books and the worshipers were seized and cast into prison. Though the release of the Nunezes was brought about by the royal need of the doctor's services, a humiliating stipulation was imposed: To prevent the backsliding of the family into the faith of their fathers, two officers of the Inquisition were to live as spiritual watchmen in their household.

Hereupon Samuel Nunez, having made up his mind to flee this persecution, adopted a plan as daring as it was romantic. With the aid of an English sea-captain, not to mention the silent persuasiveness of a thousand *moidores* in gold, the flight found a haven in London.

Nunez owned a great mansion on the banks of the classical Tagus. He was rich, and his sumptuous entertainments were considered as part of the routine of wealth. What could there be, then, out of the ordinary in his selection of a pleasant summer day for one of his banquets? From the lawn of the Nunez estate could be seen an English brigantine rocking at anchor. What more natural, again, than that the captain of the vessel, one of the physician's guests, seeking to fill in pleasantly the time before the grand repast, should invite the family on board, together with a few friends—not excluding the inquisitorial agents—for an examination of the brigantine and a little lunch? And what more natural than that they should accept?

Perhaps there was something to drink as well as to eat. The company, in any case, made merry below. Above, however, earnest business was afoot. Anchor was being weighed . . . Sails were being unfurled . . . Soon a fair wind was swelling them, sending the bark of freedom fast through the waves of Camões' hallowed stream. Before the unwitting accomplices of the escape were aware of what had happened, they were on the high seas, bound for England . . .

Back on the banks of the Tagus, in the Nunez mansion, on a table surrounded by vacant chairs, lay an uneaten dinner.

Together with the abandoned house, the servants, the equi-page, the furnishings and as much of the plate as the Nunezes had left behind, this cold meal was seized by the outwitted Inquisition. All else had been spirited along by the departing family. The jewels and precious stones had been secreted by the women. Nunez, having converted his negotiable posses-sions into gold, had divided it among the menfolk of his entourage, who concealed it in their leather belts.

The escape was as a leap into the dark, for the Nunezes were strangers to the ways and to the tongue of England.

The Sephardic congregation of London, since the opening of the eighteenth century, had achieved the leadership of the Jewish congregations throughout Europe. It stood for wealth and power. It was natural that Portuguese refugees should turn to it for aid and counsel. German Jews, lower than the Sephardic Jews in the economic, and therefore in the social, scale, were at this time beginning to pour into England and to look to the Sephardic congregation for help. That congregation, before the arrival of Dr. Nunez in London, had appointed a Committee to apply to the British govern-ment for some of the land grants that were being distributed to prospective immigrants into Georgia. Practical results had not been forthcoming; this was, undoubtedly, one of the reasons why Jewish leaders were compelled, as will presently be seen, to take the law into their own hands.[1]

In London, the Nunez party, once settled among their fellow Sephardic Jews, must soon have heard of the project to establish in America the select colony of Georgia. The

[1] See the account of the Jews in Georgia, by Leon Hühner, in *Publications of the American Jewish Historical Society*, vol. x, pp. 65–95. These Publications will be referred to hereafter in the notes as *AJHS*.

Wesley brothers, John and Charles, were speaking of Georgia as of an Eldorado. Its climate and soil were ideal. And select, indeed, it was to be, despite early and unfounded notions that this settlement was populated by a beggar's opera of runagates. It excluded, for example, only Papists among the religions; it frowned, though later relaxing this prohibition, upon rum; it looked with a sour eye upon lawyers. On the commission empowered to solicit contributions in aid of the colonization were three Jews: Alvaro Lopez Suasso, Francis Salvador, Jr., and Anthony Da Costa.

Not that Georgia held out any special welcome to the Jews, or that they entered the colony in the regular process. Messrs. Suasso, Salvador and Da Costa were authorized collectors; they were not administrators. Nevertheless, they must have reasoned in this wise: We have gathered considerable funds for the founding of a specially exacting colony; these moneys have come *from* Jews and *through* Jews, therefore why not some of it *for* Jews? Accordingly, instead of handing over these sums to the Trustees, or depositing them in the Bank of England, they assembled forty of their own faith, on their own initiative, without the requisite authorization of the Common Council, chartered a vessel and shipped this cargo of suffering and hope to Savannah.

The date of sailing, as the date of arrival, is uncertain. The ship was commanded by Beverly Robinson, and struck trouble from the moment that it sustained an injury in the Thames, thus being long delayed by the necessity of repairs. One gale after another it weathered, finally escaping shipwreck off the coast of North Carolina. Delayed in the beginning, now again she was delayed for several weeks in the inlet where she had taken refuge.

2. GEORGIA

These activities, long before the Jewish emigration to Georgia, came to the ears of the Trustees, who demanded, on January 31, 1733, the surrender of the commissions held by the three high-handed, if high-minded, Jews. Suasso, Salvador and Da Costa refused to capitulate. The forty Jews landing in Savannah in July must have found Christian welcome in the heart of Oglethorpe; for when that gentleman reported the arrival of the Jews and was notified, in response, that the Trustees disapproved of the whole affair, he proceeded as if nothing irregular had happened. In vain the Trustees' committee protested to the public that they did not propose "to make a Jew's colony of Georgia"; that the presence of Jews—who, in all likelihood, had not been excluded together with the Papists only because it had never occurred to the Trustees that Jews would seek out their settlement—was calculated to injure trade and human relations; that these Jews deserved no encouragement. Oglethorpe replied that the Hebrews had by no means proved a detriment to the colony. Especially, he singled out the valuable contribution of Dr. Nunis, or Nunez.

The Nunez party, then, was among this Jewish immigration from London to Savannah. The Trustees were willing that Dr. Nunez should be paid for his services, but they were against the distribution of grants of land to Jews. Again Oglethorpe disregarded the instructions of the founders, for, among the grantees of town lots, gardens and farms mentioned in the conveyance executed on December 21, 1733, besides Dr. Samuel Nunez Ribeiro[1] are found Abraham Minis,

---

[1] Ribeiro is a matronymic. Portuguese usage, like Spanish, often adds to the family name of the father that of the mother.

Isaac Nunez Henriquez, Moses le Desma, Benjamin Sheftall and Abraham Nunez Monte Sano.

The record of the Jews in Savannah was excellent. They aided the plans of the Trustees to make profits from wines and silks. They were industrious and largely self-supporting, inclining rather from agriculture to commerce. They opened, of course, as soon as they could, a modest house of prayer in Savannah,—a rented house on Market Square—named it Mikveh Israel (Hope of Israel), and in order to economize, dispensed with the services of a minister by having the members alternate, gratis, in the conducting of the Sephardic ritual.

With the Nunez party had come David Mendez Machado, upon whom the Inquisition had weighed as heavily as upon Dr. Nunez.

Another member of the Nunez party was Nunez's daughter, Zipporah, whom David Mendez Machado married shortly after their arrival in Savannah. Within a year he is found in New York City, as *Hazzan* (Reader) of the first synagogue to be established there: the Shearith Israel (Remnant of Israel),—a synagogue patterned, like all the very early synagogues in this country, after the Sephardic ritual.

A veritable exodus of Jews from Savannah was to occur. This is not to be interpreted, however, as a symptom of oppression. As a matter of record, the Jews left Georgia largely for the same reasons that many Christians were leaving: they were not permitted, for one thing, to own Negro slaves, and were thus placed at a commercial disadvantage in relation to the inhabitants of nearby colonies where the rules were not so strict.

Nunez was prosperous for a while; he had received six

farms. He left Georgia for Charleston, nevertheless, on August 31, 1740. Between this date and 1750 there was a considerable shift of Jewish population from Savannah to South Carolina; but by the extreme date many had already returned.

To David Machado and Zipporah Nunez were born two children,—Rebecca, on November 17, 1746, and Sarah, date of birth unknown. Sarah married a Mr. Moses of Charleston. Rebecca, on November 10, 1762, married Jonas Phillips in Philadelphia, thus founding a line that has flourished to this day with a cultural distinction equaled only by its multiplied fruitfulness.

In the story of the Nunez immigration there are several caveats to be entered. For example, whether the Nunez party arrived with Oglethorpe or later is not clear. The available records suggest the later arrival. Even more important: the coming of David Mendez Machado, a relative of Dr. Nunez, together with the physician and his daughter, Zipporah, whom Machado subsequently married in Savannah, is not authenticated by any records. Hühner, commenting upon Mr. N. Taylor Phillips's account,[1] suggests that Machado and Zipporah Nunez came to Georgia after Dr. Nunez, as several Portuguese Jews seem to have followed the first importation within a few months.[2]

N. Taylor Phillips recalls a curious anecdote from the stories of his father, Isaac Phillips. For years after the coming of the Nunezes and their friends and relations, the women of the family could not repeat their prayers without telling them off on the Catholic rosary. So ingrained had this habit become through usage in Portugal,—a usage in-

[1] N. Taylor Phillips, *AJHS* vol. ii, p. 46.
[2] Hühner, *AJHS.* vol. x, p. 73.

tended to deceive sudden visits from inquisitorial agents. Our own Noah was fond of recounting that his ancestress, Abby de Lyon, who died in Savannah, carried to her grave the marks of the ropes that the inquisitors had fastened around her wrists when, at the time of the persecution in Lisbon, she had been strapped to the wheel and, as the euphemism of that day phrased it, "put to the question."

From any but the strictly genealogical standpoint it is not so important to us whether Dr. Nunez was a great-great-grandfather of Mordecai Manuel Noah, or, what amounts to the same thing, whether the woman that Machado married was the daughter of the Lisbon physician. In the absence of documentary evidence, this is the weak link in the demonstrable genealogical chain of Noah. For Nunez, beyond a doubt, if not one of the biological progenitors of Noah, stands among his salient psychological forbears.

Noah treasured the tradition of the Nunezes,—of their trials, their romantic escape, their coming to the United States. He used it melodramatically in his public speeches. He took from it spiritual sustenance for his own projects, now lucid enough, now quixotic, for the rehabilitation of his people. Proud of his country, proud of his race, he found in the tradition of Dr. Nunez and the Portuguese Inquisition a veritably theatrical background for that self-dramatization which, through life, was to him a necessity of the body and of the spirit.

3. JONAS PHILLIPS

Jonas Phillips was born in Germany, Rhenish Prussia, near Aix-la-Chapelle, in 1736, the son of Aaron Phillips. Brought early to London he was trained, among other things, to the skill of the *Shohet*, or ritual slaughterer. In November, 1756, he landed at Charleston, then Charles Town, South Carolina. Of independent character, he early involved himself in the separatist activities of the American patriots. He was, or very soon became, a Free Mason. Freemasonry, leaning so heavily upon the Hebrew ideology, held out a strong attraction for the Jews, and they were, if not in too great numbers, identified with that organization from the time of its first appearance in this country.

Phillips's activities, once he arrived in America, appear to have veered from the sacred to the profane. In his business he handled almost everything. His evident belief in advertising makes it rather easy to reconstruct his commercial activities. He notifies the readers of the *New York Mercury*, August 1, 1761, that in a short time he intends to leave Albany, where he has been established, and asks for the settling of his accounts by September 1st. Among his stock are European and Indian goods, wines, brandies, teas, raisins, Florence Oyl, biscuits. "N.B. He takes in payment Beaver and Deer Skins, small furs &c. at the New York market price . . ."

He is soon, as we discover in the *New York Mercury* November 23, 1761, established in New York, "Opposite the Fort, next door to Mrs. Moore's."[1]

He is found, in 1769, as a retailer in New York; in 1771 as an auctioneer. In the period immediately following he identifies himself, in the synagogal debates as to policy, with the new patriots. It being pointed out to him by some of the Tory sympathizers among the Jews that flight and abandonment of the synagogue might mean the scattering, once more, of these Remnants of Israel, he replied that it were better for the Congregation to die in the cause of Liberty than to live at the cost of submission to tyranny.

[1] *AJHS* vol. iii, pp. 82–83.

Between 1775 and the time of his entrance into the Revolutionary army Phillips advertised steadily. Characteristic notices in the *Pennsylvania Packet* (September 11, 1775; September 17, 1776; December 18, 1776) and in the *Pennsylvania Evening Post* (October 24, 1776) reveal him as a Vendue Master (i. e. auctioneer) and as dealer in such a miscellany as dry goods, Geneva, Mamsy, Frontiniac and Claret Wines, sweet oil, best French and Carolina Indigo, mace, cinnamon, nutmegs, pepper, best Northern Beaver and Raccoon Skins, "with sundry other goods all exceeding cheap, for ready money only."[1]

Phillips had signed the Non-Importation Agreement in 1770, together with Samuel Judah, Hayman Levy, Jacob Moses, Jacob Myers and Isaac Seixas. As late as 1894 it was brought to light that he had addressed, on September 7, 1787, to the Federal Convention of that year, which framed the Constitution of the United States, a curious document in respect no less of its petition than of its orthography. Dr. Herbert Friedenwald, at the time he made public a transcript of this letter, pointed out that it was sent ten days before the Convention rose, and that three weeks before it was written, "that clause of the Constitution, as finally adopted, providing that 'no religious test shall ever be required as a qualification to any office or public trust under the United States', had been considered and, after scarcely any debate, unanimously adopted. Beyond what Mr. Phillips himself states, nothing, I believe, is known as to the reason why he, a prominent citizen of Philadelphia, should have written such a letter."[2]

[1] *AJHS*. vol. vi, pp. 50–54.
[2] *AJHS*. vol. ii, pp. 107–110.

Phillips's intention, however, was clear. He maintained "That all men have a natural & unalienable Right to worship almighty God according to the dictates of their own Conscience and understanding & that no man ought or of Right can be Compelled to attend any Religious Worship or Creed or support any place of worship or Maintain any minister contrary to or against his own free will and Consent, nor can any man who acknowledges the being of a God be Justly deprived or abridged of any Civil Right as a Citizen on account of his Religious sentiments or peculiar mode of Religious Worship, and that no authority can or ought to be vested in or assumed by any power whatever that shall in any case interfere or in any manner Controul the Right of Conscience in the free Exercise of Religious Worship."

When the Shearith Israel faced, at last, the very choice that Phillips had foreseen, the patriotic party won out, and Philadelphia was selected as the city of refuge. The valuables of the Congregation, together with the Scrolls of the Law, were entrusted to the Reverend Gershom Mendez Seixas, *Hazzan* of the Shearith Israel, with instructions to bring them out of retirement to Philadelphia as soon as it should seem safe to resume services in that city. When Seixas went into temporary withdrawal at Stratford, Connecticut, on August 22, 1776, many of his congregants removed to Philadelphia. Jonas Phillips was among them. His wife's family already lived there, and he took up his residence at 110 North Second Street. The original of his license to trade in Philadelphia is still in existence; it is dated September 24, 1778.

Phillips was not one to confine his rebellion to talk. On October 31, 1778, he enlisted in the battalion of Philadelphia militia under Colonel William Bradford, company of Captain

John Linton, and a few days later was mustered into the service. His record in the fighting forces has not come down.

The scattered remnant of Israel had been worshiping, since their flight to Philadelphia, in a rented house on Cherry Alley, between Third and Fourth Streets. In March, 1782, a committee was appointed, with Jonas Phillips as member, to purchase ground for a synagogue. Land was bought of Robert Parrish and Henry Hill in Cherry Street, west of Third, and the contract for the building was let out to John Donohue and his associate, Edward McKegan, bricklayer. Work was begun on April 1; on June 19 the corner stone was laid, with the Reverend Gershom Mendez Seixas, returned at last from official exile, officiating. By September 13 the simple one-story brick structure, seventy feet by forty, was ready for occupancy by a congregation of two hundred souls.

It was officially dedicated as the Kahal Kadosh Mikveh Israel,—the Holy Congregation of the Hope of Israel. The first president of the new congregation was Jonas Phillips. The Trustees: Michael Gratz, Solomon Marache, Solomon Myers Cohen and Simon Nathan. The Treasurer: Benjamin Seixas, brother of the *Hazzan*. Phillips, accustomed to dedicating epistles to the conscript fathers, addressed a letter to General George Washington, inviting him to be present at the consecration. Washington, with his accustomed generosity, sent a cordial reply.

Two years later, when the Revolution had triumphed, there was a natural trend of some of the New York Jews back to their first city. The Reverend Gershom Mendez Seixas having at last been persuaded to return to New York, and to help in restoring the original Shearith Israel, Phillips too returned, intending to resume his commercial activities. He had written himself too deeply into the communal life of his fellow Philadelphians, however, and by June of 1789 was back, there to remain until his death on January 29, 1803.

A fighter he was, and a fighter he remained, even after death. For, having engaged shortly before his last illness in a quarrel as to the management of congregational affairs, he withdrew from membership and forbade his remains to be buried in its cemetery. Hence it was that he was interred in New York, in the burial ground of his first synagogue, the Shearith Israel, on Oliver Street. His widow, the mother of his twenty-one children, outlived him by more than twenty-eight years, living in Philadelphia until her death, on June 21, 1831. Early marriages, many children, anonymous domesticity: such was the lot of Jewish womankind—of womankind in general—in our mid-eighteenth century and later. The widow of Jonas Phillips left a numerous band of descendants to carry the name like a waving banner into the history of Philadelphia and New York.

II

A PHILADELPHIA BOYHOOD

1. His Grandfather's Son

PHILADELPHIA was rich in historic associations. Here the
Declaration of Independence had been signed; here, the
Constitution of the new republic drawn up. The men who
had guided the fortunes of the emergent nation still walked
these streets in the flesh, for wide-eyed children to gaze upon
in wonderment caught from parental eyes, and for opponents
to bespatter with vilification. History had not yet been
buried in books. It was alive.

In the great overturn the Jews had played a part far
greater than the ratio of their numbers to the entire population. Robert Morris had been plentifully helped with Jewish
money. To Washington and the Cause many a Jew had given
his life. One of the numerous traditions of the Noah family
is that George Washington attended the wedding of Manuel
Mordecai Noah to Zipporah Phillips, daughter of Jonas, and
that he witnessed the *Ketubah*, or marriage contract, with
his signature. It is not impossible. Washington is said to
have been a warm friend of Jonas Phillips. Manuel Noah,
too,—father of our Mordecai Manuel—during the War of
the Revolution, to which he sacrificed almost everything he

possessed, is supposed to have been sent North from the staff of Francis Marion to serve as an aide-de-camp to Washington. The father of his country, moreover, was from the first a friend of the Jews . . . All that we know of Manuel Noah's origin is that he was a native of Mannheim on the Rhine, Germany. At the time of his son's birth he was, like his father-in-law, a merchant. The Colonial Jew had engaged in multifarious activities,—shipping, whaling, planting, furs. To commerce, to the law, or to books, the post-Revolutionary Jew most naturally turned.

Here, at almost the beginning of the son's career, is a family mystery. He was born on July 19, [some accounts give the 14th], 1785, in Philadelphia, the first child of his parents. (There was to be but one other, Judith, born sometime in 1789; she never married, and died on August 24, 1868.) His full name has come down to us as Mordecai Manuel Noah; for a long time there were many who, supposedly on good authority, persisted in using, as his middle name, Menasseh. None of his available letters contains a signature in full; always the initials alone of the given names appear.

When Noah was but a child of less than six and a half his mother died, on November 18, 1792, in Charleston, South Carolina, where she was buried. His father seems to have been stricken with melancholia and, for a long time, to have disappeared. According to another account he was in Europe when his wife died. The circumstances of his discovery, many years later, read like a melodrama,—like a recognition scene, in fact, out of the plays that his son was one day to write.

What was the nature of this melancholia? What, indeed, was the temperamental condition of the elder Noah? Just when did he disappear, and whither? As will be seen, the atmosphere of his return to this country from France, where he is supposed to have been found by his son, is equally misty. The questions, I believe, are important because a certain eccentricity in the son may have derived partly from the psychology of the father.

For the rest, Noah's dominant qualities seem to have been inherited from his mother's side,—from the strain of the remarkable Phillips family. In a very real sense Mordecai Manuel Noah was the son, not of his parents—neither of whom he really knew as a child—but of his maternal grandfather. I do not find, in all his writings, any mention of his father or of his mother. There is much, on the other hand, about his grandfather, and about such of his ancestry as he must have learned about from that genial, talkative old gentleman. Spiritually and intellectually, Noah was the child of Jonas Phillips . . . [1]

---

[1] In *AJHS*, vol. xxvii, pp. 55 and 57, I find record of Mordecai Noah's attendance, between 1793 and 1794, right after the breaking up of the family, at the Boys and Girls' school of the K. K. Shearith Israel, New York City, under the tutelage of Gershom Seixas. He is listed together with a Uriah Noah, and leaves school together with the same Uriah. In the only extant letter of Noah's mother, which is hereby appended (the original is in my possession) there is mention of a Uriah as being "verry sick with a cold." Mrs. Noah speaks of Uriah and of "my dear Sammy" as she might of her own children. She names March as the month in which she expects to give birth. Mordecai, we know, was born in the middle of July, 1795. Judith was born in 1789, month unknown. This letter, then, which is undated, must have been written just before Judith's birth. Who were Sammy and Uriah? May they have been brothers of Mordecai, born between his birth and that of Judith?

The letter, sent by Zipporah Noah to her sister Phila(h), follows:

New york   sunday

I was verry happy to see by My dear philah's Letter that all the dear family injoys health as this Leaves us—you Cannot form an idea how unhappy I am about My dear Aunt sally I Can say she is not a moment out of my thoughts God send the next Letters may bring an account of her recovery which is my hourly

It was grandfather Phillips who, upon the child's bereavement, took him into his populous household and gave him a place at the table. It was Grandpa who took the tot to the opening of Congress, where the spectacle of Washington became the ground tone of life-long reverberations. It was he who pointed out the aged Franklin and his wife strolling through the streets of Philadelphia. From Phillips, and from the inevitable competitions of crowded domestic existence, Noah absorbed those Franklinian virtues that were to guide him for the rest of his life. In Jonas Phillips, too, is the living source, in example and in precept, of that patriotism for Israel and for America which was to be the dual motif of Noah's career.

pray'r poor Uncle Moses I pity him to have his wife and child, sick at once I hope we shall have Letters soon from our dear david heavins send him a safe and quick voyage I suppose we shall hear all about his reception—you I make no doubt have heard the fine piece of work they made before they left here Hannah never bid adieu to her father nor Mrs Henricks Sunday morning before they went Jacob abused them all round & Hermon send him a challenge Hannah Complains much to Mrs Gomez of the bad treatment of Mrs Hendricks She says when she was at dinner she help'd her to the Leg & thigh of a fowl which is a part she never eats had she not reason—enough to be angry— My dear sammy begins to stand much stronger than he did Uriah was verry sick Last week with the Cold, I have had several attacks tho not so violent as the first it continues verry bad in this place I desire you all not to forget my baby-cap—as the time fast approaches— tell my dear mama I long much to see her and think the middle of march not an unpleasant month to travel as I dont expect to Lay in before the later end of the month do my dear philah try & persuade her to come If I can't so conveniently Come to see her as she can come to see me I shou'd have been there before this my Love to my dear papa tell him I have nothing particular to write But what he knows my Love to grandma & pa & all the dear Childrin God Bless you pray your affectionate sister   Z Noah
Mr Noah joins in Love to all the family
My dr philah Mr Romberg will give you two shillings which you will buy for me six'd worth of worsted the Colour of the paterns and six pence worth of Black for mr dicxon Let it be fine

Out of his double bereavement, young Noah, blessed with health, won a stout independence. It was a personal rather than an intellectual self-reliance. If Noah became a fond lover of the past, sometimes reactionary, often sentimental, ever ready to revert to grandfatherly guidance, it was largely because the phantom of Jonas Phillips still walked beside him, holding a sturdy, wide-eyed grandson by the hand . . .

From Jonas Phillips, and from the necessary economies of the household in which he was reared, Noah early acquired, and never lost, a sense of budgeted existence that at its occasional worst might suggest parsimoniousness. In all things susceptible to accounting, whether money spent upon food or time spent in the pursuit of higher living, measure was imposed upon means. There was an insistence, too, upon a hardihood that had been impressed upon him in youth. Noah grew into generosity, into eccentricity, into sentimentality— which may be a generosity of the emotions—, but rarely into softness, particularly where children were concerned.

He never forgot, in the tumult of his paradoxical career, the lessons and the experience of the Phillips household. He remembered the very simplicity of his breakfasts, eaten with seven others and consisting of milk and water, or very weak coffee, placed in a large earthen pan, served to each in his tin cup and complemented with two generous slices of buttered bread. There were delicacies to be had, but only after the school day was over.

At night the children were permitted to join the family party, but evidently to be seen rather than heard. The system of his domestic upbringing he afterward made his own. It was, by principle, a harsh system, regarding it as a sacred parental duty not only to feed and clothe the child but to preserve his mind and morals pure. Prudence, Economy, Industry . . . And these virtues were to be imposed by the dogmas of precept and example. The child was to be ruled by fear, that he might learn to obey and respect. He was to be kept at a distance, and, during those stated periods when he was admitted into the parental presence, was to be improved by rational and affectionate conversation. Above all, any attempts to be witty, "or, what is called smart sayings," were to be crushed ruthlessly, as being the "precursors of insolence, rudeness and ill manners."[1]

By which token the rising generation of the early nineteenth century, fast careening toward Noah's middle age, when, of course, "wholesome doctrines have become unfashionable", had its forerunners of our "wise kids" and our "wisecracks." *Plus ça change* . . .

Noah was all for a hardy childhood . . . for simple, nourishing food . . . for teaching a child the value of money by making him earn it . . . for letting him have little of that money, or none . . . for inducting him early into a trade or profession . . . for *compelling* children to obedience . . . Seven-eighths of the bad characters of the world, he argued, were reduced to extremities by the "culpable neglect and unpardonable indifference of parents."

Harden the young idea. Rather than spare the child, spoil the rod. The orthodox Jewish father still bore, though with a much-enlightened severity, a close resemblance to the stern-faced Roman paterfamilias. Noah was to be of this breed.

---

[1] These quotations, and those that follow upon similar themes, are taken from a collection of articles made by Noah from editorial writings in *The National Advocate*, printed between 1818 and 1820. The collection was originally published as *Essays of Howard on Domestic Economy*, New York, 1820. In 1845 Noah published, under his own name, *Gleanings From A Gathered Harvest*, which is almost identical in contents with the *Essays of Howard*.

All this was a projection of his own childhood, shadowed forth upon a subtly changing age. The theological era of the child nation had drawn, except for the inevitable prolongations of history, to a close. The political era had begun. The Jewish heritage of Noah belonged to ethics and theology. His American heritage belonged to politics. These two categories, life long, he would drive in tandem.

2. PRENTICE DAYS

Just when young Mordecai, in his determination not to be a burden upon the Phillips household, apprenticed himself until his twenty-first year as a gilder and carver, is not known precisely. That he did, however, we know from his own writings.

What time could be rescued from his prentice days, Noah spent in the Old Franklin Library, at the Philadelphia theaters, and with a group of youngsters who yielded themselves gleefully up to amateur theatricals. At the Library, which was a rendezvous for the political figures of the day, Noah, silently watching as he read, got to know men as well as books. It was here that his earnest studiousness attracted the attention of the officials, and of the gentlemen who foregathered to debate the destinies of a nation. It was here that he was discovered by Robert Morris, who rescued him from his indentures. Morris found for his protégé a position as clerk in the office of the only auditor that the United States Treasury of that day could boast.

Noah was launched. Wolf records that, in the regular course of his duties, he prepared the actuary tables on the eight per cent loan, and that Congress, in recognition of this service, voted him a bonus of one hundred dollars. When, in 1800, the national capital was removed from Philadelphia to the muddy wilderness of Washington, Noah resigned his clerkship and accepted a job as reporter of the sessions of the Pennsylvania Legislature at Harrisburg.[1]

The chronology at this stage of the youth's career is somewhat uncertain; the activities, on the other hand, and their importance to his development, are clear enough. He had won for himself notice from national leaders; he had received his first political appointment; he was learning to watch men of state, high and low, at their jobs, and to report upon their doings. There is reason to believe that this had been achieved with the substantial aid of his uncle, Naphtali.

For the grown-ups the Phillips household was a place of simple contentment and a certain well-tempered austerity. It was a small house, but commodious. There was, on the tables, enough to eat, but never too much. Evenings were spent at the cheery fireside, or in pleasant walks. Income left a comfortable assurance against expenditure. The tempo of life was leisurely.

A friend or two would send word that they would spend the afternoon with Mrs. Phillips. They would arrive, say, at two or three in the afternoon, shortly after dinner, in elegant attire, but nevertheless bringing along a ruffle to hem, or a handkerchief to mark, while light conversation played a merry counterpoint to busy fingers. There would be five o'clock tea, by which time the menfolk would be dropping in, released from the duties of the day. Talk was free, but modest. The men were polite without ostentation; the ladies, delicate without affectation.

---

[1] I should like to have better documentation for this period. Noah, after all, was only fifteen years old,—even less. Wolf is so full of misstatements that this information must be received with caution.

Night would bring music on the spinet . . . general conversation . . . anecdotes, but without the fetid breath of
scandal, mark you . . . the chronicle of marriages and births
. . . business talk . . . It was at such visits as these, no
doubt, that many a business venture was inaugurated, and,
certainly, many a match arranged to add to the vital statistics. In the relativity of time, eight o'clock, socially, was as
midnight to us. At this advanced hour the gentlemen, with
proper gallantry, would see the ladies home.

Noah looked back at it all through the haze of nostalgia
. . . "The ladies with water tabby silks so stiff and lasting,
laced ruffles and fardingales, high-heeled shoes and silver
buckles, fine cotton stockings of their own knitting; the
gentlemen with superfine coats which lasted three years, and
other parts of dress to correspond." Not the lesser part of
beauty, then, whether in women or what they wore, was
durability. And if Noah, harking back to these days, could
exclaim, "Now, how changed is everything!" it was because,
upon this stage, already as a boy he had been cast as a
gentleman of the old school.

The younger generation that succeeded his own he never
ceased to measure, not against the changing conditions of
American life, but against the austerities and the depriva-
tions of his childhood. His condemnation of the sapling fops
to be met with in his New York of the first quarter of the
nineteenth century was in great measure moralistic—nor was
it always primly so—and perhaps only in lesser degree a
retrospective envy.

He catches sight, for example, of a pair of sixteen-year old
dandies. They are wearing "blue coats of superfine cloth,
buttoned tight over a pair of (I am ashamed to name them)
corsets, so that not a wrinkle was seen; but they appeared to

be squeezed to a proportion which prevented the free circulation of breath and blood. Wide pantaloons, short boots, gold seals and chains, and a white cravat around their throats tight to suffocation. I regarded them with pity and regret; pity at their useless, forlorn, and neglected situation, and regret at the delusion of their parents and guardians. In short time they gave me a greater cause to lament the folly and extravagance of the times, the unthinking and dangerous partialities of friends. These boys seated themselves at a table, lighted a segar each, loudly rapped with their rattans, and vociferated for the waiter, who at length appearing, they ordered *a glass of brandy and water each*, with *little water in it*!! and a dozen of fried oysters. While they smoked and drank, their conversation was loose and vulgar, and not unmixed with oaths. What a scene for moral community! and what an example for a rising generation! . . .

"Thirty years ago a boy never considered himself at liberty, either to dress in the fashions, to expend money, or participate in amusements, until he was of age. In those times the value of money was known; for boys were permitted to have but a trifle; they were compelled to attend to their studies, to pursue their mechanical business; they were justly considered as bound to parents or masters until they were twenty-one. Now, unfortunately, they are scarcely released from the nursery before they assume the airs and dress of men; plunge into the extravagance of the times, and have bank notes given to them as if they were blank paper of no value; and before they can *earn a shilling by honest industry*, they expend hundreds! . . .

"Let any person visit the third tier of boxes in our theatres, and among that class of beings so awfully numerous in populous cities, they will see a vast number of these fashionable boys, figuring with fine clothes, and money in their pockets, in the lobbies with these persons, and imbibing all the vicious propensities, manners and language, inseparable from such connexions. Deprive them of means to make this show, to obtain entrance into bar rooms and theatres; confine them to their studies, and to their daily labor, watch them with vigilance, and punish them with promptness, and the evil ceases."

Noah's ideal young man—it is a recollection of his own youth, as well as a program—was to be a Franklin model. He would get up early in the morning, with clear head and invigorated mind. He would, if other business did not claim him, devote some time to a foreign language—French, Spanish—"for languages are a species of capital to a man in business." He would eat sparingly—Noah came to believe in but two meals a day, though in the rotundity of his prime he did not look like the sincerest advertisement of the abstemiousness that he enjoined—and drink nothing of an injurious nature. An hour with a favorite author, a walk through the suburbs . . . "At night, let him seek cultivated and respectable society, improve his mind, soften his habits, and give spirit, animation and chastity to his conversation, by associating with discreet and sensible females, whose society, when judiciously selected, is ever calculated to temper those feelings and passions inseparable from nature, and give to real pleasure a salutary impulse."

Of course, he went to bed early, this Franklin model — modeled after Franklin as Poor Richard, not after the Franklin who wrote the Letter of Advice to a Young Man About to Choose a Mistress!—with a pure mind, and a healthy frame, to deliver himself up to the sweet dreams of continence.

Is it strange, then, that Noah's ideal of womankind should have been patterned after the Griseldian virtues of the classical Jewish wife and daughter? Noah's strictures were not always unfounded; nor was his moralism inevitably a mere Hebraic passion of passionlessness.

24

At best his Griseldis grew into an ambidextrous muse of kitchen and culture, alternating between the apron and the blue stocking. She got up early in the morning, and before she left her room—it was a chamber in those days—she set it in order, adjusting "all those little domestic objects which require care, while they encourage industry." Before breakfast she studied, perhaps a chapter in history, or a lesson in French. At the breakfast table she did the honors. Whereupon, after clearing away the meal she resumed her studies: music, languages, drawing, perhaps dancing. Nor did she forget the fascinations of a good handwriting . . . Noah, later in life a good Jeffersonian, was of that noble statesman's opinion as to the importance of calligraphy to a lady. To the very end of his days, in his letters to his daughter Zipporah, we find him urging upon her the cultivation of a fine hand. Whereupon, back to domesticity. For, "like Portia and Lucretia, she is not unmindful of, nor unskilful at, her needle." Noah was never a firm believer in boarding schools for girls, fearing, among other things, the implanting of stiff and unsocial doctrines. A good home training, he maintained, included the advantages of a boarding school, and added to these an excellent preparation for wifehood.

If the problem of the rising generation troubled his thoughts, so did that twin "evil," the "new woman."

"Alas!" he apostrophized, thinking back from the New York of his first editorial days to the Philadelphia of the Phillips household, "what is fashion to bring us to? A young and lively female casing herself in steel, flying from the elements, binding and compressing her delicate frame and blasting her fair skin by the rude embrace of a vile black substance, checking respiration, obstructing the free use of her lungs and muscles, laying the foundations for cramps,

MAJOR NOAH: AMERICAN-JEWISH PIONEER

pain, and consumption, and courting death, disguised in the alluring and illusive shape of Fashion! 'Fie on't! O, fie!' "

The brightest jewel in the female casket, of course, was virtue. Next came an amiable temper. And if, despite the rapid growth of the country, marriages were—even then!—falling off in number, and the churches were to be seen populated more and more by old bachelors and old maids, it was because, no doubt, of the "new woman." For, "men have not the same confidence, nor women the same moderation in their views, as in former times." Women are no longer so economical, industrious and content as in the good old days. Parents have indulged their daughters in notions of extravagance and fashion; these young dragons maintain a distance, a coldness, a stateliness, that scares off the very gentlemen "whom they should judiciously and modestly encourage."

It sounds, like so much ancient history, strictly contemporary. For the past has a sardonic habit of plagiarizing the future.

Noah's experience of apprenticeship, peculiarly enough, was not to leave him with a too lively sympathy for youth thus bound. Youth, indeed, before it was indentured to a master, was indentured to a father.

Many years later, as Counselor of the Supreme Court in New York City, he will be defending the master of an abused apprentice. The counsel for plaintiff Joseph Oakley will justify young Oakley's application for a discharge from his indentures on the ground of ill usage,—being beaten upon the head and otherwise injured. The master will allege, in justification, that the apprentice has been a "worthless, idle, intemperate, bad boy". Plaintiff's counsel will rebut: the truth of these allegations can not serve as excuse for such brutal punishment. Whereupon Mr. Noah will arise to side with the law, order and authority. Such discipline is necessary, he will maintain. He ought to be permitted to know something on this subject, as he himself had been an apprentice and had often been beaten and flogged. It had been a wholesome discipline.[1]

3. THESPIS

What Noah read, during his ardent Philadelphian nights, may be surmised from his literary productions of the time, and from advice that he was later to give to the rising generation.

History and politics he considered obligatory. "Nothing", he asserted, in a speech of his middle years, after enjoining upon his listeners the avoidance of all intemperance, and urging upon them religion, morality and economy, "betrays a loose course of reading than to be familiar with the history of every other part of the world better than that of your native land. Commence, then, at *home*, and in addition to the discoveries in America, familiarize yourself with the history of the United States, its early struggle for freedom, its laws, government, soil, climate, productions and manufactures; the names and populations of states, their mountains and rivers. Once thoroughly informed on these subjects, the mind may pursue its inclination. The history of Rome, of England, France and Spain, and every work containing useful information of foreign countries, or ancient or modern events together with voyages and travels, which blend novelty with instruction, and amusement will always be sought after with avidity. If a taste prevails for the higher department of literature and Belles Lettres, you will find the

[1] New York *Commercial Advertiser*, May 20, 1823.

Spectator and *Rambler*, and the sketches of Lord Kaimes, the essays of Burke, the lectures of Blair, together with the admired writings of Johnson, Robertson, Hume, Gibbon, Ferguson, Gilles, Horne Tooke, Ramsay, Gordon, Marshall, Warren, Jefferson, Madison and Hamilton."[1]

Noah, as a youngster, was symptomatically drawn to the theater. Drama fascinated him. He read it, followed it, studied it. Shakespeare was a second Bible, asking commentary upon commentary. The circumstances of his life had been leading him, from the first, toward a psychology of self-dramatization. When, therefore, the necessity of forging a career presented itself, it was an easy transition from strutting upon the scene to the posturings of the politician and the orator. Patriotism, too, was ingrained in him; he was equally sure, then, once he had tried his hand upon the adaptations of foreign plays current in his day, to embark upon a very definite theatrical Americanism.

Opposite the South Street Theater, the old American Theater of his native Philadelphia, was a tavern whose sign depicted the historic Federal Convention. He recalled it in later years as "an excellent piece of painting of the kind"; it represented a group of famous patriot founders debating matters of public moment. Just such a group, indeed, as he might have seen any day at the Old Franklin Library . . . Under the sign ran the following couplet:

> These thirty-eight great men have signed a
> powerful deed,
> That better times, to us, shall very soon
> succeed.

[1] *An Address delivered before the General Society of Mechanics and Tradesmen of the City of New York*, at the opening of the Mechanic Institution, on November 25, 1821.

The shield has a peculiar attraction for the boy; he had gazed at it so often that the scene was etched upon his memory, especially the commanding head and bespectacled eyes of Dr. Franklin, then but a few years dead. It was this couplet that was responsible for young Noah's first lines, written as prologue to a play. This pair of verses, and a society of amateur actors to which he belonged, and which produced its pieces at the theater on South Street . . . The lines of what he himself called "sorry doggerels" have not come down to us. Noah, however, did recall, for William Dunlap,[1] something about the Thespian Club that was responsible for his contributions to the American stage.

"In our Thespian corps, the honour of cutting the plays, substituting new passages, casting parts, and writing couplets at the exits, were divided between myself and a fellow of infinite wit and humour, by the name of Helmbold; who subsequently became the editor of a scandalous little paper, called *The Tickler*. He was a rare rascal, perpetrated all kind of calumnies, was constantly mulcted in fines, sometimes imprisoned, was full of faults, which were forgotten in his conversational qualities and dry sallies of genuine wit, particularly his Dutch stories. After years of singular vicissitudes, Helmbold joined the army as a common soldier, fought bravely during the late war, obtained a commission, and died. Our little company soon dwindled away; the expenses were too heavy for our pockets; our writings and performances were sufficiently wretched, but as the audience was admitted without cost, they were too polite to express any disapprobation. We recorded all our doings in a little weekly paper, published, I believe, by Jemmy Riddle, at the corner of Chestnut and Third Street, opposite the tavern kept by that sturdy old democrat, Israel Israel.

[1] Noah's letter to Dunlap was dated New York, July 11, 1832, and was incorporated by the very versatile William in his *History of The American Theatre*, vol. II, pp. 316–324.

"From a boy, I was a regular attendant of the Chestnut-Street Theater, during the management of Wignell and Reinagle, and made great efforts to compass the purchase of a season ticket, which I obtained generally of the treasurer, George Davis, for eighteen dollars. Our habits through life are frequently governed and directed by our early steps. I seldom missed a night; and always retired to bed, after witnessing a good play, gratified and improved: and thus, probably, escaped the haunts of taverns, and the pursuits of depraved pleasures, which too frequently allure and destroy our young men; hence I was always the firm friend of the drama, and had an undoubted right to oppose my example through life to the horror and hostility expressed by sectarians to plays and play-houses generally. Independent of several of your plays (i. e. plays by Dunlap, to whom Noah is writing) which had obtained possession of the stage, and were duly incorporated in the legitimate drama, the first call to support the productions of a fellow townsman, was, I think, Barker's opera of *The Indian Princess*. Charles Ingersoll had previously written a tragedy, a very able production for a very young man, which was supported by all the 'good society,' but Barker, who was 'one of us', an amiable and intelligent young fellow, who owed nothing to hereditary rank, though his father was a Whig, and a soldier of the Revolution, was in reality a fine spirited poet, a patriotic ode writer, and finally a gallant soldier of the late war. The managers gave Barker an excellent chance with all his plays, and he had merit and popularity to give them in return full houses."

It was a miscellaneous repertory that Noah followed during the period[1] when he was trying his hand at dramatic

---

[1] For this period I have consulted chiefly the clippings, pasted into bound volumes, in the possession of the library of the Philadelphia Company, comprising Charles Durang's *The Philadelphia Stage. From the Year 1749 to the Year 1855*. This account was compiled partly from the papers of John Durang, father of the author, and was annotated by the editors of the Philadelphia *Sunday Despatch*, where it ran serially.

composition and, as we shall presently see, at nothing less ambitious than the criticism of Shakespeare.

More to Noah's taste than such offerings as *Douglas*, *Alexander The Great*, *The School of Reform*, *The Honey Moon* and other light fare must have been Fennel in *Hamlet*, *Macbeth*, *Othello* and *Richard III*; or Cooper, toward the end of that season, in those same plays, as well as in *Coriolanus*.

There were jolly Dibdin operettas, too—*Thirty Thousand*, *The Blind Bargain*—and these must have had their importance in the young man's education. For in the years of his prominence in Gotham Noah fancied himself as a critic of opera.

In 1806 Noah, at his old stamping ground, the South Street Theater, may have had an opportunity of seeing Mr. and Mrs. Poe in repertory. "Mr. Poe", reports Durang, "came from Virginia circuit. Mrs. Poe is known to most of our readers as Miss Arnold, who was a member of this company for several years. She was good in light parts, such as Little Pickle, and in smart chambermaids."

From an American point of view, the outstanding performance this season at the Chestnut Street Theater was Barker's *Tears and Smiles*. There had been, of course, the regular array of English importations—farces, musical pieces, melodramas and an occasional classic. *Tears and Smiles*, however, though it played but two nights, served further to dramatize the emergence of native playwriting. Noah must have been among those who felt the indignation of the historian at those "certain *native borns*, with foreign feelings, brimful of prejudice against the literary bantlings of their own country," who tried to laugh the comedy down.

4. FIRST FRUITS

At the time that Noah wrote his reminiscences for Dunlap, James Nelson Barker, who had been a captain in the "late war"—that of 1812—had also distinguished himself as Mayor of Philadelphia (1819), thus repeating the political success of his father, General John Barker. As early as 1816 the versatile gentleman had begun to be called "the American dramatist". The Barker piece in question, however, was not, as Noah writes, *The Indian Princess*—the first of our plays based upon native Indian themes—but *Tears and Smiles*, first acted at the Chestnut Street Theater, Philadelphia, on March 4, 1807. *The Indian Princess* was not given until April 6, 1808; it is supposed, incidentally, to be the first drama by an American dramatist to have been played in England, where, under the title *Pocahontas*, it was produced at Drury Lane in 1820.

Tears and Smiles, a comedy owing a number of suggestions to Tyler's *The Contrast*, and revealing the contemporary interest in those Mediterranean pirates that were to play as large a rôle in Noah's life as in his plays, may well have been the direct incitement to the composition of Noah's first play. Its prologue, too, echoing the independent Americanism of the prologue to Tyler's comedy, may equally well have left a deep impression upon the mind of Barker's young associate in theatricals.

Our superior native, in his preference for things and thoughts foreign—foreign, in this connection, would be virtually equivalent to English—looked down upon nativism in life and art as evidences of an uncouthness to be sneered at. In Noah's youth such Americanisms were being cried down as "Columbianisms." Barker, circumspectly, invoked his audiences:

Good, gentle trav'lers, do not then, I pray,
Like some ungracious tourists, curse the way,
From Dan to Beersheba, and back to Dan,
As vile, simply because American.
But, if some humble beauties catch your sight,
Behold them in their proper, native light;
Not peering through discolor'd foreign prisms,
Find them but hideous, rank Columbianisms . . .

Possibly inspired by the excitement surrounding the production of *Tears and Smiles,* and certainly stimulated by
such local events as the publication of the first volume of
the *Dramatic Works of William Dunlap,* in September, 1806,
and the growing success of Barker, Noah set about composing
his first play. He did not at once plunge into the American
scene; though certainly not a contemner of "hideous, rank
Columbianisms", he did peer, for plot and form, through
certain "discolor'd foreign prisms."

The Fortress of Sorrento, completed in the immediate period
of *Tears and Smiles,* acknowledged, as the source of its
"leading features", a "french (sic) opera", *Leonora.* The
play was never performed; the author, among other things,
as he averred, lacked sufficient influence to have it acted.
Nor had he sufficient money to have it printed. Happening,
however, to be on a journey to New York, with the precious
manuscript in his pocket, he paid a visit one day to Longworth's Dramatic Repository. To have kept silent about
his new drama would have been superhuman. Noah mentioned his firstling; Longworth evidently thought it worth
printing, if not paying for; and finally a bargain was struck:
Noah would surrender the manuscript to the publisher in
return for a copy of every play he had already published.
It was probably a good exchange on the part of the young

man, for he went home to Philadelphia with a neat little library of dramas in his possession, among them such contemporary Longworth publications as Dunlap's *Abaellino, The Great Bandit*, translated from the German and adapted to the New York Theater; his *Bibbemont, or The Feudal Baron*, tragedy in five acts, as performed at the same playhouse; L. Beach's *Jonathan Postfree, or The Honest Yankee*, a musical farce in three acts; Charles Breck's *The Trust*, comedy in five acts, and the same author's five-act comedy, *The Fox Chase.*[1]

Shortly, Noah had the thrill of beholding his first coveted title-page:

The
Fortress of Sorrento:
A Petit
Historical Drama
in Two Acts

———

"Hos natura modos primum dedit"
Virgil

———

New York:
Published by D. Longworth,
At the Dramatic Repository
Shakespeare-Gallery

———

1808

The Fortress of Sorrento, in all conscience, was a poor thing and not even Noah's own. Its plot is practically identical with that of the only libretto to which Beethoven set

———

[1] These are the titles entered by David Longworth in the Clerk's Office of the United States District Court, District of New York, between November 4, 1802 and January 25, 1808.

music for an opera: *Fidelio*. If, however, it is not American in theme, there is nevertheless a passion of libertarianism that runs through its brief course. This, for Noah, is symptomatic, and will remain so. When he comes to treat of American history, he will remember this tale of the faithful wife who donned masculine disguise to outwit her husband's enemies and rescue him from a foully unjust imprisonment.[1]

Noah's defense of the theater, in his letter to Dunlap, is another evidence of the independence that he had acquired as a youth. It does not seem, at this distance, to harmonize with the rather sober morality to which he had been subjected in his grandfather's home, and so much of which he absorbed. Life is not logic, however, and even the most simple of us finds it easy to discover reasons for liking what he likes.

Noah's presentation, then, of the stage as a moral influence is at wide variance from the attitude at first current in the infant republic,—an attitude by no means abandoned more than a century later. The clergy fought the theater from the beginning. It was the house of Satan,—a brothel in gauzy disguise,—a nest of corruption,—the gateway to Hell.

And all these things, among others, it really was. In our late eighteenth century the feuds that flamed up between the rival actors were reflected in the riots that erupted in the audiences. If theatergoers came to their seats grossly intoxicated, it was but the way that the actors themselves frequently came to the "boards". There were reserved boxes for prostitutes, who have always had, for the theater, an affinity that the theater has reciprocated.

[1] That young Noah took his libertarianism seriously is attested by his political affiliations of the time. I find, in the *Philadelphia Aurora* of Sept. 10, 1808, his name listed among some eighty "Democratic young men," members of a "Committee of Vigilance for the City."

5. SHAKESPEARE

Noah, having relished his first taste of printer's ink—it was ever thereafter to flow warm as wine against the buds of his tongue—promptly returned for another.

His next book—one of the rarest of Noah items—was no meager playlet that one could stuff into one's pocket and forget. It was an octavo volume, with an eloquent title page and immortal associations:

Shakspeare Illustrated;
or, The
Novels and Histories
On Which The
Plays of Shakspeare
Are Founded.

———

Collected and Translated from the Originals
By Mrs. Lenox,
Author of The Female Quixote, &c.

———

With Critical Remarks
And
Biographical Sketches of the Writers
By M. M. Noah

———

In Two Volumes
Volume I

———

Published By
Bradford & Inkeep, Philadelphia: Inskeep and Bradford,
New York; William M'Ilhenney, Jun., Boston; Coale &
Thomas, Baltimore; And E. Morford, Charleston.
Printed by T. & C. Palmer, Philadelphia
1809

The book, as much of it as Noah was responsible for, was dedicated to the Rev. James Abercrombie, D.D., "whose pursuits as cultivator of science, are eminently calculated to call forth that justness of taste and elevation of mind, which must ever tend to the embellishment of society."[1]

Preparing his readers for such strictures as he would venture to voice against the immortal Bard, Noah, author of the unproduced *Fortress of Sorrento*, proceeded to chide Will for the wildness of certain native wood notes.

"Every thing relative to this great poet," he wrote in his brief Introduction, "is calculated to excite curiosity, and will be sought after and read with avidity. It is known, that, whilst his merits have never been overrated, his faults have been excessively indulged. To censure him for these faults is both necessary and proper. It prevents taste from being vitiated by extravagant praise or blind admiration; for, where

[1] I have found this early work of Noah's listed only in the Boston and the New York Public Libraries. I discovered it in the Barton-Ticknor Collection of the Boston Public Library. Volume II never appeared. The rare copy in the Barton-Ticknor Collection has a pasted-in manuscript letter addressed by Noah to Thos. P. Barton, dated New York, December 28, 1842. "Sir," it reads, in part, "It would afford me great pleasure to send you a copy of the work referred to in your favour of the 26th the only copy I had was stolen within a few months past It was entitled" (hereon follows the full title) . . . "I only published one volume not being able to collect the materials for the other It was dedicated to the Rev Dr. Abercrombie and a copy will be found in his collection or in the old bookstores I have long cherished a wish to complete the work but have been prevented by the pressure of other occupations."

undistinguishing commendations are profusely applied, it will always retard the improvement of dramatic composition. Every reader of the plays of Shakspeare should consider himself capable of commenting on them; for every reader, without possessing a ray of invention, must feel the effect, and discern the excellencies of his writings; but to check the exuberance of fancy and the progress of indiscriminate praise, it is necessary to direct the judgment, and cause them, whilst feeling these excellencies, to discern their nature and origin . . . "

The plays considered in Noah's volume are *Romeo and Juliet*, "illustrated" by the ninth novel of Bandello's famous collection; *Othello*, "illustrated" by the source-tale of Giraldi-Cinthio; *The Winter's Tale*, prefaced by Green's story of Dorastus and Fawnia; *The Comedy of Errors*, deriving from Plautus's *Menaechmi*; *Cymbeline*, "illustrated" by the ninth novel of the Ninth Day of Boccaccio's *Decamerone*, and *Macbeth*, for which a like service is performed by the Hollingshed *Chronicles*. Noah's biographical notes upon the writers assembled by Mrs. Lenox are of the scantiest and most perfunctory sort.

Patently, the youth's very patient commentary upon the dramas was of far greater importance to his own intellectual development than to the canon of Shakespearian criticism. But that it was patient and conscientious is attested by the particularity of his remarks. It was, under the circumstances, something of a feat, and suggests that, had matters taken a different turn at this point in Noah's life, or had he been able to achieve the financial independence for which, life long, he was to yearn unsuccessfully, the drama and belles-lettres might have become for him rather an aim in themselves than the embellishments of a career that was predominantly political.

It is to the young man's credit that he was not awed by Shakespeare's reputation into uncritical acceptance of that reputation. Whether his strictures upon the dramatist turn out to be well-taken or ill-taken, there is, in them, a certain healthy independence of spirit that engages our sympathy, and that is of an importance quite distinct from the defensibility of his findings.

We find him thus regretting that Shakespeare did not know the original of the Bandello tale, having had to rely upon a faulty translation. There was little invention in the great Englishman; the only original incident in *Romeo and Juliet* is the death of Paris.

As for *Othello*: Shakespeare, by making Desdemona the only daughter of a senator, makes thereby highly improbable her devotion to a man of Othello's color. In Cinthio she is but the daughter of a plain citizen. The incident, absurd in the tale, is augmented in the drama. And the famous handkerchief: Cinthio makes the lieutenant privately steal the token from Desdemona; nobody else knows of it. The dramatist, on the other hand, very improperly alters the case . . . "The Moor is represented by Cinthio as a man of extraordinary valour, and Shakspeare calls him the valiant Othello. After the guilt of his wife is supposed to have been made clear to him, he determines to destroy her. This task he assumes to himself, whilst he orders Iago to kill Cassio. It may well be doubted whether a brave man would have resorted to such unjustifiable measures, even when convinced of the infidelity of his wife."

Any writer other than Shakespeare, asserts young Noah, would have found some other means for his heroine's deliverance, but, as a review of his celebrated tragedies discloses, he was hardly one for distributing good and evil with a sense of justice. Too often he blends the destruction of the most amiable with that of the most depraved. *Othello*, to be sure, is replete with high poetry and peculiar tenderness, and even certain noble sentiments, brilliantly expressed, but it is "crowded with improbable irregularities, and founded upon inconsistent and offensive principles."

The chief criticism of *The Winter's Tale* is that the plot, in contrast with the tale that suggested it, is forced in design. Shakespeare, beginning with an extravagant case of jealousy in Green's story, immoderately augments it. In *The Comedy of Errors* there is heaped-on abuse of credulity. For, in the matter of ambiguous appearances, Shakespeare out-Plautuses Plautus, adding, to the Latin dramatist's miraculous brothers, a pair of servants miraculously similar to those brothers.

As for *Cymbeline*, Noah disagrees with Pope that Boccaccio was the only source, and accepts Steevens's assertion that Shakespeare knew also Kit of Kingston's *Westward for Smelts*. The circumstances were taken by the dramatist from Boccaccio; the scene and the manners he borrowed from Kingston. Nor did he improve upon a single incident that he lifted. Taking his material much as he has found it, he arranged, adapted, transformed it, but "betrayed little or no desire to expunge the indelicate and offensive principles on which the novel is founded."

Of *Macbeth*, Noah had little of consequence to say.

It will be seen, from these suggestive extracts, that Noah's approach to Shakespeare was, in a measure (and observing proper distances!), almost Voltairean. The poet, he held, lacked order, proportion; he spilled over. He did not conform to the Hebraic feeling about crime, punishment, retribution. Now Shakespeare *was* something of the savage with genius. For the Englishman's ample embrace of our common living,

—for his high seat above good and evil and the delimitations of moral codes,—for his elevation of lower ethics into that higher ethics of which one aspect is esthetics,—our youngster had little appreciation. This, too, was a symptom, for it pointed to the attitudes that Noah was to carry into his own life.

For us, Noah's criticism of Shakespeare is important because it is Noah's youthful, dogmatic, inexperienced criticism of existence. His own plays, despite this early allegiance to the master dramatist, were to lack many of the Shakespearean qualities even in low degree, but they were to supply that morality which the divine Will did not possess.

III

PORT OF CHARLESTON

1. POLITICIAN "ON THE MAKE"

POLITICAL life, for the Young Democrat that Noah had become, was wedging toward another international crisis. Every peace made between diplomats contains the germ of the next war. It was to be Noah's belief that the War of 1812 was really an extension of the Revolution . . . Three presidents had now occupied office, and their heads had lain as uneasily as those that wore a crown. Washington, from 1789 to 1797, had a cabinet that contained the personal patterns of the forthcoming party alignments: Secretary of State Jefferson, Democrat, strict constructionist, opponent of the Federal Bank, agriculturalist; Hamilton, aristocratic, conservative, patron of "implied powers", defender of the Federal Bank, spokesman of the industrial powers. Here, *in propria persona*, are the Republican-Democratic and the Federal parties of the early tomorrow.

The war between England and France . . . the insolence of Genet . . . the black journalism that vilified Washington as the abettor of monarchy . . . the stupid policy of England, alienating the gradually rising sympathy of this country by

impressment and marauding upon the high seas . . . Further
stupidity of our own rulers, under the Federalist John Adams
(1797–1801), with Jefferson, as Vice-President, a notch nearer
to the Presidency . . . The Federalists favoring England;
the Republicans (to whom the name Democrats was being
applied as a term of scorn, much as liberals in the early
1900's were called Socialists, in 1915 Bolsheviks, and today
Communists) adhering to France . . . The Alien and Sedi-
tion laws, stifling the utterance of independent opinion . . .
The removal, in 1800, of our capital from Philadelphia to
Washington, then a distant mud-hole of half a thousand in
population . . .

The triumph of Republicanism in the election of Jefferson
(1801–1809) to the Presidency . . . The growth of the States:
to Vermont (1791), Kentucky (1792) and Tennessee (1796)
the addition of Ohio (1803) . . . The motto of Madison, now
Secretary of State: "Peace is our passion" . . . The far-
sighted purchase, in April, 1803, of Louisiana, for $15,000,000
. . . The illusion, just before this, that we had, with our little
navy, frightened the Barbary pirates out of their Mediterranean buccaneering . . . The threat of the New England
Federalists against the Union, in their fear that oncoming
Democracy would destroy government of, by and for the
respectable . . . The defeat of the plot by Hamilton's exposure of Burr, followed by Burr's challenge of Hamilton to a
duel, and the assassination—quite ethically, of course, in the
code duello—of Hamilton upon the field, so-called, of honor
. . . The wisdom of "Fulton's Folly", in 1807 . . . Napoleon
in Europe . . . England and France contending, with the
United States as the helpless scapegoat . . . The disgrace of
the Leopard and the Chesapeake . . . A world at war, mock-
ing at Madison's motto . . . England, according to Jefferson,

a den of pirates, and France a den of thieves . . . The Embargo Act, followed by repeal and the Non-Intercourse Act . . . The election of Madison and George Clinton in 1808 . . .

That Noah was following this political kaleidoscope with the passion of participation was soon to become evident. He was twenty-five; not old, certainly, but no longer young, especially in a day when maturity seems to have come earlier than, for all our sophistication, it comes today. Already he had ventured into most of the pursuits that would engage him for the rest of his life: government employ, theater, letters, politics, journalism. The obvious question now, for a young man who had no financial independence against which to cushion his ambition, was: which of these should he make his vocation?

There is evidence, from letters recently discovered, that his uncle, Naphtali Phillips, twelve years his senior, had become his mentor and benefactor. Philadelphia, since it had ceased to be the seat of the government, seemed to hold out less attraction for a youth with political and commercial ambitions. Charleston, ancestrally and paternally, loomed as a fair promise. It was one of the few Jewish centers on the littoral. A young fellow might, for example, put up there with his relations, study law in a successful office, try his hand in the local newspapers, and, especially, try out his voice in the political meetings.

Passions again were running high. Peace, however, was not Noah's passion any more than it was then Madison's. And there is no doubt that he needed money badly. Well before the end of Madison's first term he had acquired friends in high places and had begun to cast his eyes upon possibly lucrative foreign posts.

By summer of 1811 wires have begun to be pulled by Joel Barlow and are audibly jangling in the office of the President of the United States. A document—one of an important batch now first brought to light—gives a contemporaneous account of Noah's progress; it is reprinted as nearly in Noah's hurried epistolary style as typography permits:

Mr N Phillips
  Merchant
    New York

Baltimore Monday 10 June 1811

Dr Uncle

Your two letters are received with the dft on Waite for which I cannot be too thankful be assured that in every situation in life I shal always remember with gratitude the friendship & affection you have always manifested towards me I promised in my last to give you particulars respecting my application__ On calling on Mr. Monroe with Mr Barlowes Note & explaining my views, he desired me to address a note to him that my Documts should be laid before the Prest and specifying which Post I should prefer I accordingly wrote the note & mentioned either of the Barbary Powers—Nantz, Riga or Bayonne I sent it in to the Secy & took my leave I then went home & wrote a long note to Joel Barlow setting forth the peculiarity of my claims & requesting him to make such statement to the Prest as would ensure success I contemplated calling with my Docmts on Mr Madison myself which on reflection I declined, as all business of such nature must be transacted through the Secy of State both as a matter of form and civility__ So you will observe that throughout the whole affair I have not seen the Prest calling however a few days afterwards & sitting alone in Mr Grahams room the Prest walked leisurely in & seeing me & thinking I was engaged made a bow & was retiring I got up and told him I was not engaged & that Mr Graham whom he wanted was in the next room I retired— Next day Mr Graham told me that Mr Madison had asked him if I was not Mr Noah & told him that Mr Barlow had a long conversation with him respecting me & that he was very much disposed to make the apptmt as my Documents were very strong calling a few days after on the Secretary he told me that the Prest was disposed to appt me to the consulate at Riga that it was under consideration, asked me a number of questions respecting its situation &c & desired me to call on Saturday which I did but the Secy was out Mr Graham however told me he would see the Secretary & I should call on him Monday— I went early & saw Mr Graham who told me the Prest had concluded that I should have the consulate I told the Secy to have my letters &c made out, after considerable conversation Mr Graham told me I might go home & that my Commisn instructions &c should be forwd to me at Baltimore in the course of a week to the care of Levy Solomons— As they have not yet arrived I write this day to Mr Graham I request him to forward them to Philada

The Prest said that he would prefer appg me to the Barbary powers & had I waited until next Session I should have got it but situated as I was an appt was necessary to be immediately made & the remote situation of Russia affords a fine field for the exercise of some abilities & I shall make it of such importance as to justify a speedy promotion— Riga is nearly as large as Baltimore & has annually 600 ships of all nations loading and unloading Mr Smith tells me it is a better Port for general business than St. Petersburgh & the only port where we can rely on a good trade—besides which the City of Rival & other maratime towns are in the limits of my jurisdiction in which places I shall appt Vice Consuls——— Uncle Benny says he made some arrangements with my friends in Philada & I can return I shall leave this tomorrow——— My object is to go from NYork or Philada a ship for Riga or St Petersburgh——— Enquire among the merchts who ship to Russia if they will send out with me—My appt will enable me to give great facility to the unloading of a cargo & procuring a fresh one & every advantage which a residence will produce such as purchasing articles for exportation at low rates in Winter & shipping them in Summer I can possess besides in the article of Looking Glass Plates I can make advantageous purchases from all that I can gather every appearance is manifest that I shall do considerable business a Peace between in England & Russia will secure our property in the Baltic & immense quantities of Goods will be shipped from Russia to the US . . . Mr Graham tells me I must enter into a bond for $2000 as a matter for form. Two are forwarded in my instructions one filled which I must get signed by some creditable person the other I retain as a Copy From Philada I shall again write to you

Aaron is here & returns tomorrow wh me came to see the place My love to Aunt Rachel & the children Remember me in the most friendly manner to Mr (illegible) & return him my sincere thanks for the letter he favoured me with Should be happy to reciprocate in any manner advantageous to him

Very affectionately yours

M M Noah

Just when Noah arrived in Charleston is not established. Hardly was this letter written, however, when he received his appointment as Consul for the United States at Riga . . . and eventually, for all his high hopes, declined it. Why? Conditions in Russia had assumed a new, more somber, aspect. Napoleon, by the rupture of Alexander the First with France, had been turned into an implacable foe of the Slav empire. Noah beheld now, in Russia, more chaos than commerce. So, despite the precarious financial condition in which he found himself, he decided to wait until the Barbary appointment should, if ever, materialize.

Once in Charleston, our Young Democrat plunged into

the political turmoil of the day. The city, during the year 1812, was a hotbed of meetings. Sentiment was generally Republican, which is to say that it favored war with Great Britain. We had whipped her once; we should have to whip her again, to show her that our sailors were not to be trifled with nor our hard-won national sovereignty insulted. This is not to say that there was no sentiment against the declaration of war. There was, and in the heat of its expression it served to prove that men bent upon the preservation of peace between nations could not keep it between themselves.

Noah, as one of the headstrong "war hawks", did more than his share of eagle-shrieking. Melodramatically he made his entrance into Charleston,—as melodramatically as he was to make his brief stay and his departure. An air of theatricality already enveloped him, and it would not be Noah if he did not take full advantage of the opportunities that the day afforded. The final meeting before the declaration of war had been called at the Exchange; spacious as was its hall, however, it could not contain the crowds that responded. The meeting was adjourned to the circular church, under the speakership of Mr. Geddes.

Behold: the first orator who rises to ask the floor . . . A young gentleman already verging upon corpulency, twenty-six years old, with sandy hair, a generous Roman nose, and equally generous whiskers of red . . . A buzz drones through the hall. Who is he? Where did this fellow come from?

Colonel Keating Lewis Simmons bends over to his pew partner, E. S. Thomas, editor of the *Charleston Gazette*, and asks whether the journalist knows this stranger. No, he doesn't. But soon, in the excitement of the young man's passionate address, the question of his identity is for the nonce forgotten. He speaks noticeably well . . . Indeed, well enough to win, after he is through, the compliments of Colonel Simmons, orator for the opposing Federalists. And well enough to inflame the next speaker, the young Joshua W. Toomer, also a Federalist, into casting slurs upon the Republican party, which comprises, in addition to Mordecai Manuel Noah, at least two thirds of those present.

The war resolutions, however, are passed, and the meeting is adjourned.

Among the principal Republican speakers has been a Dr. Ramsay, who rushes forward to shake young Noah by the hand. Not since the Revolutionary War, exclaims Dr. Ramsay, has he heard so classical and eloquent a speech. "The fact was," as Noah wrote to his Uncle on June 8, 1812, "the subject was popular and I made the most of it. My few friends were delighted . . . In short, I was the city talk for a long time after."

He was, indeed, "followed by a mob home looking at me with the greatest curiosity."

And now, really, who was the red-whiskered young fellow that had the meeting by the ears? Editor Thomas pursues his inquiries. He learns that Noah has been staying for the past few weeks with a relation. The fellow has made few acquaintances. He has been engaged in legal studies. And he has been writing, under a pseudonym.

Noah, indeed, is none other than that Muly Malak, whose letters, ostensibly Oriental, have been enlivening the readers of the *Charleston Times* with their thinly disguised account of social and political life in contemporary Charleston.[1]

---

[1] This account is based upon *Reminiscences of the Last Sixty-Five Years*, by E. S. Thomas. Hartford, 1840, vol. II, pp. 57–61. Thomas is in error when he dates the recollection 1811, as is proved hereinafter, not only by the dates of the Muly Malak letters, but by a manuscript letter of Noah, which describes the selfsame

2. "MULY MALAK"

Noah, voracious reader that he is, has been spending much
of his spare time at the Charleston Library, just as, in Philadelphia, he divided his evenings between playhouse and
bookshelf. He has become acquainted with Goldsmith's
Citizen of The World, and, as he aspires to become just such
a citizen, he reports his first impressions of the city of
Charleston with the pen and through the eyes of the supposed
visitor from the East, Muly Malak. It might have been
Mordecai Manuel Noah writing to Mr. Naphtali Phillips,
now of New York[1] . . .

meeting and gives the details of one of the duels caused by his political and epistolary activities.

This is as good a place as any other to correct misstatements that have crept
into print about Noah and his Charleston period. He was not, as Wolf asserted in
his monograph of 1897, and as has been frequently reprinted from this often unreliable source, editor of the *Charleston City Gazette*. His new friend, Mr. E. S. Thomas,
was. The Muly Malak letters were written, not for the *New York Times*, as it is
stated in Hervey Allen's excellent life of Poe, *Israfel* (vol. ii, page 884), but for the
Charleston Times.

[1] The brief series of letters begins in the *Charleston Times* of Thursday evening,
April 16, 1812, page 2, under the headline *Oriental Correspondence*. "Copy of a
letter from Muly Malak, agent for the House of Said Hamet at Aleppo, to Caled
the Elder, Aga of the Janizaries; giving a Description of Charleston, the manners
and customs of the Inhabitants. (Translated from the Arabic)."

The second letter was printed in the *Times* of Saturday evening, May 9, 1812,
from the same to the same. The third, on June 2, 1812, ditto. On June 4, there
appeared, in the *Times*, a letter from Joshua W. Toomer, objecting to the report
given by Muly Malak concerning the town meeting at which war was debated so
hotly. Two days later Caled the Elder, one of Noah's masks, replied to Muly
Malak, the other. Then, on June 13, the Oriental Correspondence suddenly shifted
from masters to servants, and Selim Baba, the confidential servant of Muly Malak,
wrote to Yusef Kahn, chief cook to Caled the Elder. There was a reply from Yusef
Kahn to Selim Baba on June 23 (the issue erroneously carries, on the outside, the
date of the 29th).

Another manuscript letter of Noah, now freshly unearthed, shows that at this period of political warfare in Charleston he had not lost touch with the politics of the Northern States. Charleston, at the time, was also one of the chief centers of Jewish population, and Mr. Muly Malak, as it appears, could not keep out of the very human brawls incidental to synagogal activities. It should be observed, moreover, from this letter, that Noah, almost a year after his appointment to the Riga consulship, still had it in mind, though he had declined it.

Charleston May 10, 1812

Dear Uncle,

My several letters to you are without reply, a circumstance I regret very much as a private opportunity has occurred whereby I could hear of you and family in a satisfactory manner I pray you will drop me a few lines and give me every information— I read the old Public Advertiser which I perceive is edited with spirit and talent The war is carried on between the two parties as vigorous as ever Surely Clinton must have already seen that the people of the U. S. are not prepared to change their officers. This State with North Carolina & Georgia gives a unanimous vote for Madison— I have approved of the energetic conduct of Gv Tompkins in proroguing that intriguing Legislature—I do not see your name among the Committees as usual I am as well persuaded as ever that you have not abandoned the old cause and general opinion states that yr friend Tompkins will be promoted shortly in the U S Service—great complaints are preferred against Congress their measures press heavy on the people—I feel it as much as any person it has completely deranged my plans am now doing nothing waiting with my usual patience for a change of times and friends In my last I enclosed to you a bill of fare relative to a singing match established by Mr Carvalho within this last week the Congregation has been in a state of warfare sanctioned & approved by that gentleman unheard of in the annals of religion—It appears he had taught the children to sing the concluding psalms of the Sabbath Morning Service in a very handsome manner which in a measure did away the discordance which attends every Synagogue for a whim or caper he discontinued this ceremony & forbid the children to sing The private adjunta conceiving it to be his duty to continue a system which was generally approved of respectfully requested him to allow the children to continue which he refused to do and on application for some other branch of his duty he treated the adjunta with disrespect & they suspended him for five days which suspension terminated on Saturday at 10 oclock when he performed the prayers—Saturday evening being a meeting of the adjunta in general body he collected a rabble composed of all the vagrant Jews & had a petition signed by them to give him redress this petition was handed the Parnass who could not act upon it being in express violation to the constitution Mr Carvalho in person aided and abetted the confusion & riot which took place in a short time the whole meeting parnass & all were battling with clubs & bruising boxing &c during which his reverence & brother & friend Lipman came off with a few thumps this outrageous & disgraceful produced by the interference & co-operation of Mr Carvalho terminated without any serious injury The result has completely destroyed the small remnant of respectability & character yet left for Mr C his duty was not to take the law in his own hands but to submit with respect to the conduct & resolve of the private adjunta who are composed of the most respected & indeed the most enlightened part of the Congregation Mr C should have taken a lesson from Mr Seixas book & studied the character & views of a man who after 45 years public Service retains the respect the esteem & regard of his Congregation & holds a place in the general estimation & opinion of the public

Aunt Hetty talks of going to the northward this Season and if she makes up her mind will go to New York She wishes much to see you & always desires when I write to send her love to you & Aunt & Children begs (?) you will let the boys write to her— her four children are beauties but she is in very bad health Mammy Hannah complains not hearing from you I hope the pressure of the times is not felt by you as severely as formerly— I perceive by a letter from Uncle Elias that Mr Hart has an auctioneers Commess & he has a share I fear they will do little I have had some excellent letters given me to merchants in Russia God knows when I shall be there— I leave nothing untried by my friends not not (meant for *to*?) anticipate my wishes I pray you to write to me all news foreign and Domestic giving my love very sincerely to Aunt Rachel & children & believe

always affectionately yrs
M M Noah

By the end of June, 1812, the pseudo-Oriental prose of the Malak letters had lost its novelty, both with Noah and the public. But the youth had caused his nine days' sensation, and for years thereafter was to be known, among Journalists, as Muly Malak. He had helped the Charlestonians to see themselves through Northern eyes, and had already begun to train those eyes in the perception and description of peoples and policies.

In Charleston there had been a Hebrew congregation since 1750,—the Kahal Kadosh Beth Elohim (Holy Congregation of The House of God). Such names as Cohen, De Costa, Tobias, Sheftall, Lazarus and Cardoza are found at the beginning of a Jewish chronicle that grows with the growth of the Republic. Nor is it surprising that when, on Friday, September 14, 1793, the corner-stone of a new syngaogue—

stone, and not, like the first, wood—was laid, it was laid by the Masonic fraternity.

Noah, writing in his Oriental disguise as Muly Malak, found a neat and comfortable city, free of wandering beggars. The ladies—and wherever Noah traveled he always had an

eye for the fair sex—"suffer the rude gaze of the passing throng to light on them, without horror or concern: they neither pencil their eyebrows, nor dye their cheeks; and exhibit in their appearance a simplicity of attire and a modest mien, that fails not to surprise . . .

"They are very devout also, and never fail attending the Mosque on Sunday, and are most scrupulously attentive to a little book which they hold in their hand, occasionally lightening the labor of their eyes, by casting an expressive look around them . . .

"The people here read much; aye, and good books Caled; yet Science is circumscribed, and the Fine Arts languish . . . There is a large Hall filled with works instructing and amusing; and an old Mufti, good and engaging, serves up the intellectual repast. O, Caled, what cements the bonds of society, strengthens and improves the mind, warms and affects the heart, like Science? It sheds its beams like the evening Sun, brilliant and irresistable . . .

"Amusements are various and change with the seasons, like the *Upas* of the East. Running of horses (be not surprised, dear Caled) forms one of their popular and prominent pursuits; they have an extensive plain set apart for this amusement, to which all the beauty and fashion resort— the Ladies appear to take great delight in these equestrean pursuits; and what may appear singular to you, they bet upon the fleetness of a horse, whose qualifications they must, for the best of reasons, be strangers to. Gloves, purses and smiles are thus indiscriminately distributed; while the Gentlemen stake sums which not infrequently involve their whole capital. All is confusion, heat, dust, joy and dismay. Ladies of quality, demi reps, and demi devils, judges, counsellors, physicians, soldiers, sailors, black legs, and lame ducks are mixed and commingled with all their armorial bearings and distinctions—these, together with horses, dogs, whips, barouches, roly-polys and raree-shows, in all their sad variety, fill up the checquered scene—and all this is called spirit, taste, elegance, and fashion.

"The system of education which a few young ladies of this country are known to have availed themselves of, is at once strange and incomprehensible; they are not like the pupils of the good Irad, instructed in the useful branches of knowledge . . . Instead of the useful and important they are taught the tedious and unnecessary branches of education—they are carefully instructed by a variety of professors, in Mensuration of Superficies and Solids; Longimetry, alimetry, algebra, trigonometry, surveying with solar, lunar and astral observations; rhetoric, composition, logic, history, chronology, mythology, philology, natural philosophy, and astronomy—good prophet, defend us, what a medley. These, together with reading, writing, dancing, music, drawing and languages, fill up the vacuity of the brain, if any such vacuity exists, at an incredible and useless expense. In short their minds present a confused mass of extraneous and garbled science, so sedulously mottled and confounded, that it requires an age to extract the gold from the rubbish in which it is hidden; and when found, it is hardly worth the trouble of looking for."

3. CODE DUELLO

Noah, to be sure, will ultimately get down to his political ruminations. He will inform Caled as to the country's growing determination to avenge foreign aggression . . . of its forty years' journey through the wilderness of domination to the promised land of deliverance and true independence . . . Already, in 1812, he will be regarding with moralistic uneasiness the unexampled prosperity that is deadening the sensibilities of his fellow-citizens. "Wealth and luxury has choked (sic) up the channels of their hearts; energy and enterprise can find no entrance."

Muly, however, is after all a Turk, and you may be sure that sooner or later he is back at the contemplation of the local beauties, if only for the pleasure of comparing them with the Northern sirens and reproaching them for the dear foibles of femininity.

It is in the Muly Malak papers, indeed, that there first appears in Noah a certain old-fogyishness that never left him. Later, as editor of the *National Advocate*, when, in his armchair style he will inveigh against the fashions, for both men and women, he will but echo the humorously pompous observations of Muly . . . "the strange mode adopted by the ladies, to display their figure to advantage, by bracing their delicate bosoms with certain ligatures into various forms, convex and concave, octagon and diagonal" . . . Minds, too, may be corseted . . .

In this same letter we discover Muly, upon his introduction to the naval and field officers of the infant nation, commenting upon their ardor to distinguish themselves. ". . . And for lack of employment, they continue to kill time, kill care, and kill one another on the most petty and frivolous occasion." For Noah is a War Hawk, and would have these dashing fellows staining their uniforms with English blood. Soon Charleston will be asking whether Noah's veins run with red blood or with printer's ink. He will have an answer.

This sort of thing was not calculated to maintain the peace of Charleston, and it is hardly to be wondered at if Noah, in his eagerness to embroil the United States in a war, first started a war of his own. Joshua W. Toomer, the young advocate of peace, at the meeting that Noah had addressed, was held up to metaphorical ridicule in Muly Malak's latest Oriental communication. He promptly replied to the editor of the *Charleston Times*, defending his fellow citizens from the unjust and misrepresenting aspersions of "a writer in your paper, who bears the character, as well as the name, of an unchristian Turk."

Noah countered with "a flaming letter under the signature of Fabius"—I quote again from the letter of June 8, 1812— and was to receive, this time, from Toomer, a reply more direct than the coldness of print.

The war of 1812, in the calm perspective of history, appears to have been neither noble nor necessary. Personal bravery, of course, it did call forth, as do all wars, just or unjust. Nor can Noah's bravery, under the circumstances, be questioned. He hated monarchical England. Thrones had begun to totter, and this young American Jew, with the ardor of prophecy in his veins, foresaw the century of democratization.

This was, in history, an apocalyptic moment. Upon three continents a vast holocaust shot forth the flames of an old order that was burning to the ground. Heraldic figures cast giant shadows against this cataclysm . . . Washington . . . Napoleon . . . Bolívar . . . A free America, North and South . . . A free Europe, marshaled by *la belle France* . . . The heroes of the ancient republics, with Hannibal at their head, rose out of Noah's readings to companion these epical contemporaries. Beyond the boundaries of the accumulating national problems Noah had joined this internationale of advancing hope. This impassioned youth, sternly addicted to the Lord of the Old Testament, found in the Scriptures— as, indeed, the Puritans and the Dissenters had found on this soil before him—warrant for resistance to oppression. It is not a debasing morality, and it added stature to the young Noah.

No sooner had he been introduced to Ebenezer S. Thomas, who was later to prove so good a friend to Poe, than Noah was suggesting for the *Charleston City Gazette* still another contribution that was not exactly a libation of oil upon the troubled waters of the municipality. Thomas knew what it meant to publish the article, and forewarned the firebrand of the possible consequences. There were optimists who had thought that the tragic duel between Burr and Hamilton would do away with this antiquated method of settling disputes. Thomas knew better. And, shortly, Noah would find out.

The Toomer insult rapidly assumed the nature of a blot on the Federalist escutcheon that must be wiped out in Republican blood. Noah's ancestors had come up from the South; his mother lay buried in Charleston; he had yet, however, to make his acquaintance with Southern chivalry . . . Nor was he too much perturbed when, a few days after the appearance of his offensive writings, he was called out—i. e., challenged to a duel—by Mr. Toomer. This was a mere formality, he explained to himself. The proper explanations and adjustments would be made, and he could go on with his fulminations, his studies in the law, his quiet and serious reading. Having been called out, then, he did nothing more violent than to repair, as usual, to the City Library.

Suddenly his perusal was interrupted by the delivery of a note on vellum paper, in the hands of a gentleman who first accomplished two or three very graceful bows, and now stood waiting for reply. The note introduced Major Hamilton, afterwards to be General, and Governor of South Carolina. Major Hamilton would make all necessary arrangements for the affair of honor. What was there for Noah to do but to rise and return, as handsomely as he could, the bows that had prefaced this very earnest business? Hereupon they sat down in close converse, Noah holding forth upon wind and weather, the war, palmetto forts, rice birds, cotton crops, and what not else except pistols for two. It appeared, however, that this *was* a serious business, and that Major Hamilton, however flattered he may have felt at Noah's evident pleasure in making his acquaintance, had come to reach agreement upon the preliminaries of private murder . . . Very well, he would have Noah's answer in an hour.

Hastily Noah summoned the leaders of the Republican party to a conference. What course should he follow? Only one, they replied, as a man: Noah must fight. "It was the usage of the country, and no leader of a party of such high and patriotic pretensions, could evade an invitation in which the dignity of the party was so vitally concerned." That settled it; the very destinies of the United States, so Noah was made to feel, depended upon his honor in this encounter. A high dignitary was named as his second, and a note was at once despatched to the challenger, accepting the call and leaving to his own representatives the settling of all preliminaries.

That afternoon a carriage drove up to Noah's door; it was two friends who were taking him for a ride. The exhilaration of a drive behind two spanking greys was soon abated, however, by the sight of two pistols lying at the bottom of the carriage. Noah's friends, it appeared, harbored certain doubts as to his marksmanship, and the afternoon was to be devoted to target practice. Noah needed it. He had never held a pistol in his hand. But when a card was pinned to a tree and the novice, at ten paces, cut through its heart, it was considered an auspicious beginning. "You're a first rate shot!" exclaimed the one. "Poor devil, he will be killed!" cried the other. And "Pray," asked Noah, at last, "what kind of a person is this whom I am to meet?"

"A very clever fellow," was the answer, "of great promise and a gentleman of fortune and character, of a large and ancient family, highly esteemed and respected." It all seemed stupid to Noah, now. What ill will had he against this unnamed gentleman, personally? They were differing on principles. Was this a cause for slaughter? Couldn't the difficulty have been adjusted just as well, and to the honor of their respective parties, over a bottle of south side Madeira, with the shedding of nothing more bloody than wine? But no. Even the Police spread the news that the duel was to come off at four that afternoon, over on the race track, whereupon the sports of Charleston bought up every gig in town for transportation to the great event. And the ladies, God bless them, after the first few tears that youth should be cut off in its flower, were swept into the excitement.

It could hardly have made Noah feel any better when he heard that some of the leading Republicans intended, if he fell, to bury him with all the Civil and Military honors.

The duel—the first to which Noah had been challenged—never took place. Thomas, who, indirectly, had got him into it, got him out of it. He saw that, at a moment when concerted action in a higher cause was needful, such a quarrel could only result in unfruitful dissension. Accordingly, Thomas called early the next morning upon Keating Lewis Simmons, head of the Federal Party. A meeting of the high contracting powers was arranged, and after four hours of deliberation it was decided to call off the duel. Not until

the etiquette of adjustment had been gone through did Noah
learn that his opponent-to-have-been was Joshua W. Toomer.

"I was entirely satisfied with the issue, having no desire
to kill my antagonist . . . Nor had I any wish to be killed
myself. But the dear public, it seems, was not so well satisfied with the result . . . Pompey had harnessed the bays
in the Buggy—whips, spurs and trotting horses were all
ready for the race course, to see two promising fellows shoot
each other, and so the affair is settled—the pistols are returned
to the case—and the Doctor was not called upon to prepare
lint, probe stick, and plaster."

The dear public, however, chatted. Noah was like all of
these young Republican-Democrats; he'd rather eat than
fight . . . He'd have to show them. So, a few days after the
Toomer affair, he got into another newspaper row, this time
with a fellow named Crafts. The comedy of interchanged
billets began anew. Here was Noah, headed again for the
race course and honor, when Mr. Crafts had the kindness—
perhaps the good sense—to fall sick. *Ergo*, no bullets flew,
and the matter was adjusted even as the Toomer affair had
been. And again a public that was spoiling for a fight
resumed its sneers.

Noah was afraid, they whispered, not too softly.

Noah, to be sure, was sensible. Duels struck him as out-
moded. More, he was, as it took a certain bravery to confess
to oneself, not by constitution brave. He hadn't the slightest
inclination to shoot or to be shot at, this hot-headed proponent of war between Great Britain and the United States.
He was no bully or braggart. But this did not mean that,
under proper provocation, he would not fight . . . Federal
Charleston, aroused by this sharp-tongued Northerner, and

wishing to silence him, meant to see that he was put to the test. He had made too many enemies with that free pen of his, and that free tongue, to escape his baptism of fire.

4. THE CANTOR AFFAIR

It was a Southern Jew, Cantor by name, who now made up his mind to rid the town of this too-aspiring politico. Picking a trifle as excuse, he delivered a challenge to Noah in terms that could not be rejected. He desired, this new challenger, neither explanation nor apology. Cantor, though of good family and of respectable character, was nobody of any special importance. He was not even a politician. Nothing would be served by their meeting, except to glut the popular appetite for brawl and scandal. Thus, for a third time, Noah was victimized by the code of honor.

This time there *must* be a fight, or there would be an explosion of damaging mockery. Noah's friends gathered once more about him with their *vivas*. His opponents circulated the taunt that he would "creep out of it" *again*. Cool and determined, he set about the business with despatch. He even felt a certain indifference. After all, though nothing yet had happened, he had been twice prepared to die on that now familiar battling ground, and the apprehension had lost something of its chill. He had no property to leave, no family to provide for, no will to draw up.

Noah's good friend, Geddes, now Speaker of the House and later to be Governor, lent him horses and carriage, and a case of fine hair triggers. Noah engaged a surgeon to attend him. The night before the day of the duel he stayed at a friend's, amid the solemnity of a discussion that resembled nothing so much as a wake in which the corpse did not have the politeness to lie still. He slept but fitfully, racked by nightmares. He was awakened by the sound of the servant downstairs grinding coffee. His lips were parched, his head feverish. A cup of the strong beverage, and they were off to the field.

He looked around at the beauty of the day as one who is bidding it farewell. For a third time the futility of this dishonorable *honor* mocked him. It was too late for fear, but he did feel for himself a great sorrow. There were his friends, eyeing him in the carriage beside him, with farewell in their looks . . . A miscellany of humans greeted them in the beautiful valley, dotted with two or three cottages, where the encounter was to blot the landscape. Men in gigs, on horseback, others who had walked, a parcel of darkies, groups of neighbors. In a few minutes Cantor and his suite appeared.

Noah, as the challenged person, had the choice of weapons, position and distance. He chose ten paces—the parties to stand back to back at this distance and to wheel and fire at the word. "I chose this mode", he recalled, thirty years after, from a memory upon which the flamboyant period had been deeply etched—"for several reasons. It was in consonance of the rules of honor, which did not necessarily claim a victim by a direct and deadly aim; it also gave a chance for both or neither to escape; besides, I did not wish to incur the stern gaze of my antagonist:—a deadly scowl, tossing off the hat, and some melo-dramatic action for effect, to throw me off my guard or shake my nerves . . . Not seeing my man until brought face to face by the word *fire*, and the sudden wheeling gave no advantage to either, and was deemed by all, considering the slight cause of offence, as proper and expedient."

63

Noah watched his second nervously as that assistant measured off his ten paces. What short legs this fellow had! Why, ten of his paces were surely but six of normal length! Noah and Cantor took their positions back to back. Noah looked around and discovered that his man was not in direct line with him. He moved a step to the right to bring him on a level.

"Gentlemen, are you ready?"

Two clear, strong voices answered: "Ready!"

"Wheel and fire!"

Noah wheeled with an expertness that surprised him. There, before him, stood Cantor, in the fraction of a second before the trigger was released. The challenger reeled and fell. Noah remained frozen to the spot in self-forgetfulness and in self-accusation. He had killed the man! *He was a murderer!* The blood of the first Abel was upon his head. His knees were knocking together and horror rippled through him. The spectators were dashing hither and thither, and a crowd had formed about Cantor's body.

All at once, to his vast relief, Noah realized that Cantor was alive. Not only alive, but filled with vindictiveness. "I'll have another shot," Noah heard him say.

He was hardly in condition, however. Noah's bullet had entered below Cantor's knee, and penetrated the calf of his left leg, which was bleeding profusely. Here was cause for double rejoicing: not only was Noah alive; he had not slain his opponent. It was his own surgeon that extracted Cantor's bullet. And, since Cantor could not stand up to fire or receive "another", the affair was considered as having been settled with all deference to the code. Cantor rode home in Noah's—that is, Speaker Geddes's—carriage.

Well, he *could* fight as well as eat. Friends and foes shook hands with him. The police—they had come to witness the fight, not to prevent it—departed on their mounts. The gigs and buggies and carriages and chaises began to roll off. "And thus ended the whole *humbug*", was Noah's signature to the deed, italics and all.[1]

What the situation—personal, political, municipal, international—looked like at the very moment these events were taking place may be gauged from two letters written by Noah on the spot, within a week of each other, to his benefactor, Naphtali Phillips. They supply details not to be procured elsewhere, and serve to correct erroneous impressions still current.

It would have been altogether unnatural that, for all the mixed emotions of this dashing from one field of honor to the next, Noah should not, in view of the outcome, have achieved a new sense of his importance. He detested duelling, to be sure; he lost no opportunity, in later years, to inveigh against the mad mode, and could speak with the confidence born of experience successfully overcome. Nevertheless, he

[1] This is not, even in its conversation, a piece of the so-called "historical reconstruction" that has been too common in contemporary biography; that is, unless the "reconstruction" was done by Noah. My account is based, in part, upon an article, *My First Duel*, written by Noah for *The Union*, New York City, and there printed on Wednesday evening, July 20, 1842, together with comment upon the duel between Marshall and Webb that prompted the recollections.

To show how careful one must be in accepting evidence: I have a letter from one of Noah's grandsons in which he tells me that "I have heard my father speak of his father fighting a duel with a man named Catron somewhere in South Carolina. Alfred Lewis in his book on Peggy O'Neal makes Noah fight the duel with Catron over Peggy, but I am told the duel arose from a quarrel of different character." The cause of the duel we have seen. Catron is the name that Lewis gave to Noah's opponent in his much romanticized novel about Andrew Jackson's friend, Peggy Eaton. And the name of Cantor passes on to the Noah family itself in its fictionized form!

had been tried and had found himself not wanting. In his own mind, and in that of others, he was a bigger fellow. The episode, moreover, had confirmed his party importance.

Yet he was hardly the dangerous killer that later anecdotes, multiplying vague report with Falstaffian gusto, have made of him. He did not engage in a round of duels. There was no notch in his gun. The near-duels and the one authentic affair were but incidents in the campaign that had brought Noah to Charleston: much-needed political advancement. Noah's letter of June 15, 1812, disposes of his duel with Cantor in three lines.

Dear Uncle,

I wrote to you by Hayman Levy at some length an opportunity occurring I write a few lines in addition—I find that your State has nominated Dewitt (sic) Clinton for Prest in opposition to reason, hope delicacy honor or good faith The faction (of which thank God you are not one) has completely disgraced the State in the eyes of the Union and of the world. I find here that the Republicans in the Southern Parts of the U S think (?) little of Dewitt and if they vote for him they will ground their support on what New York that is (illegible) Southwick says. Presuming that I had some knowledge of the man many Republicans of high standing have come forward and requested me to give a public statement of all I know concerning Clinton in order to set his claims to public view in their just light I now apply to you for every minute information at length concerning Clinton—No man knows him better than you— No man has watched his political career more attentively and no one is better calculated than you to give an history of his actions—I wish you therefore to sit down and favor me with an account of his whole course of political exercises—his intrigues his nomination for different offices his influence in the Councils—his denunciation of

Cheetham Dyde Tupper—Burr—in short give me a long
account of his political life Refresh your memory by a
recurrence to the Public Advertiser   Write me all about
him I will give it to the world in a Pamphlet form You owe
him no favours (a passage is here crossed out) You will do
your country your party yourself & myself a most important
Service by this information Send it by the first vessel & be
quick for they may be stopped or by private oppor^{yi}—if I
could get a file of the good old public advertiser I would
return it in Safety a file about the periods of the elections
. . . The people look to me for this information and I will
give it—War thank God is at last declared everything will
go on well—business will once more be brisk— In order to
prevent any uneasiness I state to you that a puppy by the
name of John Cantor had the insolence to send me a Challenge to fight him. I accordingly met him on Sunday last
and plump'd him the first Shot in the leg to the joy of all
Charleston— Hyam Cohen was my Second My friends were
all out on the ground and I was very cool and comfortable
on the occasion—Give my Love to Aunt Rachel & all the
Children I beg your attention to the foregoing request &
assure that

I am always affectionately yrs

MMN

5. Greenroom Interlude

Not all was battle that was Charleston. Noah, it appeared,
had a reputation, more than local, as a dramatic critic and
as a man of the theater. Sometime during this eventful year
of 1812 Mr. Charles Young, husband of the beautiful actress,
approached the young blade with the suggestion of writing

---

[1] That is, opportunity.

a play with his wife especially in mind for the leading feminine rôle. In this, her heyday, she was a blonde beauty of
dazzling fair skin and rosy cheeks. Her tendency toward a
slightly evident fleshiness did not interfere with the grace
of her carriage. The age of boyish femininity, of the lank
limbs and haggard cheeks that Gilbert's poet, Bunthorne,
pretended to admire, was more than half a century in the
future. Mrs. Young was one of the favorites of the day.
Though she appeared to be successful in every female type,
she had ambitions—or her husband, for her—to play what
the greenroom of that time called a "breeches part".

Writing a play, for Noah, was but an interlude in the
serious Republican-Democratic-Federal turmoil. Quickly he
concocted a tear-drainer that he christened *Paul and Alexis*;
or, The Orphans of the Rhine, with Mrs. Young in the rôle
of the hero. It was hardly what one might have expected
from the gentleman who had signed, recently, those moral
and realistic strictures against William Shakespeare. Nor
was it, if Noah's political enemies had any say in the matter,
to stand any chances of success. On the night of the performance they forgathered in considerable numbers, but either
their interest in the proceedings caused them to forget their
arrangement to hiss the piece, or else their courage failed
them until the last curtain fell, when suddenly they remembered and hissed too late.

Paul and Alexis was, for the day, a stage-worthy piece.
Mr. Young appears to have sent the manuscript on to London, where it was subjected to mild revision, emerging finally
as *The Wandering Boys*; *or, The Castle of Olival*, fathered by
John Kerr, and produced at Covent Garden on February 24,
1814.

Mr. Quinn has pointed out[1] that Noah's first acted piece was founded upon the most popular of the melodramas by Pixéricourt, *Le Pèlerin Blanc ou les Orphelins du Hameau* (1801), which was founded in turn upon Ducray-Dumesnil's *Les Petits Orphelins du Hameau,* which, in *its* turn, was founded upon Marsollier's opera *Les Petits Savoyards*. Pixéricourt's version of the hackneyed plot enjoyed a record of 1533 performances.

Noah's material did not have even the thesis of impassioned libertarianism, which had inspired his unproduced *Fortress of Sorrento,* to recommend it. Again a poor thing, and not even his own. Heroism and villainy and innocence are bodied forth in primary colors. The disguised Count de Croisy, father of the outraged sons, Justin and Paul, is every millimeter an angel guardian; his boys are paragons, whether of suffering or of stupidity; the Baroness Olival, their designing cousin, is unmitigated fiend. And all alike speak a dropsical prose that, when the swollen periods subside, leaves nothing but water.

Comparison between the printed versions of the Noah piece and that of Kerr—Noah's was published anonymously in 1821—shows very little difference in the manuscripts as acted. Historically, the Gothic melodrama by young Noah is important as being "probably the second play by an American to be performed in England after an initial production in America."[2] We shall meet it again on March 16, 1820, when, under the English title, it is produced at the

---

[1] *A History of the American Drama,* From the Beginning to the Civil War. By Arthur Hobson Quinn. New York, 1923. Pp. 193–194.

[2] Quinn, ibid. Page 194. Curiously enough, the first was—See page 32—the much altered *Pocahontas, or the Indian Princess,* by Noah's friend, James Nelson Barker.

Park Theater, New York, initiating thus a popularity of many years.

It was Noah's political ardor that got him and his friends into trouble. At the risk of stirring up another affair of honor, the hotheaded War Hawk now induced editor Thomas to print a long letter couched in the most violent terms against Joseph Alston, then Governor of South Carolina. Alston was married to Colonel Burr's daughter, and Noah charged him with a treacherous part in the famous Burr conspiracy. To this, among other things, he added the accusation that Alston, in order to gain his election to the legislature, had bribed the voters of All Saints parish. Thomas, as was to be expected, was prosecuted by Alston for publishing the letter; nothing further came of the matter.

6. "Jimmy's War"

The War of 1812 was hardly a popular war in this country, nor does it appear to have been altogether an inevitable one. To be sure, between the blockades that France and Great Britain attempted to enforce against each other, at the expense of the neutral nations, American trade, especially in New England, suffered heavy losses. Yet the New England traders, rather than become embroiled with their chief customer, Great Britain, were content to mark up the capture of their vessels to profit and loss.

As a matter of record, when war was at last declared there was frank opposition to enlistment in New England on the part of the Federalists; they were the principal sufferers from the state of affairs and, politically, pro-British in their sympathies. The Democrat-Republicans, of course, were pro-French. England did not desire war with us. Five days after we declared war, indeed, the long objectionable Orders in Council, to which Napoleon had replied with his Berlin and Milan Decrees, were revoked by Great Britain. Communication was very slow in those days; England did not know that the United States had declared war, nor did we, for a long time, know that the Orders had been revoked.

From June 18, 1812, a state of war had existed between England and America. Impressment of American sailors by Great Britain was not advanced as a *casus belli* until after the war had started and President Madison had learned of the revocation of the Orders in Council. "Thus, strangely enough, the War of 1812 was fought in spite of the protest of those for whom it was presumably fought."[1]

It was a war waged at the behest of our southern and western states in opposition to the will of the northeastern section of the country. Eager expansionists envisioned a United States enlarged by the annexation of Florida below and Canada above. The Canadian dream, indeed, had originated during the Revolution and claimed ardent sponsors in such leaders as Washington, Franklin, Jefferson and Governor Morris of Pennsylvania . . . Noah had hitched his wagon to these stars . . .

Still waiting for his Barbary appointment, with nine months already passed since our declaration of war, Noah sent another letter of appeal to Naphtali Phillips.[2]

[1] See *The War Myth in United States History*. By C. H. Hamlin. New York, 1927. Pp. 29–41.

[2] In the letter of June 8, 1812—which may be read in full in my article on Noah, *The Menorah Journal*, Autumn issue, 1936—Noah wrote to his uncle Naphtali, à propos of the Toomer argument, just before it reached the stage of a duel, "Throughout the whole I have been spoken of in terms too flattering for an individual & am afraid that I could procure the unanimous [sic] vote of all the Republicans for any situation I may require I must now use it to some advantage & shall unite their influence to prevail on the President to send me to the Barbary Powers through the delegation at Congress——" Of Clinton, Noah wrote in the same letter that "he never will be President."

Georgetown D C—March 11 1813

Dear Uncle,

I have not lately received a letter from you although the mail brings me the National Advocate. I am forcible impressed with the talents of Mr Wheaton—He appears perfectly conversant with the affairs of Govt and particularly intimate with the points of dispute existing between the two Govts as his remarks on the Non importation law and the Prince Regents proclamation clearly developes . . .

The secretary of State has informed me that the President has been so engaged in regulating appointments in the new army and with other concerns that he has not had the time to decide on my application but assures me of his favourable intentions and from what I can learn and that too in a very direct way from the Secretary—the Prest has made up his mind to appoint me Charge des affaires at Tunis and Mr Gaillard has been so positive of the fact that he has presented me his printed documents relative to the annual disbursements in that Regency. It will put me in possession of handsome funds a very desirable object for what with delays &c I am reduced to a low ebb— Should the Prest not have time before Wednesday to make the appt accompanied with all the instructions—I shall that day set off for Charleston and let the documents follow me— Should that be the case I may run short of money before I get to SCarolina— If it is convenient with you lend me $20—for fear I may run short or be detained on the road— I will return it to you and at the same time beg you to let me know how much I owe you I have some memorandums but they fall short of the amot— If I get liberty to draw on the Treasury I can very conveniently pay my debts and none will I pay more gratefully than yours—no favour or affection will I so long and earnestly remember— I dine on Saturday with Mr Madison I have not pressed my suit—feeling a little dignity with my strong recommendations and I believe he is aware

of it— If you do not write me by Sundays mail I shall not
receive it as that mail arrives here Tuesday evening— Love
to Aunt Rachel & Children & believe

mt affectionately yrs

MMNoah

The coveted appointment was signed in short order, nine
days after the letter was written, and came as a godsend. In
fewer than three months Noah was on his way to the Barbary
states. The Riga appointment he had declined because he
feared the chaos of a Europe arrayed against Napoleon. In
the Barbary States he was to fall into just such conditions
as he had sought to avoid in Russia. And, as in Charleston,
to the warfare that was rending the nations he was to add
another little war of his own.

During the period immediately preceding his appointment,
Noah seems to have traveled between Charleston and Philadelphia. For, some time in 1813, he received the title Major.
It was bestowed at an election for militia officers, "which,
as he afterward told with glee, was attended only by himself
and two other persons."[1]

---

[1] See *History of Philadelphia*, 1609–1884. By J. Thomas Scharf and Thomas
Westcott. Philadelphia, 1884. 3 vols. Vol. ii, p. 1137.

IV

INNOCENCE—AND GUILE—ABROAD

1. THE BUCCANEERS OF THE MEDITERRANEAN

IT was every inch a determined gentleman who, on May 28, 1813, strode at daybreak across the deck of the schooner *Joel Barlow*, Captain Buchanan in command. As the vessel weighed anchor, the young gentleman pointed, together with its prow, the prow of his own high ambitions France-ward.

The portfolio of his hopes bulged with a strange miscellany.

Imprimis: a stout heart, already proved by adversity and the conflicting passions of man.

Item: a foundation of broad and solid reading, awakened by an alert curiosity and awakening new curiosity in turn.

Item: a brief experience in the governmental auditing division, brghtened by special reward, and by contact with leaders of the nation. Young Noah meant to lay the groundwork of his fame and fortune. Circumstance and temperament would combine to cheat him, but they, like other failures, lay yet ahead with other storms of sea and land. Money would slip through his fingers, but rarely into his own pockets.

Item: reportorial experience of law-making bodies.

Item: proud authorship of two plays, a literary commentary, and a series of pseudonymous letters to the press that had stirred hot discussion and added size to his political personality.

Item: a sudden reputation as a budding orator, which had increased his self-confidence and his self esteem.

Item: a baptism of fire that came to companion his baptism of printer's ink. He had proved his courage under the threat of duel and in actual participation.

Mordecai Manuel Noah . . . United States Consul . . . Virtually protégé of the President . . . Twenty-eight years old . . . This schooner was not merely the *Joel Barlow*. It was the Ship of State. In Noah's hands lay the credit of his race, the reputation of his country, both to be enhanced by the manner in which he should acquit himself of the difficult mission that had been entrusted to his diplomacy.

No longer under the protection of a foreign power, our infant republic was compelled to treat directly with the pirates of the Barbary States, who had been swooping down like vultures upon the Mediterranean for hundreds of years. Only a strong navy could protect national rights, and our navy, like our republic, was in its infancy. There was nothing to do but follow the policy that had been forced upon even the ancient kingdoms of Europe: to buy off sea-robbery with disgraceful tribute.

Treaties, of course, were concluded with the various Regencies, and representatives of our country were established at the important cities of Algiers, Tangier, Tunis and Tripoli. At Algiers, immediately after the successful outcome of our Revolution, had been Joel Barlow, lately so active in behalf of Noah's appointment. He had died on the eve of the War of 1812; the very vessel that was now carrying the young Consul to his duties had been named after him. An early error of policy, though perhaps not at that time unavoidable, had been the appointment of non-Americans to consular posts. They could hardly have been expected to execute their duties with anything beyond administrative perfunctoriness. The United States, therefore, became a target for insult and extortion, with its representatives yielding, on the whole, a ready compliance.

Capt. O'Brien, an ex-captive of the Algerines, alternated his payment of tribute with urgent suggestions that we resist the aggressor. In 1798, President Adams appointed James Leander Cathcart Consul at Tripoli, and the eccentric William Eaton Consul at Tunis. A Monsieur Famin, named by Mr. Barlow to watch over our affairs at Tunis, had got us into a peck of trouble by signing a treaty that threatened further to degrade the nation. Our Senate rejected the treaty and looked to Cathcart, Eaton and O'Brien to uphold the national dignity. Their arrival at Algiers with over-generous gifts of vessels, ammunition, jewels and money, naturally excited the cupidity of the Tunisian rulers; the result was that Famin's treaty, with a few excisions purchased by more presents, went into effect.

From now until 1801 Consul Eaton lived a hellish life at Tunis, resisting the piratical demands of his hosts with a firmness that even the ardent Noah, retrospectively, considered to border on indiscretion. Meantime our peaceful relations with Tripoli, in the consulship of Cathcart, were rent by her Pasha's violations of our treaty. Even now, the policy of tribute and propitiatory gifts was not abandoned; afraid lest the other Barbary States pounce upon us in case of a declaration of war, our government was ready with bribes for Tunis and Algiers. The Pasha made the one natural inference: the United States was afraid, and should be treated with renewed contempt.

Consul Eaton, at Tunis, looked on at our shilly-shally policy in enraged helplessness. He quarreled passionately with the natives; he quarreled as passionately with our naval commanders. What these barbarians needed, he kept proclaiming, was the taste of American vengeance.

It was not Eaton's fault, or the lack of American courage on land and sea, that his plan virtually came, at the very last moment, to naught. Two rival brothers contended for the Tripolitan throne: Yusef Carramalli, the reigning Pasha, and Hamet, exiled in the Regency of Tunis. Upon the declaration of war by Tripoli against the United States, Hamet saw an opportunity to use the situation: by aiding the United States to defeat Yusef, Hamet would be restored, and a suitable treaty drawn up between the contending nations.

Our small navy was distinguishing itself in these foreign waters. Decatur and his party, by their unexampled bravery, had cheated the Pasha Yusef of his accidental capture, our frigate *Philadelphia*, by boarding it, burning it to the water's edge and retreating without loss. Commodore Preble, greatly outnumbered, had attacked the Tripolitan batteries, destroyed several of the enemy's gun boats during four or five hours of fire, inflicted heavy damage upon their town and fortifications, and slain many of their men. During the blockade there were many sudden incursions into the harbor by the Americans; one of them was so disastrous that the Pasha sued for peace, renouncing every claim except that of $500. payment for each United States prisoner. The suit was sharply rejected.

The romantic General Eaton, in the meantime, had returned to the United States with the plan of Hamet, and Jefferson's message to Congress had concurred in the plot. Hamet's position, during the absence of Eaton, had been strengthened. On February 23, 1805, Eaton, authorized by his country, signed with Hamet the treaty of alliance by which we were to aid in restoring the exiled brother to the throne of Tripoli, in return for which service we were to be indemnified by a transfer of the tributes stipulated to be paid by Denmark, Sweden and Holland. Not least of the satisfactions to William Eaton must have been his appointment as General and Commander-in-Chief of all the land forces.

A week later Eaton, together with Hamet and a small staff, was on the march for Derne, which, according to Yusef's broken pledge, should have fallen to Hamet as Governor. The steady progress of Eaton filled Yusef with concern; though rushing the defense of Derne, he was prepared to yield to America's terms. The Governor of Derne, however, was in no such conciliatory mood. When, before attacking in force, by land, with the *Argus*, *Nautilus* and *Hornet* within gun-shot of the town, Eaton sent a message for the Governor under flag of truce, he received an iron reply: "My head or yours." Eaton, in the attack that followed, received a ball through the wrist; fourteen Christians were killed, and many Mussulmans on both sides. The Governor took refuge in a mosque. But the town was taken by assault. In the thirtieth year of American Independence, Noah proudly and italically records, "the American flag was displayed on the walls of this city, in the *Lybian desert*."

Colonel Lear, Consul-General to the Regencies of Barbary, was on board the blockading squadron. It was through him that the fruits of victory were snatched out of brave, eccentric Eaton's hands. For, with the reigning Pasha eagerly suing for peace, Lear, on May 26, in the frigate *Essex*, opened communications. Under the circumstances we could, and should, have made our own terms. It was the Pasha's strategy to renew his original propositions of payment for a treaty and the prisoners, amounting in all to $200,000. It was for Lear firmly to reject and let the Pasha return in humbler mood. Instead, Lear, out of the generosity of his ignorance, himself suggested our payment of $60,000. and deliverance of the Tripolitan prisoners, in exchange for adjustment of the difficulties and the release of our captives. The Pasha hastened to assent.

Eaton withdrew from Derne in disgust. In two weeks he could have had Tripoli at his mercy. Subsequently he came back to America and proceeded to drink himself to death. He was replaced in Tunis by Dr. George Davis, a naval surgeon. Colonel Lear repaired to Algiers, where, as a result of the anti-climactic close to our war with Tripoli, we were regarded with increased respect but not yet with fear.

Nor was Lear's policy calculated to avert the war with Algiers that seemed inevitable, once we should be delivered from the hostilities that engaged us with England even as Noah sped across the Atlantic on the good ship *Joel Barlow*. Lear was all for buying peace. The Dey was all for greed. Why not, if United States money was so easy?

For Lear's consular subservice the Pasha of Algiers had a rod in pickle. Compliance was repaid with increased insolence. The capture of the brig *Edwin*, of Salem, Massachusetts, provoked the inevitable outbreak.

Algerine piracy had changed but little in the more than two hundred years that had gone by since the enslavement and the fortuitous ransom of one Don Miguel Cervantes y

Saavedra. Algiers, as Noah afterwards described it, was
"the great depot, the sink of iniquity and the curse of humanity. The European powers have much to answer for, in
permitting their citizens to be thus enslaved, by a small
piratical band . . ."

2. JULY 4, 1813

We were at war with England; the Mediterranean was
therefore closed to our vessels. Our captives were sending
up prayers to their countrymen for release from this horrible
slavery. Through ransom or through war? War, until we
should have settled accounts with England, was out of the
question. One thing, however, Noah felt before he left this
country: He saw that because Britannia ruled the waves,
Britons never, never would be slaves. He wished Americans
to be proudly free. There was a logical deduction, and hence-
forth he would never cease from proclaiming it: the United
States must build up a navy and use it to inspire the respect
born of fear.

Algiers neither feared nor respected the new republic. To
the injury of capture she had added the insult of dismissing
our Consul without ceremony. The United States, at the
moment, was reduced to the expedient of attempting to purchase the freedom of the *Edwin's* crew through indirection.
This delicate commission was not the least of the duties
with which Consul Mordecai M. Noah had been entrusted
by his government.

These were his instructions in this regard, as forwarded to
him by Secretary of State, James Monroe:

"On your way to Tunis, perhaps at Málaga, or Marseilles,
you may probably devise means for the liberation of our

unfortunate countrymen at Algiers, whose situation has excited the warmest sympathy of their friends, and indeed of the people generally of this country.—Should you find a suitable channel, through which you can negotiate their immediate release, you are authorised to go as far as three thousand dollars a man; but a less sum may probably effect the object. Whatever may be the result of the attempt, you will, for obvious reasons, not let it be understood to proceed from this government, but rather from the friends of the parties themselves. As yet, we have information only of eleven persons; the crew of the Brig Edwin, of Salem, being confined at Algiers, and it is to be hoped that no addition has been made to that number. If success should attend your efforts, you will draw upon this department for the necessary funds for paying their ransom, and providing for their comfortable returns to their country and friends."

Other prospects opened up before him as he paced the deck of the *Joel Barlow*. For long, as a result of his readings in the history of antiquity, he had cherished a desire to visit the country of Dido and Hannibal; "to trace if possible the field of Zama, or seek out the ruins of Utica: but travellers in those regions, now inhabited by barbarians, must be strongly protected . . ." He had another motive: "I was desirous of obtaining the most authentic information, in relation to the situation, character, resources and numerical forces of the Jews in Barbary, part of whom had been banished from their colleges at Cordova, and part were emigrants from Judea and Egypt. The only Jewish traveller in those countries whose works are extant is Benjamin, of Tudela in Spain, who travelled in the 13th century."

The *Joel Barlow*, formerly a privateer, was a schooner of some 160 tons, long and narrow, and, though originally pierced for fourteen guns, now carried but two nine pounders.

She was a letter of marque, with a cargo of cotton and a crew of eighteen men who struck Noah as being remarkably fine-looking. The small trunk cabin, which would have held two in comfort, housed for the voyage, besides Noah, the captain and his mate, another American gentleman, a little Frenchwoman who appears to have been a busybody, an old French lady and her somewhat demented son of twenty-five. Noah smiled wryly at the disappointment of the old French lady with America, based upon exactly ten days of residence in Charleston. She might have been a foreshadowing of certain contemporary visitors from abroad.

The sea was afloat with prize money, and Captain Buchanan of the *Joel Barlow*, after they had been some fifteen days out, and had been blown by favoring winds to the eastward of the Bermudas, was tempted into the chase of a promising quarry. Almost too late he discovered that she was a British gunboat convoying the fleet of merchantmen sailing toward the southeast. He was lucky to avoid capture himself. The incident, indeed, inspired him with a caution that was to prove, after all, unavailing.

For, when they had been thirty-five days out, delayed by calms, and considered themselves in the Bay of Biscay, within sight of their destination, an ominous sail arose on the far horizon,—a brig of war accompanied, as it turned out, by a cutter, apparently in pursuit of the American vessel. They made no gain on the *Joel Barlow*, and it began to appear that Noah's captain, once night had set in, could change his course and evade the pursuers. A black spot on the crimson disc of the setting sun disillusioned them. Another few hours and a British frigate was at their stern, firing a volley into their rigging. At the bow of the frigate the captain hailed the American vessel through his speaking trumpet. Where were they from?

"From Charleston", replied Captain Buchanan.

"Haul down your jib, sir, immediately."

The *Joel Barlow* had been captured by Sir Thomas Staines of the *Briton*, a ship attached to the blockading squadron off Rochefort, in command of Admiral Durham. The passengers of the American boat were transferred to the *Briton*, and Noah, swinging in the cot that had been slung for him, had time to ruminate upon the caprices of fortune. He had chosen France as his first stop because it would have been convenient for him to purchase there the consular gifts that he had been instructed to bear. Had he sailed in a licensed vessel for Spain, he could have avoided capture by the British, but would have exposed himself to the Algerines, who were haunting the Rock of Lisbon. It was better, after all, that England rather than the pirates should have got him.

It was the Fourth of July,—an ironical date for the marine imprisonment of a proud American freeman. Captain Staines, however, was the soul of courtesy; he showed the prisoners his ship, discussed with Noah their respective navies, ordered a stoup of wine for the *Barlow's* crew in honor of their Independence Day, and allowed his special guests to repair to the cabin, select their own music to be played by the band and even drink to United States victory.

Noah could see the peasants at work on the French coast; the sight filled him with a yearning to land and be on his mission. Lord Keith, however, politely informed him, in reply to an optimistic note, that he had no communication with the coast of France. There was no help for it; Noah would have to proceed to London. Shortly, after a couple of weeks of this marine shunting, they docked at Plymouth; here Noah was directed to report himself to the agent for prisoners of war.

The delay was not without its compensations, and Noah emerged from the experience with some very definite notions as to the requirements for a bigger and better United States navy. He admired the system by which boys of between seven and twelve years were trained on board ship for a midshipman's warrant; he approved British discipline and nautical science. He beheld the American sailor, however, as a volunteer, while too many of the Britons were impressed, under compulsion, brave but indifferent.

British officers were not so good as they had been in the days of Rodney and Drake. They were already exhibiting the quasi-effeminate character that Gilbert, sixty-five years later, was to satirize in his *H. M. S. Pinafore*. With a continuance of this tendency, predicted Noah, "a race of puny spirits will spring up . . . and instead of tar and turpentine, we shall have Cologne water, lip salve and essences."

Our Consul's progress to London seemed a translation, in terms of land, of his many-vesseled transportation from the scene of his capture to the Plymouth dock. Here he was, a gentleman of some importance, in the country of the enemy upon whose head, but a few months before, he had been hurling the defiance of his outraged Americanism. "Jimmy's" War . . . Noah's War . . . Was he surprised, even slightly disappointed, that England refused to regard him in the light of a dangerous alien? Surprised rather than disappointed, one would say.

3. LONDON TOWN

London at last, and the Angel Inn behind St. Clement's Church. *Laus Deo*, Noah sings, in Latin, appropriately. After a night of that troubled sleep which afflicts even so many experienced travelers on their arrival in strange places, he awakes to awakening London, and goes at once in search of lodgings to Adam Street, Adelphi. Thence to the Alien Office, in report as prisoner of war. How long will he be detained in England? And what disposition is to be made of him? These problems he deposits with Mr. Beasly, American agent for prisoners. For the present, he must appear every fortnight at the Alien Office. The rest of the time he may fill in as he desires. It is easy to predict what he will desire: people, pictures, institutions, books, theaters, traditions.

Westminster Abbey crowds him with the majesty of its evocations. He is not so blinded by hostility as to overlook that these glorious names, in part, "were the ancestors of our nation, and while we should endeavour to produce parallels, advance science and literature, and reward merit of our own, we have no occasion to be ashamed of our origin; there is much to admire and imitate."

Westminster Hall, and meditations upon the courts of justice in Great Britain, where "that equality which is denied to men in other situations, is enjoyed to the fullest extent; he participates equally in the benefits of the law, and has no cause to fear the uplifted hand of power (except in the admiralty court), when shielded by a jury of his peers" . . . The Strand, the Thames, the Exchange, each tagged with an appropriate observation . . . Unfortunately, neither Drury Lane nor Covent Garden was open, but some of the minor playhouses were, and from this American visitor they drew forth characteristic observations.

"The Lyceum is a small and somewhat confined theatre, being opened only in the summer. It was fashionably filled, but not crowded; before me on a front seat sat four black gentlemen elegantly dressed, and comporting themselves with attention and respect; they were agents from St. Domingo, on business for the government, and were treated with great deference. A South Carolina friend, who was with me, eyed them with some curiosity, but without much complacency; he was not familiarized to such scenes; habit is difficult to overcome. It would be highly honourable to us, if our policy in the south, could, with safety, hold forth a greater equality of rights to the Blacks. The organization of the government of Hayti, the talents of the monarch and the cabinet, and the general system of morality and good faith, are examples highly creditable to the inhabitants; and is at once a proof of that sound intellect, which for ages was denied by some writers to exist among them."

This was 1813. The contemporary war was regarded by Noah, as we have seen, in the light of an inevitable continuation of the Revolution. The Civil War, too, had already begun to sink its roots deep into American life.

In his own roundabout manner Noah comments upon the plenteous prevalence of prostitutes, gay and beautiful, in the Lyceum. English theaters, like our own, could be anterooms to the bordello . . . He pauses to remark that with the increase of civilization and learning, "the British sway in India must eventually be checked."

Returning to his lodgings he finds a note from Mr. Beasly containing welcome information: the government would find it quite agreeable for Consul Noah to leave the country. He speeds up his program; dashes off to visit the painter,

Benjamin West, now venerable and venerated, but much too old to fulfill his promise to visit the United States. In the figure of West he beholds, symbolized, the opportunity in the new republic, for the fostering of young talent . . . Noah, on the eve of departing from the mother country, contrasts the parent with the offspring.

Owing, perhaps, to the difference in climate, the American —he finds—is more "etherial" than the Englishman; English liberty is enjoyed largely in the imagination, being "empty and evanescent", except in the matter of individual movement. Wealth is the criterion,—"a blind passion, a diseased infatuation, which considers money as the sole desideratum . . . In England, the poor man is the poorest creature in existence, the mere cypher in society. The cultivated and accomplished mind, and the splendid genius, receive no deference if clothed in rags; hence persons are induced to assume appearances they can ill afford . . ." Noah feels keenly, before it is finally stigmatized by Lowell, the well-known condescension of this foreigner. As for the English woman, she is superior in many respects to her man. But "to complexions the most dazzling, and faces generally beautiful, they unite a disproportion of figure, an awkward gait, and ungraceful mode of dress."

Noah was, on the whole, not sorry to take English leave. "To an American . . . after visiting the principal objects of curiosity, this city ceases to be interesting." Back now to Falmouth, that crooked and dirty town, to take sail for Cadiz. Arrived there, he learned that it would be a week or ten days before a packet would be available. He hunted up Robert Fox, the Quaker, formerly American Consul for the port of Cadiz; although Noah was a Philadelphian, not until this moment had he found the opportunity to study the maligned sect, and to indorse, with qualifications, their stubborn adherence to mildness, tolerance and pacifism.

4. IBERIA

England, present enemy of the Americans, lay behind. Spain, ancient enemy of the Jews, greeted our Consul in the harbor of Coruna and a few days later was gleaming at him whitely from Cadiz. Noah had not desired to visit either of these countries; his ancestral prejudices fanned his dissatisfaction at capture and delay. As we northern Americans had risen against our oppressive motherland, and were now reënforcing the victory of the Revolution, so were the former Spanish dependencies at this very moment in self-assertive rebellion against their motherland, their stepmotherland, forging a new America of the south to companion our own liberties.

Of course, our Consul, who was once a Turk, Muly Malak, has an eye for the Spanish ladies. They constitute, he finds, especially in Andalusia, the important and influential part of the nation. Unconventionally, Noah blunts the celebrated Spanish point of honor. Suspicions, duennas, grated windows, bars and bolts? Pure romance. "There is less jealousy in Spain than in any other country I have visited. There is no fastidiousness in their families; a husband introduces you to his wife, with the most perfect confidence; and to his daughter, if single, with a perfect reliance, which is never shaken, in her virtue, and your integrity. There are seldom instances of an aberration from virtue on the part of unmarried women; and it is strangely irreconcilable, that after marriage, all restraint being removed, women are seldom found without a lover, or, as he is called, a *cortejo*; and what is most extraordinary, the lover and husband are affectionate friends, frequently inhabiting one house, and exercising an equality of jurisdiction. Spanish women have, generally, dark or olive complexions, large black piercing eyes, fine teeth . . . and a noble and majestic walk, for which they are eminently distinguished. They cannot be called beautiful, but they never fail to interest. Their vivacity and sensibility, the unaffected ease of their manners, their general politeness and address, joined to the advantages, resulting from the most rich and copious language in the world, give to them the most surprising advantages, and evidently place the men, in a secondary rank and condition."

Shades of Lope de Vega, Calderón, Tirso de Molina and Rojas y Zorrilla![1]

. . . Noah is delighted to behold, over the door of the Cadiz theater, a slab commemorating the constitutional admittance of actors to the status of human beings . . . He finds Spanish a language better adapted to tragedy than even French . . . The Spanish dances—*bolero, fandango, cachucha, zapateo* (to pronounce their names is in itself a dance) delight him . . . There are no blue-stockings, alas; in fact, these *bellas españolas* are but mediocre conversationalists and they know little or nothing about books . . . He is delighted, on meeting in Cadiz some deputies to the Cortes from South

---

[1] Franceso Rojas y Zorrilla, for example, in his famous play *Del rey abajo, ninguno* (*None Beneath The King*) has a husband who slays his lily-pure wife, whom he knows to be absolutely innocent, merely because she has been gazed upon covetously by another man. That man, for a time, the husband mistook for his king; only the king could so have betrayed him with impunity. No one beneath the king, however . . . Hence the title. Spanish classical drama abounds in like instances of the "point of honor." It is doubtful whether, in actual life, the point of honor (much more exigent than our own "unwritten law") was as imperative as on the stage.

America, to hear them call themselves, not Spaniards, but *americanos.*[1]

In Spain, Noah was to have little time for the speculative idling that was forced upon him in England. Serious business—he little knew how serious—lay immediately ahead. There was the strategy of ransoming those American sailors, without revealing to our enemy, Algeria, the hand of the United States government. There was a Tunisian ruler to be appeased with gifts . . . and how was one to proceed to Tunis? The young American needed guidance badly. The natural thing to do was to call at once upon our consul at Cadiz, Mr. Hackley. This he did.

5. COMMONER'S RANSOM

At Hackley's home lived Richard R. Keene, a native of Maryland who had become a Spanish citizen. Keene, having learned of Noah's special mission to Algiers, offered his services. He appeared to be the ideal man for the difficult business. As one born an American he would appreciate the government's motives; as one recognized in Algiers, and elsewhere, as a naturalized Spaniard, he could carry through the plan without revealing our official hand. On October 2, 1813, Noah addressed to Mr. Hackley a letter outlining his requirements and his readiness, under state authority, to pay as high as $3000., preferably less, for each man ransomed. The very next day Hackley replied, strongly indorsing Mr. Keene. Accordingly, after almost a month and a half of negotiations, Messrs. Noah and Keene drew up an agreement:

[1] In our own carelessness, we are accustomed even today to call a Colombian, a Cuban or a Chilean, let us say, by the general term Spaniard. It is as if a foreigner, forgetting the Revolution, were to call an Oklahoman, a Texan or a Dakotan, by the general term Englishman!

"Whereas, Mordecai M. Noah, consul of the United States of America, for the City and Kingdom of Tunis, in virtue of competent authority on the part of his government, proposes to Don Ricardo R. Keene, a Spanish subject, to effect the release, from Algerine captivity, of a certain number of citizens of the said United States, and to convey them to the most convenient place of safety, so as to facilitate their return to their country: And whereas the said Ricardo R. Keene agrees to attempt the accomplishment of said purpose: Now, it is hereby understood and settled between the said parties, that the following are the terms, to the observance of which, they mutually bind and pledge themselves, in reference to said negotiation.

"Mordecai M. Noah, as a remuneration to said Don Ricardo R. Keene, agrees to pay him in advance, one thousand dollars, for all the personal expenses which he may incur in this negotiation. If said Ricardo R. Keene does not succeed in securing the release of said captives, nothing further is he to receive; but in the event of success, the said Ricardo R. Keene is to receive a further compensation, to wit, of three thousand dollars, and any surplus that may be above the prices to be paid for the said captives, out of an allowance at the rate of three thousand dollars for each man, to be furnished by the said Mordecai M. Noah, as the ultimatum of the purchase money; so that there being, as is now understood, twelve, and twelve only,[1] of said captives, the amount of said purchase money to be thus furnished by said Mordecai M. Noah, on behalf of the United States, will be thirty-six thousand dollars.—Consequently, the said eventual surplus, will be the sum short of, or under, thirty-six thousand dollars, which may remain above the actual disbursement, in effecting said purchase.

"In the event of obtaining the release of said captives, funds are to be provided by said Mordecai M. Noah to effect their conveyance to a place of safety as aforesaid.

---

[1] The instructions of Secretary of State, James Monroe, mentioned eleven persons, not twelve.

"In testimony whereof, the said parties have interchange-ably affixed their hands, this 13th November, 1813, in the 38th year of American Independence.

M. M. NOAH,

(Signed)   R. E. KEENE."

While Keene awaited further orders, Noah was compelled, because of the war, to go to Gibraltar, there to establish those credits for the release of our seamen that he could not arrange in Cadiz. This settled, Noah, on January 20, 1814, wrote to Keene, authorizing him to draw upon Horatio Sprague of Gibraltar, through whom the credits had been arranged, at thirty or sixty days sight. He cautioned Keene against the usurious Algerian brokers, and authorized him further to procure for the released prisoners conveyance to any port in Spain. One strongly suspects that Keene received other instructions making of him, virtually, a spy in American service. For, while Noah filled himself with the sights and sounds and traditions of Gibraltar and Algeciras, evoking the pageant of Spanish history, Keene was bent not only upon ransoming slaves, but upon discovering the best manner of subjecting the Regency to attack.

After four months of silence, Keene sent to Noah, who had in the meantime been compelled to return to Cadiz, a letter dated Algeciras, May 22, 1814. Keene had, through compli-cated strategy, reached the ear of the Dey of Algiers . . . The Dey tartly replied to his offers that not even two million dollars could buy back the American slaves. Keene, about to return defeated, learned that one Charles Walker, escaped from an English frigate, had embraced the Mohammedan religion to prevent his recapture. Despite this conversion, the English consul, Mr. Hugh MacDonald, determined to claim him. And now it appeared that Walker was a native American. Mr. MacDonald, convinced of this, decided to help Keene rescue Walker. The Dey, at first obdurate, relented to this extent; he would deliver, instead of Walker, two of the American slaves. The two turned out to be the least important of the captives from the brig *Edwin*: William Turner of Salem and John Clark of New York.

Upon the heels of this episode four seamen, claiming to be Louisianians, were landed in Algiers from another English frigate, the *Franchise*. Though we were at war with England, and though impressment was one of the major issues of the conflict, MacDonald offered Keene the same service that he had given in the Walker case. The six Americans were in due season safely transported to Algeciras.

It had been a costly as well as a tricky business. For Turner and Clark $4000. had been demanded; this left, for Keene, $2000. But he spent so much of it in other objects connected with the rescue that almost nothing remained to him for his efforts. For the rescue of the four Louisianians, Keene charged half the price allowed for Turner and Clark. To be sure, his instructions did not cover this case at all; humanitarian principles, and obedience to the spirit rather than the letter of his authorization, had prompted him. Whether he should be paid in full he left to Noah and to the United States. He had been away from Cadiz six months in all, had risked his life as the secret agent of a hostile power, and had been forced to defray almost all his own expenses.

His letter ended with a long report upon the advisability of fighting the Algerines to the bitter end, in which, together with historical data, he offered practical advice as to topography and strategy.

Keene followed shortly upon his important communication. Here was for Noah a delicate problem. Should he, by indorsing Keene's claims, himself appear to be stepping beyond the limits of his official instructions? He decided that he would. "If any error is to be committed, let it be done on the side of humanity" . . .

"Besides", he afterward set down in self-exculpation, "I had with me the accounts of Col. Lear, late consul-general at Algiers, and though extremely cautious in my expenditures, and keeping within the purview of my instructions, yet when referring to his presents of jewels, his valuable donations in money, his eighty dollars for a cup of coffee, and other approved disbursements, which in the course of his administration, covered nearly a half million of dollars, I was satisfied, that the government would make no objections to a sum, disbursed by their orders, and for the protection of our seamen, for whose rights we were then waging war with a powerful nation. For the two seamen of the Edwin, Mr. Keene had paid $6000; these two sums, together with an exorbitant premium paid at Algiers, with the charter of a vessel to convey them to Spain, with provisions, clothing, travelling expenses, &c. swelled the account to $15,852. Had a charge been made for the six seamen, agreeable to my instructions, they would have amounted to $18,000. The sums had already been drawn for on my agent, and I received the men, provided for their comfortable return home, paid their passage to the United States, and drew bills on government at a loss of 18 per cent for all the disbursements, amounting to upwards of $18,000. I am thus particular in detailing the events of this negotiation, in consequence of the impressions, very generally circulated, that I went beyond orders, or that no part of my instructions authorized the mission. It will be seen by a reference to those instructions, and the result, that they have been adhered to virtually and substantially."

The business of the ransomed captives settled—or so Noah thought—he turned his eyes to France, the next stage in his progress toward Tunis. He took Spanish leave with as little regret as had accompanied him out of the right little, tight little isle. But not without the usual apostrophe. "Spain, Spain! . . . Arouse yourself! Shake off your insolence! and give your prejudices to the winds! . . . tolerate all religions; call back the Moors and the Jews . . . declare your provinces in South America, Sovereign and Independent; and establish a profitable commerce with them, founded on equal and exact justice . . . let industry, science, and the arts be encouraged, let honour and good faith prevail . . ."

It would require but ten years to prove that Noah, with regard to the Spanish colonial wars, was right. Predicting the independence of Spanish America, he predicted, too, that the genuine freedom of the colonies would depend upon "their rejection of Spanish laws and customs, a perfect system of religious freedom . . . Without these indispensable attributes of liberty, they will only be released from foreign chains, to put domestic shackles on themselves."

6. AMERICAN BEARING GIFTS

France, the sweetheart of Noah's Jeffersonian dreams, as England had been the stepmother of his political hatred, none the less did not detain our Consul to Tunis. Here was no enforced junket such as he had enjoyed in Great Britain and, in lesser degree, Spain. This was the threshold to his official duties, the first port-of-call of his intentions, whence he had been shunted by the accident of captivity. Naturally, on his progress, he would miss no opportunity to feast upon sights and sounds, upon theater, roads, historical associations and . . . the French ladies, who, it appears, more esteem the gift of a flower than a present of greater monetary value.

The Bey of Tunis, unfortunately, was not to be pleased so easily as these ladies of Marseilles. He desired, as Noah had been duly warned, something more substantial, if less fragrant, than pinks, violets, narcissus, roses, and sweet scented shrubs. At Tunis, indeed, there was considerable excitement over the heralded arrival of a new consul, and Noah's advisers suggested that he had better not leave France without a veritable shipload of perquisites. Having been instructed officially to appropriate $4000. to that end, Noah laid in a stock of cloth, cambric, brocades, watches, jewels, and even arms. Once again, because of the war between England and the United States, he found it difficult to negotiate a bill of exchange upon his country. Only at Paris, where we had a Minister and a banker, could this be arranged. It was either this, or wait in Marseilles until the end of the war.

Impatiently, Noah sets out for Paris, where he learns to his patriotic displeasure that he will have to wait, after all, until the conclusion of the war before he can negotiate his bills. He "does" the town,—the Louvre, the Palais Royal, the obligatory *et ceteras*. He finds the French to be great lovers of amusements, of music and the dance. They do not allow business to interfere with their pleasures, as do the English . . . Back to Marseilles, where, in the midst of his financial perplexities, a Mr. Belknap of Boston comes to his rescue, by procuring the needed funds through guaranteeing their repayment by the United States government. At once the Consul purchases his gifts, procures passage to Tunis on the Swedish storeship *Forsoken*, Captain Hesh, sailing in company of a brig of war under the same colors. He leaves France with paradoxical gifts, to a virtual enemy, of cannon, timber and balls.

No *civis Romanus* was ever prouder of his citizenship than was our Consul of his Americanism as he landed in Tunis. His theatrical eye was properly appreciative of the effect that he made as he drove in his cabriolet through the city, amidst the waving of consular flags. Here had not Hannibal once dwelt? And Scipio? And Charles the Fifth? Now followed Noah . . . His theatrical ear, having heard the salute from the ship, missed a salvo from the batteries. "A disgraceful article had crept into our treaty, by which we subjected ourselves to pay a keg of gunpowder for every gun fired in compliment; consequently, no interchange of such civilities ever took place." Comic operas, for all their extravagance, do not lie.

If, however, insufficient gun-fire greeted our Consul, before the week was over he had been welcomed with—a revolution. The Bey had been indisposed, and Noah had not yet had opportunity to convey to him our nation's gifts. Lo, at daybreak of the sixth day the American Consul was informed —officially—that the Bey, Ottoman Pasha, had been assassinated, together with Mariano Stinca, his Christian Secretary, and some sixteen others. For horrors, vengeances, and spectacular deaths, it was an Oriental overturn in the best tradition of melodrama.

The next day our Consul made arrangements to pay his respects—and his gifts—to Ottoman's successor, Mahmoud. Through no fewer than six gates, each heavily guarded, the

97

American party passed. Our Consul found new cause for patriotic indignation. Here, amid slaves, water-carriers, cooks, Arabs, janissaries, in the marble patio, Noah must wait for his audience with the ruler. " . . . No Bey of Tunis has ever thought proper to appropriate an apartment for the use of the foreign Consuls." What some of his unconscious attitudes must have been we may gather from his report of the scene. For, his man, Abdallah, having been relieved of his *attaghan*, or small sword, by a guard, "I imagined that they would make the same request of me, and held the hilt of my sword with a firm grasp." Noah was allowed, however, to pass armed into the Hall of Audience,—a gloomy space, topped by a fret-work roof over heavy pillars of marble, at the end of which, on an ottoman a few inches above the floor, nestling against his cushions, sat the Bey, Mahmoud.

It wounded Noah's pride to stoop and kiss the Pasha's hand; "a degrading and humiliating custom", he protested. But when in Tunis, do as the Tunisians. To be a diplomat is to bide one's time for revenge . . . and, in the Barbary states, to be forever handing our *douceurs* to officials, from the highest to the lowest. Two bands assailed his ears and went off with their payment in gold *maboobs* . . . then came the *bowebs* or door-keepers, then the guard of the wardrobe, then the slaves, until the Consul ran out of patience—and money . . .

Trouble, since Noah had departed from the United States, had come to him in shipfuls. Another ship was even now on the way . . . On January 17, 1815, our Consul wrote home to his government that the private armed schooner *Abaellino*, Captain Wyer, of six guns and seventy-six men, had anchored in the Bay.[1] She had captured the English schooner *Nancy* bound from Liverpool to Sicily with a "valuable cargoe of dry Goods", and had ordered that vessel to the port of Tunis. The *Nancy*, at the time of Noah's writing, had not yet arrived. The *Abaellino*, records Noah in his travelogue, with his usual patriotism, proudly italicized, was "a beautiful coppered brig, of surprising swiftness, and, if I am not mistaken, she anchored near the ruins of Carthage, completely armed and equipped, and had taken a valuable prize, *in less than sixty days after her keel had been laid in America*! What nation can boast of equal enterprise? What efforts in ancient or modern warfare, bear comparison with his?"

At once an important question arose: Would the United States be allowed to sell the prize? The English Consul contended that this was in violation of Great Britain's treaty with the Bey. The Bey was hardly ready to risk war with England. English prizes might be brought into the Bay of Tunis, was the·interpretation, but not sold. Noah, on the other hand, examining the treaty upon which this decision was based, discovered the stipulation that none of the *belligerents of Europe* was to dispose of British prizes in ports of the kingdom. Clearly, he argued, the American people was not included in this article.

This established, the Bey posed a more difficult problem. The United States could not sell prizes in any of the ports of the European nations. "Why, then, do you ask of me a privilege which no European power will grant you?" Noah needed all his wits to answer this one, and he directed his rebuttal not to the Bey's reason but to his cupidity. Each of the European powers, he pointed out, had received a

[1] The original letter, addressed to His Excellency H. W. Crawford, is in the private collection of Mr. Leon Hühner.

valuable consideration for the exclusion. Why had not the Bey been similarly paid? "What?" exclaimed that potentate? "Do the English pay other powers to exclude American prizes, and give me nothing for the same privilege? I, who am a great Prince. Consul, you may sell your prizes . . ."

The merchandise was soon landed, brought to Tunis and prepared for disposal. In his first diplomatic encounter, Noah had won . . .

Revolution, which had raised the Bey to this thorny throne, now sought to depose him. This time the *Sapatapa* (Prime Minister) Sidi Yusef, who had been promoted to power by Hamouda, predecessor of Ottoman, and had been continued in his ministerial office, attempted to do away with the present Bey, Mahmoud. Mahmoud had made him a freeman, and had given him his daughter in marriage, most likely as reward for his services in the assassination of Ottoman. Sidi Yusef, indeed, was virtual ruler. Yet Sidi Yusef, not content with the reality, lusted for the title that proclaims the rank. The conspiracy, betrayed by an underling, ended in the cunning slaughter of the over-ambitious *Sapatapa*. Seized by the beard, slit through the throat, stripped, he was eventually torn apart, literally, by a mob eager for vengeance upon a hated oppressor. From the terrace of his house, Noah beheld the magnifico, so arrogant but a moment before, trailed through the mud of Tunis, over rock and stone, to the din of a savagely shrieking populace. "Such is the fate of a sanguinary ambition, when evinced among barbarians."

Meantime, the *Abaellino* was cruising the waters for more prizes, and more trouble for our Consul. She had added to her captures a brig and a schooner, both laden with valuable cargoes; they had been manned and ordered to Tunis. The English brig of war, *Lira*, under Captain O'Reilly, had been instructed to cruise just outside the harbor, so that it might intercept the prizes and recapture them beyond the Bey's jurisdiction. The prizes, however, safely entered the Bay of Tunis, Noah watching them from the terrace of his consulate. O'Reilly, nevertheless, managed to take possession of both, sending them on to Malta. At once, under date of February 22, 1815, Noah addressed a protest to the first Minister of the Bey. Here was a clear violation of the treaty between Tunis and the United States. For the value of the vessels thus retrieved by England, Tunis was responsible.

The Minister regretted the "accident", but ridiculed the idea that his country was financially answerable. It was the United States that had been in the habit of purchasing Tunisian friendship and forbearance, not the other way around. Incensed, Noah replied that American rights would be insisted upon. As the *Abaellino* was at the moment bottled up in Tripoli by an English brig of war, it would be necessary to wait until she was released.

This did not happen until the beginning of May, when in conformity with the stipulations of the Treaty of Ghent, the English had raised their blockade. According to the declarations of the prizemasters, the two vessels illegally recaptured in the Bay of Tunis were valued at $46,000. Noah again demanded payment; again the Ministry refused to pay in full or in part.

While thus occupied in maintaining the dignity of the United States on the seas Noah did not surrender our dignity upon land. He had discovered, upon his arrival, that for nine years past Americans had been suffering all manner of insult. He determined that at the first opportunity he would impress the Bey with a new state of affairs. Shortly that opportunity arrived in the person of an Italian merchant, a signor Curadi, who entered the American Consulate one day, informing Noah that bills of exchange drawn on Leghorn for 20,000 piasters had been returned protested, and that his creditors were about to seize him and his property, which was worth double the sum that he owed. Curadi's rightful protector, Mr. Nissen, the Dutch Consul, was too completely in the Bey's power to be of any avail. Would the American Consul come to his aid?

Yes, replied Noah, but in one way only, since he could not very well usurp Mr. Nissen's powers. If Curadi desired to claim the protection of the American flag, he should have it. Whereupon Curadi made of our Consulate his sanctuary. Surely enough, next morning the Bey made demand for the surrender of Curadi as an evading debtor. Noah, who would not willingly miss a melodramatic effect, replied that no one had ever been given up who had taken refuge under the flag of the American Consulate. For several days this little comedy of demand and rejection was played. One morning, however, it came to Noah's ears, through his terrified drago-man, Abdallah, that the Bey threatened to send twenty Mamelukes to the Consulate, to cut the Christians to pieces. Abdallah's terror invaded Curadi. The effect upon Noah, on the other hand, was to increase his determination.

Curadi's creditors, who could have settled their affairs with the Italian under Noah's roof, had preferred to bribe the Bey to get the man out of the Consulate; the Bey, assuming that Noah did not know his own rights in the matter, had accepted . . . Our Consul was supplied with arms and ammunition. Up went the United States flag, shut went all gates and doors. Bring on your Mamelukes!

Curadi, it appears, now lost courage completely. Let Noah, he entreated, take him to the Bey at Bardo and permit him to present his case to the ruler. Confronted by our Consul demanding an explanation of the projected attack by the Mamelukes, the Bey denied ever having said such a thing. And poor Abdallah, to whom the Bey had made the threat in person, was compelled to deny the story. Curadi was allowed sixty days in which to dispose of his property and make payment to his creditors. Noah returned from the seat of the palace to Tunis, again triumphant in his vindication of American rights.

It was not long, however, before he was back at Bardo, again in the rôle of national vindicator. For Curadi had been tricked into a dungeon of the palace. Let him be instantly released, demanded Noah, now more wroth than ever. The Bey's son, Hassan Bey, author of the plot, was implacable. Whereupon our Consul replied that if Curadi were not at once brought forth, he would strike the American flag and end on the spot the peaceful relations between Tunis and the United States.

Return tomorrow, suggested Hassan Bey.

Now or never, countered Noah.

It was now. From a dismal dungeon, stifling, infested with vermin, Noah for the second time within the week delivered Curadi, this time to eventual prosperity. The American flag had been preserved inviolate. The other Consuls rejoiced. It was the first time that such a case had been crowned in Bardo with such a victory.

7. CARTHAGE . . . THE JEWS OF TUNIS

Among Noah's personal interests in the territory of his Consulate were the historic past of Carthage and Hannibal, and the historic present of the Jews of Barbary. Between the various excitements of his office he found time to examine both, not to speak of Mohammed, the women of the Bey's harem, national customs and commercial statistics.

Carthage speaks to him from its destruction, pregnant with lessons for all civilization, but especially significant to "an American, to a citizen of the only Republic on earth." It is a lesson in the blessings of liberty, and in the curse of materialism. Hannibal rises from the ruins, the greatest hero of antiquity, yet second after all to Napoleon.

As for the Jews of Barbary, Noah did not approach them with the unstinted tenderness of a coreligionary. Indeed, during the troubles over the vessels captured by the *Abaellino* he had noticed that commerce in Tunis was centered in the hands of the Jews, and that they managed by hook or crook to stifle any competition. Yet he saw, for this state of affairs, reason (which is not necessarily justification) both historical and psychological.

The skill of the Jews in business, he found, and the advantage that they take of Christians and Moors, "have been the subject of severe and just animadversion; they will, if not narrowly watched, avail themselves of opportunities to overreach and defraud; for this the world has showered upon them opprobrium and insult. But has the world ever held out proper inducements for the Jew to be honest, except in countries where they enjoy equal privileges? If they are just, they are not credited for it; if they do a good action, approbation does not follow; proscribed and insulted, their virtues denied, public opinion attaching to them the odium due to bad men of all persuasions, no friend, no solace in misfortune, hunted, despised, and shunned, it is still asked of them to be honest, when they receive no reward or gratitude for their honesty, when no man will give them credit for one good action!—What is the incitement to virtue? The approbation of conscience and the world; the Jew in Barbary has no friend but his wealth; *that* purchases protection and toleration, and he is very zealous and active in the accumulation of it, and if he is not fastidious in his mode of acquirement, he is not singular—exclusive honesty is the property of no sect."

Noah relates without enthusiasm an anecdote illustrative of the Jews' power in Tunis. An American Consul, having beaten a Jew, and having been complained against by the Jew to the Bey, was ordered by the ruler to humble himself by kissing the Jew. The kiss was duly given and, what is worse, received.

In Noah's day the Kingdom of Tunis contained some 60,000 Jews, of whom a third lived in the city of Tunis. They had their own quarter, and were governed by an appointee of the Bey, thus enjoying a certain self-rule. The men were permitted to wear no colors, except the blue of their collarless and sleeveless frocks; stockings they wore only in winter; black slippers, a small black skull-cap over their shaved heads and a blue silk kerchief, together with loose linen sleeves and drawers of the same material completed their costume. Their houses were low and mean; they cared for their own poor, supporting them by applying to this purpose half of the doubled fees that the rich were charged for luxuries. Education was limited to instruction of children in Hebrew.

Polygamy, not forbidden by Mosaic law, was very rare among the Jews here . . . The Jewish women were fat, and awkward in their yellow and purple trousers and their colored silk head-kerchiefs. "Those who are single have their hair plaited in two or three rows, to the end of which they suspend coloured ribands; they wear no stockings, but slippers, with silver cinctures around their ankles; and the soles of their feet, their hands, nails and eyebrows, tinged and coloured of a dark brown, from the juice of an herb called *Henna*. When they walk they unloosen from their neck a piece of black crepe, with which they cover their mouth and chin, leaving the upper part of their face bare. As to their living and domestic concerns, I can say nothing, never having visited any of them."

One finds it difficult to account for these six last words . . .

When these Jewish belles were dressed for a ball at the American Consulate, in celebration of Washington's birthday, their host, our Noah, found them tasteless beneath all their jewels, brocades, tissue, lama and gauze. Those corpulent, unwieldy figures,—the Oriental conception of beauty, which weighs what it woos! The women rarely met except at the burial ground, where, each Friday afternoon, with their little jar and brush, they cleaned and whitewashed the tombs of their dear departed, addressing the dead with the concerns of the living, as is done the world over.[1]

---

[1] Commenting upon misconceptions as to the Barbary Jews, Noah refers to a Narrative by Captain Riley in which that author writes, "The Jewish women are considered by the men as having no souls, nor are they allowed to enter the Synagogue but once a year, nor do the women partake of their sacraments, which consist of bread, wine and circumcision." To which Noah makes reply that the women

Moorish gentlemen, it appeared from Noah's experience, were rather more jealous of their ladies than the Spaniards had seemed to be. Once, visiting a country house near Carthage, Noah had been required to state his business and his position. American Consul? At once the Moor cried out, "Run and tell the women to get out of the way. The American Consul is coming!"

The Consul managed nevertheless to catch a glimpse of the sequestered beauties—who had "waddled to their alcoves" —peeping at him through their curtains. As for the ladies of the harem—real Turkish beauties, not the imitation belles of Muly Malak's imaginary Orient—they dressed very richly; they devoted their day, indeed, to their persons, which they adorned in velvets, silks, gauzes, "beautifully embroidered at the bosoms and cut up in caftans and robes, without taste"; their feet were bare, shod with embroidered slippers; their hair, loose, aglitter with jewels; their ears weighed down by rings, their arms encircled in bracelets, their ankles girt with cinctures. "They use abundance of otto of roses, which is manufactured in Tunis of the first quality, and powder their hair with pulverized cloves."

But ah, the perishable standards of aesthetics! The Turkish girls, for marriage, were *fattened* with the famous dish, *cooscoos*: a "species of granulated paste, made of flour, and dried on the terrace . . . steamed down, with beef, fowls, vegetables of several kinds, eggs, marrow, saffron and cinnamon . . . really an excellent dish."

---

freely visit the synagogue, that they partake generously of bread and wine . . . "And as to the *other* part of the sacrament, I should be happy if the learned navigator would point out how the *women* could partake of that."

Behold now another ship sailing over the waters and laden, like so many ships before it, with a cargo of new trouble—this time climactic—for Consul Mordecai Manuel Noah.[1]

[1] The account in this division is based chiefly upon Noah's book, *Travels in England, France, Spain and The Barbary States in The Years 1813-14 and 15*. The book was published in New York and in London (see Bibliography) in 1819. In 1816 Noah wrote, for the *Democratic Press*, Philadelphia, and for several other Gazettes that he does not name, "Sketches of the Barbary States," taken from his travel Journal. These, for the purposes of his book, he later recapitulated. (See *Travels*, note, page 247).

As to the Jews in the Barbary States, he speaks (*Travels*, page 308) of a small volume, "the publication of which may be dangerous to them, while the north of Africa is in the hands of Barbarians, and I am not without hopes that the time will come, when some civilized power, capable and determined, will wrest that fine portion of the world from the hands of the assassins, and relieve an unfortunate race, who only require mildness and tolerance to make (them) useful and beneficial." That small volume he appears never to have published. Some of the material may have gone into his later speeches on the restoration of the Jews.

V

RECALL AND VINDICATION

1. PEACE AND WAR

FROM Gibraltar to Tunis came American newspapers containing accounts of the Treaty of Ghent and of our preparations for war against the pirates of Algiers. By the same arrival, however, came news that tempered severely the rejoicing of Consul Noah. The local British Consul politely informed the American Consul at Tunis that from Gibraltar he had received his drafts upon the American government for $18,743,—that these had been returned protested,—that, with losses and damages the amount had risen to $21,613,—and when would Mr. Noah find it agreeable to pay this sum?

Here was a pretty kettle of fish . . . The administration at Washington knew that a Consul who could not pay his bills, especially among these barbarians, at once lost caste. This could be nothing other than a hint for him to resign; that is, if under the circumstances he could avoid arrest. Richard Oglander, British Consul at Tunis, could seize Noah's person and property; and the owners of the bills had given Oglander strict orders. Yet—again a British enemy came to his rescue

—Oglander consented to keep the matter secret until the arrival of the American squadron, the commander of which, he felt sure, would redeem the credit of the United States.

Noah must have had his doubts, for at once he began preparations for leaving the hotbed of Tunis. "It is sufficient sacrifice for a citizen to serve his country in this unhospitable part of the world, without sustaining loss of credit." Surely enough, the squadron was to save the face of Noah in these Mediterranean waters, but in a way that the squadron was not to know, and that our Consul, at the moment, not so much as suspected.

At peace with England, we had declared war upon Algiers. A small force under Commodore Decatur, fit rather for protection of our commerce than for attack upon the enemy, had been ordered to the Mediterranean, where it would be required upon the conclusion of peace with Great Britain. Commodore Bainbridge, with a larger squadron, was to assume chief command and strengthen Decatur's fleet. With Decatur was Mr. Shaler, empowered together with Decatur to negotiate a treaty, and named in addition Consul-General to the Barbary States.

Decatur's mission sailed over a path of triumph. Within *forty days* after his squadron had left the United States (Noah again patriotically italicizes), and in the 40th year of our Independence (forty is a number famous in biblical history) we had won two signal victories on the sea, and had compelled the Dey of Algiers to sign, at the mouth of the cannon, a treaty that placed America on a footing with the most favored nation.

Our honor had been won with our courage. Tribute was abolished. Our captives were returned without ransom. Slavery of prisoners was relegated to the past. Compensation for American property was stipulated. "An event", crows Noah, "which for facility, energy, and promptness, has no parallel in the annals of history."

Intercommunication was, early in the nineteenth century, so slow that our declaration of war against Algiers, the departure of our squadron, its arrival, its naval victories, and the signing of the treaty, had all been effected before Consul Noah received news of it in Tunis. It was not until July 30, 1815, that the welcome sight of the United States flag greeted Noah from off Cape Carthage, flying from the flagship on whose deck, within an hour, he was received with the honors due to his station . . . Reversal, under the seal of an envelope, lay in store.

Noah was invited into the cabin by Commodore Decatur. A few formalities, and then, going to his escritoire, Decatur drew out a despatch, handed it to our Consul, and requested him to read it without further ceremony. Breaking the seal of the United States, Noah began silently to read. He could not believe his eyes. The communication came from the Department of State, and was dated April 25, 1815,—two years and twenty days after the date upon Noah's secret instructions. It was provokingly brief:

"Sir,

"At the time of your appointment, as Consul at Tunis, it was not known that the RELIGION which you profess would form any obstacle to the exercise of your Consular functions. Recent information, however, on which entire reliance may be placed, proves that it would produce a very unfavourable effect. IN CONSEQUENCE OF WHICH, the President has deemed it expedient to revoke your commission. On the receipt of this letter, therefore, you will consider yourself no longer in the public service. There are some circumstances, too, connected with your accounts, which require a more particular explanation, which, with that already given, are not approved by the President.

> I am, very respectfully, Sir,
> Your obedient servant,
> (signed) JAMES MONROE.

Mordecai M. Noah, esquire, &c. &c."

This, following so swiftly upon the protestation of Noah's notes, spelled disaster. Decatur's duty was clear: Noah was no longer Consul; the Commodore must send an officer to the Consulate, take possession of the seals and the archives, return Noah to Tunis, and in all likelihood to a dungeon such as the hole whence he had rescued Curadi . . . Noah raised his eyes from the official document to Decatur. A glance told him that the Commodore knew nothing of the contents of the letter. Oglander had given our Consul until the arrival of the squadron. He must act at once, aided by all his wits. Assuming an air of indifference, he pocketed the document and proceeded to inform Decatur upon the nature of our dispute with Tunis, bearing out his report with official papers prepared for the purpose.

The perilous instant had suggested a daring way out. Noah meant to collect, through Decatur, the prize money due from the Bey for the vessels captured by the *Abaellino*. With this money he planned to redeem the injured credit of the United States, paying the protested bills, restoring his personal honor, and chancing the consequences. His urgency, indeed, must have aroused suspicion in Decatur, especially when he suggested that it would be well for the Commodore to remain

on board until demands for payment—to be written by
Decatur in a letter to the Minister of Marine—should be
complied with.

Decatur bridled, as well he might. "You may probably
imagine," he asserted, "that I am under your orders. If you
do, it is proper to undeceive you." Under Noah's orders!
If only Decatur had known! The Commodore, who had
been pleased with Noah's report and his suggestions for ending the difference with Tunis, was with difficulty won back
to compliance. Noah spent the night sleeplessly upon the
cabin floor. Fife and drum summoned him at dawn, and a
boat and hands returned him and his dragoman, Abdallah,
to the Cape.

There, seated upon the eminence, a lone figure against
this splendor of gold—for the sun had just risen upon Noah's
despair—our Consul delivered himself up to unspoken lamen-
tations, addressed to the trilling birds that winged across
the Mediterranean water, to the sky, to the perspective of
the masts rocking gently at anchor.

Once more he read the letter from Mr. Monroe . . . "My
religion an object of hostility? I thought I was a citizen of
the United States, protected by the constitution in my
religious as well as in my civil rights. My religion was known
to the government at the time of my appointment, and it
constituted one of the prominent causes why I was sent to
Barbary; if then, any 'unfavourable' events had been created
by my religion, they should have been first ascertained, and
not acting upon a supposition, upon imaginary consequences,
have thus violated one of the most sacred and delicate rights
of a citizen. Admitting, then, that my religion had produced
an unfavourable effect, no *official* notice should have been
taken of it; I could have been recalled without placing on
file a letter thus hostile to the spirit and character of our

institutions. But my religion was not known in Barbary; from the moment of my landing, I had been in the full possession of my Consular functions, respected and feared by the government, and enjoying the esteem and good will of every resident.—What injury could my religion create? I lived like other Consuls, the flag of the United States was displayed on Sundays and Christian holidays; the Catholic Priest, who came into my house to sprinkle holy water and pray, was received with deference, and freely allowed to perform his pious purpose; the bare-footed Franciscan, who came to beg, received alms in the name of Jesus Christ; the Greek Bishop, who sent to me a decorated branch of palm on Sunday, received, in return, a customary donation; the poor Christian slaves, when they wanted a favour came to me; the Jews alone asked nothing of me. Why then am I to be persecuted for my religion?"

2. Article xi—The United States a Christian Nation?

In his perplexity, in his need for the support of principle and precedent against this attack upon his religion and his race, which, if permitted to pass unchallenged, would reverberate with evil consequences in the later history of his republic, Noah bethought himself of his political sponsor, Joel Barlow. Had not Barlow, writing a treaty for one of the Barbary States, inserted an Article XI, which was confirmed by the Senate of the United States?

"Article XI—As the government of the United States of America *is not*, IN ANY SENSE, *founded on the Christian religion*—as it has, in itself, no character of enmity against the law, religion, or tranquillity of Mussulmen; and as the said States never have entered into any war, or act of hostility against any Mahometan nation, it is declared by the parties, that no pretext *arising from religious opinions*, shall *ever* produce an interruption of the harmony existing between the two countries."[1]

Was President Madison, Noah queried, unacquainted with this Article? If Noah's religion was really an obstacle (and it was not) were we to yield so pliantly to foreign bigotry? Were we to surrender noble principles to the superstition of a Barbary pirate? The Bey of Tunis did not know that our Consul was a Jew. Had he known it, and objected to it, Noah would have made him understand in plain language that a properly accredited representative of the United States must be received and respected regardless of creed. His defense of America and of the Jew's right to his beliefs would have been one and the same, a glorification of freedom in the temporal and the spiritual spheres.

Noah had gone to Tunis as an American; his right to his creed was an article of his American faith. Whoever assailed his Judaism assailed his Americanism. Thus he reasoned. And, behold! It was not the Bey, it was the United States, that now assailed his Judaism! Clearly, he had enemies at home. Later, he came to suspect Colonel Lear, whose readiness to purchase the condescension of the Barbary pirates he is at pains, in his *Travels*, to condemn.

"After having braved the perils of the ocean, residing in a barbarous country, without family or relatives, supporting the rights of the nation, and hazarding my life from poison or the stiletto, I find my own government, the only protector I can have, sacrificing my credit, violating my rights, and insulting my feelings, and the religious feelings of a whole nation. O! shame, shame!! The course which men of refined or delicate feelings should have pursued, had there been

---

[1] Capitalization and italics follow the text of the Article as printed by Noah on page 379, and as emphasized by him for his special purpose. A few paragraphs later I discuss the authenticity of Article XI itself.

grounds for such a suspicion, was an obvious one. The President should have instructed the Secretary of State to have recalled me, and to have said, that the causes should be made known to me on my return; such a letter as I received should never have been written, and, above all, should never have been put on file. But it is not true, that my religion either had, or would have produced injurious effects."

Jews, as Noah recorded, had been serving with distinction in and for this very part of the world. Abraham Busnac had been Minister at the Court of France for the Dey of Algiers; Nathan Bacri, at the time of writing, was Algerine Consul at Marseilles, and his brother similarly in the service at Leghorn; the Treasurer, Interpreter and Commercial Agent of the Grand Seigneur at Constantinople were Jews; in 1811 the British Government had entrusted Aaron Cardoza of Gibraltar with the negotiation of a commercial arrangement in Algiers; the first Minister from Portugal to Morocco was a Jew, Abraham Sasportas, who was received with open arms and formed a treaty; Moses Massias had been sent, by Ali Bey of Tunis, as ambassador to London; Major Massias, the father of Moses, was at this very moment in the army of the United States.

"It was not necessary," argued Noah, "for a citizen of the United States to have his faith stamped on his forehead; the name of freeman is a sufficient passport, and my government should have supported me . . . There was also something insufferably little, in adding the weight of the American government, in violation of the wishes and institutions of the people, to crush a nation, many of which had fought and bled for American Independence, and many had assisted to elevate those very men who had thus treated their rights with indelicate oppression. Unfortunate people, whose faith and constancy alone have been the cause of so much tyranny and oppression, who have given moral laws to the world, and who receive for reward approbrium and insult. After this, what nation may not oppress them?"

This is one of the most important moments in Noah's life. It is the crucial experience that brings his Jewishness into sharp focus. That Jewishness, hitherto a motif of quiet, unostentatious pride, thereafter becomes a motif of proclamation, never separated from an equally proud and self-conscious Americanism.

Here he was, a young man of thirty, who had maintained the dignity of his nation through a most trying series of episodes in one of the most difficult spots in the world. He was ambitious. He had in him the stuff of which international figures are made. He had every justification for looking forward to a life of high service to his nation,—a life agreeably set against the literary and philosophic pursuits of a gentleman. And suddenly, to this grandson of Jonas Phillips, comes virtual betrayal of his race at the hands of his nation. It was a mortal wound, and Noah responded with the outcries of an animal at bay.

Article XI, invoked by Noah, has a curious history. It was for long supposed to be a translation from the Arabic of the treaty ratified between the United States and Tripoli in 1797. It turns out to have been nothing of the sort. That Article, as Noah phrased it, and as it was, up to our very day, supposed to read, is not to be found in the Arabic. How it ever appeared in the printing of our national treaties is still a mystery. "Nothing in the diplomatic correspondence of the time throws any light on the point; and it is perhaps an equal mystery why attention has never heretofore been called to the complete discrepancy between the original and the supposed translation."

It appears, from a very recent reëditing of the Treaty, that the Arabic text opposite the famous Article XI, which has long been used by those who maintain that the United States is not a Christian country, "is in form a letter, erudite and flamboyant and withal quite unimportant, written by the Dey of Algiers to the Pasha of Tripoli.[1]

Noah, then, invoked an article that was not part of the original treaty of 1797. And he invoked it, by the way, not for the clause that has been interpreted as indicating the non-Christianity of the American nation, but for its implicit protection of religious freedom. For Noah, despite the opening statement of the spurious article, expressly states that "Although no religious principles are known to the Constitution, no peculiar worship connected with the government, yet I did not forget that I was representing a Christian nation."[2]

[1] This important revision was announced late in April, 1931, by Hunter Miller, editor of the new edition of American treaties with foreign governments. See vol. II. Mr. Miller points out that ever since 1800 or thereabouts the archives of the Department of State have contained an Italian translation of the Arabic that, "generally speaking, is a reasonably fair equivalent of the Arabic text.

"The most casual examination of that Italian translation shows that in respect of Article XI it does not bear the slightest resemblance to the supposed English translation, and on that Italian translation is written a statement to the effect that the English translation of the time was extremely erroneous.

"That statement was written by James Leander Cathcart, who was one of the American captives in Algiers for more than ten years, from 1785 to 1796, and who for twenty years thereafter was a representative of the United States abroad at various posts in North Africa and elsewhere."

[2] See *Travels*, page 379. Noah never, indeed, forgot that he had been "representing a Christian nation." Toward the very close of his life he returned to the controversy, and to his peculiar interpretation of Barlow's supposed statement to the Tripolitans. It appears, from a correspondence that is reprinted and commented upon at length in *The Occident*, vol. vii, pp. 563–564, corresponding to January, 1850, that Noah had raked up the affair in his *Messenger*, and that he had been pressed, by *The Commercial Advertiser* of New York, for elucidation.

Since in the Constitution there is no recognition of any God, no authorization of any creed, we are not in any official sense, despite Noah's interpretation of his status as a representative of the United States, a Christian nation. The absence of an Article XI does not alter the logic of the case. That which is not affirmed is not therefore necessarily denied; nor is that which is not denied therefore necessarily affirmed. The spirit of the spurious article is valid, even lofty, both in its denials and its affirmations. Good authority has often been quoted for evil practice. Let it pass that Noah, in a high purpose, should in all good faith have cited a phantom text.

There was another possible cause, and a serious one, for Noah's removal: malversation of public funds. This was hinted at in Monroe's letter of revocation. It may have been, though all available documentary evidence suggests a contrary interpretation, that Noah used the Jewish question as a means of sidetracking public attention from the more material aspects of his case. If this were a substantial cause,

Noah hereupon wrote to the *Commercial Advertiser*, quoting the text that has just been commented upon, and adding that he "dissaproved the article," because it seemed to him that Mr. Barlow, being, or having become, a free-thinker, had engrafted upon it his private prejudices. "It was quite unnecessary," thought Noah, "to inform the Mussulmen of Tripoli that in effect we had no religion at all."

This looks very much as if it were Noah, not Barlow, who was engrafting private prejudice upon an interpretation. *The Occident*, taking him up, informed him that Barlow, in fact, had been for several years a chaplain in the army . . . "during all which time his ministry was acceptable to his hearers." Very properly the commentator of *The Occident* went on to say that the United States did not officially look upon Christianity or Judaism or Atheism as the law of the land. "There is freedom for all, and rights and protection for all."

Very evidently Noah, though wishing, late in life as early, to proclaim the principle of religious freedom, wished to do so in a manner that should not be offensive to Gentile citizens of his country.

asked Noah justly, why had not the government plainly indicated as much? That was a proper ground for recall. On this score he was easy. When the time came, he gave an excellent account both of himself and his finances.

This time, however, was not yet. The Bey of Tunis still remained to be convinced in the matter of that payment without which Noah would be left despoiled in a hostile foreign country, his religion aspersed, his patriotism outraged, his integrity under suspicion.

3. PAID IN FULL—FAREWELL TO TUNIS

Decatur had written to the Minister of Marine a letter demanding payment in full for the value of the vessels that had been allowed, in violation of treaty, to elude the *Abaellino*. The Minister, in a Tunisian huff, sent for Noah.

"This is not," he preambled, "a proper and respectful manner of doing business. Why does not your Admiral make his complaints to the Bey in person? Why does he demand the payment of us for prizes which the British have illegally carried away, and demand an answer forthwith? We are not accustomed to be treated in this manner. There was a time when you waited our pleasure to establish a treaty, and paid us for it, and gave us presents whenever we demanded them, and all within my recollection."

Noah, with a United States squadron off shore, calmly answered that Decatur would not land until he had received a favorable reply. Whereupon the Minister assured him, once more, that the money would not be paid. Noah, leaving Bardo in an American huff, afterwards learned from the Christian slaves that the Dutch Consul, Mr. Nissen, sent for by the Minister, advised him to resist payment, as neither

Noah nor Decatur had authority to declare war, and would not dare to commence hostilities. Whereupon our Consul dispatched "a mild and friendly note" to Nissen, urging him to keep out of the matter, and suggesting that within twenty-four hours he would lose his head for having given improper advice to the Bey.

Three or four times the Minister recalled Noah.

"What is the reason, Consul", he asked, with feigned self-assurance, "that you are so tranquil? Before your fleet was here you were loud and positive. Now that you are backed by a force, you have suddenly become very quiet and indifferent."

Why not? countered Noah . . . Algiers had just been brought to our terms. The squadron was primed for victory. Rather than a treaty that was not respected, no treaty at all . . . The Minister left Tunis for Bardo, where a report reached the palace that Commodore Decatur had been detected, in the disguise of a common sailor, taking soundings of the bay. This looked too much like earnest. It looked more earnest when Captain Gordon, Commander Jesse D. Elliott, Surgeon Kennon and some midshipmen appeared in Tunis. Gordon and Elliott had instructions from Decatur to accompany Noah to the palace and hear the answer to his demand. Crowds met them at Bardo. The Bey, deceived by the unmartial appearance of Gordon, addressed him insolently.

"Who are you?"

"I am second in command of the squadron, Sir, and I am here to know whether you are ready to do us justice."

"Why does not your Admiral come on shore, then? Why am I treated with so much disrespect by him?"

"He will not land, Sir, until you decide to pay the value of these vessels which you permitted the British to take from us."

There was a violent outbreak from Mustapha, cut short by Commander Elliott. "We did not come here to be insulted," he observed. "This interview must be cut short. Will you, or will you not, pay for these vessels? Answer nothing but that!"

"Well then," replied Mustapha, glowering furiously, "We will pay for them, but have a care, our turn comes next. Tell your Admiral to come on shore. I'll send the money to the Consul. I am a rich Prince, and don't value it. Go!"

Commodore Decatur landed the next day and, while awaiting the Bey's representation at the American Consulate, was received by the various consuls. Enter the brother of the Prime Minister, accompanied by a slave carrying the promised money. Rais Hassuna, beholding Decatur in friendly converse with the British consul, throws down the moneybags in a fury.

"See there, Sir," he roars at Mr. Oglander, "what we have to pay for your insolence, and the shameful conduct of your vessels. It is thus, Sir, you violate the rights of others, and leave us to answer for it."

"If any wrong has been done you, Hassuna," answers the British Consul, "address your complaints to the British government, and you will have justice."

It was the end of a most curious episode. Noah, in a sense, had again taken the law into his own hands, by keeping secret from Decatur the contents of the letter from Mr. Monroe. But Decatur, too, had taken the law into *his* hands. Nissen had been right; Decatur carried no instructions whatsoever about the Tunis imbroglio, as nothing had been known of it when he left the United States.[1] It was, all around, a pretty

[1] See *Decatur*, by Irving Anthony. New York, 1931. Pp. 252–254.

high-handed business, but it served its purpose. The amount
paid was $46,000, and once again Noah must have quaked
in his shoes when Decatur showed a disposition to carry that
sum off to the United States. The Commodore, indeed, was
rather pointed in his investigation of Noah's right to receive
and retain the money. All that the Consul vouchsafes us is
that "I satisfied him on this head." How, he does not tell.
Perhaps he informed Decatur that he was the agent for the
owners of the vessels in litigation. Certainly he could not
have reported the story of the protested notes, or even now
confess the contents of the document received from Monroe.
"He probably thought", relates Noah of Decatur, "that I
was to remain in Tunis, when I expected to be in the United
States before him. And from the want of explanation, probably arose some unfavorable impressions on his part, which,
however, I could not distinctly learn had existed."

Noah lost no time in depositing in the hands of the Swedish
Consul, subject to the order of Mr. Oglander, the sum of
$21,613 to cover the protested bills. Then there were duties
to pay and presents to purchase. The balance of $15,000.
was sent on to Marseilles to buy a cargo for the owners in
the United States. This they afterwards received . . . Now
to shake the dust of Tunis off his shoes.

It was almost as difficult to escape the place as it had
been to reach it. The Bey must not know that he was
leaving for good, nor learn the reasons leading up to this
departure. Noah decided to pretend that he was going on
a brief visit to Italy.

The Bey seemed to be alarmed. "Why, there is no dispute
I hope, Consul. We are on good terms, are we not?"

"Perfectly so. I leave Mr. Ambrosio to take charge of my
affairs until my return, and should I not return, you will

receive no Consul except he brings a commission from the President."

"His government," explained the Minister of Marine to the Bey, "is about to send him to a better place." This, to Noah's ears, was sharply ironical. "So far," he comments, "were these people from believing that my government had recalled, discredited, and probably intended to disgrace me. The Bey shook me kindly and affectionately by the hand; we had always been on good terms, and he had treated me with marked deference, the ministers all reciprocated (sic) their good wishes and kind remembrances, and I left the palace regretted, I believe, by all. So much for the *unfavorable effects of my religion!*"

And how much, one wonders, for the consistency of our Consul, who, at this farewell, suddenly transforms the Minister and the Bey from pirates into civilized gentlemen?

He left for France on the frigate *Fleur de Lis*, bound for Toulon. Before he could land, he was compelled to undergo thirty days quarantine as an arrival from Barbary . . . He was content with the manner in which he had fulfilled his duties. Well he might be. His most practical achievement is best to be appreciated when contrasted with the supine methods of a Colonel Lear, who was ever ready to conciliate the pirates with gold. Just before Decatur had won his signal triumph over Algiers, Lear had advised the purchase of peace from that country at the price of $300,000. Decatur, instead, paid in gunpowder, proceeded to Tunis in the same warlike spirit, and from Tunis went on to Tripoli, using like methods for like results.

At Marseilles Noah met his successor, Mr. Anderson, whose path he eased with much practical assistance. To avoid a tedious sailing on the Mediterranean at this season our ex-Consul crossed country to Bordeaux, where he would take ship. With the "turban of the suspicious and sanguinary Turk" behind him, no longer compelled to grasp the handle of his stiletto, he breathed easily once again, thanking God that he was back in a Christian land. Within a month and a half, after an uneventful crossing, he was again, after three long years, on his native soil.

4. EXONERATION

Vindicated in his conscience, Noah set out at once to affix an official stamp upon that vindication. It was no simple matter. He had enemies in Congress, and everywhere else in the party life of the nation.

For a year and a half Noah was the target of journalistic malice. A pamphlet that he prepared upon his return, in which he printed all the documents pertinent to his case, was distorted into an attempt at blackmailing a high official at Washington; Noah, it was bruited, was to be spared prosecution for embezzlement of public money or else this unnamed great man was to endure the consequences of publication. This was palpably stupid, as the pamphlet was published, and republished, and contained precisely what was needed to establish Noah's freedom from guilt; nothing more. The $46,000. collected from the Bey was magnified into $200,000., "of which you could not, or would not, give any account."

Monroe had received Noah coldly on his return. Of his religion, not a word was spoken, despite the definite allegation of the note recalling him. The Secretary of State, now a candidate for the Presidency, accused him of having gone beyond his orders, of having made himself obnoxious, of

having spent unnecessarily the public money. Let Noah
clear himself with those friends who had recommended him
for the post. It looked very much as if Monroe were acting
on the advice of President Madison, so that there would be
little use in seeking out the chief executive. And Noah, in
his naive optimism, had expected, in return for this affront
upon his integrity and his religion, an office of rank equal to
that from which he had been so summarily deposed!

The pamphlet that he had prepared in self-justification
was treated cavalierly by the Department of State. His
friends in Congress, however, stood by him. A year of morti-
fication and perplexity followed, during which Noah was put
to the inevitable expenses of delay, of three special trips to
Washington, and to the ignominy of indifference. At last,
on December 30, 1816, Attorney General Richard Rush
handed down a long review of the case, which had been sub-
mitted to his special consideration.

Mr. Rush was of opinion that Noah's powers *might* have
justified the employment of an agent, but questioned whether
they justified the employment of Keene. It appeared to him
that the engagement of Keene, and the manner in which his
agency was handled, virtually made patent to all that he
was acting for the United States government.

He believed that the two members of the *Edwin*, despite
the fact that their status as Americans was highly questionable, were entitled to be ransomed, since Noah's instructions
indicated the crew of the *Edwin*. The four alleged Louisianians, however, were in different case; there was not a
trace of evidence, beyond their oaths, that they were citizens
of the United States.

"It is difficult to banish suspicion of a design at imposi-
tion, when men, under such circumstances, were received

and ransomed as citizens of the United States, and though Mr. Noah may not be implicated, it can never, I think, meet the sanction of the Government."

Finally, Mr. Rush pointed out that Noah was the prize-agent of Mr. Lewis, and as such received his funds, paying them away without authority, applying them to meet a public object which the United States was about to meet. Lewis's case was against Noah, not against the United States. Nevertheless, he was a meritorious creditor whom, in the event that Noah could not meet the obligation, the country *might* pay through the medium of Congress.

Noah's annotations upon this document are direct, pertinent, and convincing; to be sure, he refuses to grant that he exceeded or misinterpreted his instructions, but he shows—as the entire narrative of the *Travels* shows—that not only were his motives thoroughly American and humane, but they were, wherever mere literality of interpretation was insufficient, guided by the spirit of his instructions.

If the Dey of Algiers had suspected Keene of acting for the United States, he would, contended Noah, have buried him alive as a spy. (This espionage, it will be observed, is borne out by the nature of Keene's report to Noah). As for the four Louisianians, by proclaiming themselves Americans they knowingly rendered themselves subject to a dire captivity. Why do so, if their supposedly true nationality would have made so much easier their release?[1]

[1] The full document of Attorney-General Rush, as well as many other relevant documents and annotations, may be found in the Appendix to *Travels*, pp. i–xxiv. Consult also the earlier publication, *Correspondence And Documents Relative to the Attempt to Negotiate for the Release of the American Captives at Algiers*; including Remarks on our Relations With That Regency. Washington, 1816.

The upshot was that the Department of State, under date of January 14, 1817, over the signature of S. Pleasanton, sent to Noah the following official document:

"Sir,

Your account as Consul of the United States at Tunis has been adjusted at this Department, in conformity with the opinion of the Attorney General of the 30th December last, of which you have a copy; and a balance of Five Thousand Two Hundred and Sixteen Dollars Fifty-seven Cents, REPORTED TO BE DUE YOU, WILL BE PAID TO YOUR ORDER, at any time after Congress shall have made the necessary appropriation. A sum of One Thousand Six Hundred and Sixty-four Dollars, besides a charge of thirty-five per cent. loss on the disbursement of YOUR agent at Algiers, is SUSPENDED, for reasons mentioned in the account of which you have been apprised."[1]

Of his religion, again, not a word. He was exonerated, though with galling reservations. It was averred, even now, that Noah, by back-stage manipulation, had been let off easily in return for support of the administration . . . It was, after all, a sad contrast to the gay departure from Charleston three years before. He had left in high fettle, aggressive, on the threshold of a notable career. Now, for all his vindication, he was on the defensive, and, in a serious sense, would be ever thereafter.

Did Noah return from abroad with his father?
What had become of the old revolutionary?

---

[1] The capitals, of course, are Noah's.

There is a legend that Noah, while chafing over the delay in Paris, eager to be on his way to the consulate in Tunis, entered a restaurant. His eye was caught by the strange spectacle—doubly strange in the French capital—of a soldier wearing the Continental uniform, "blue coat, buff vest, short knee breeches, with his hair done up in a queue" . . . The queue had not yet gone entirely out of fashion. It is said that Zelegman Phillips, another uncle of Noah's, never abandoned it.

Noah advanced to the stranger and addressed him in French.

But, asked the soldier, "Are you not an American?"

Noah replied that he was.

"So am I", proclaimed the soldier. "My name is Manuel Mordecai Noah".

"My God!" cried the young consul. "You are my father!"

Members of the Noah family remember hearing the tale from their elders. Yet such evidence as we have is negative, and suggests that there is an unsolved mystery surrounding the disappearance and return of the father.

If Noah made this melodramatic discovery of his parent, why is there not a word of it in his book of travels? What, in this case, became of his parent? Was he sent back to America, while Noah proceeded to Tunis? Did he accompany his son to Tunis? Again, not a word of this is to be found in any of Noah's writings. We have record of the burial of the elder Noah, in New York, in 1822. Between the date of his wife's death in Charleston, however, and his

own death in New York, there is a gap that has not yet
been filled.

I am inclined, then, to doubt the authenticity of this
melodramatic legend.[1]

---

[1] See *Selected Addresses And Papers of Simon Wolf*. Cincinnati, 1926. Union of
American Hebrew Congregations. "Mordecai Manuel Noah, a Biographical
Sketch". Pp. 108–154. The legend is given as fact in a note on page 109. The
sketch was published originally as a pamphlet, by The Levytype Company, Philadelphia, 1897. Pp. 49.

It might be well at this point to correct one of Wolf's obvious errors. To Noah,
at this stage of his career, Wolf attributes the famous motto, "Millions for defense,
but not one cent for tribute." This motto, he writes, "afterwards so completely
Americanized, had its true origin with Major Noah." I do not deny that this was
Noah's spirit during the exciting days of his consulate at Tunis and his adventures
with the Algerine pirates. The motto, however "had its true origin" with Charles
Cotesworth Pinckney, Ambassador to the French Republic, in 1796, when Noah
was a child of eleven.

VI

SAINT TAMMANY AND THE PROMISED LAND

1. Odium Politicum

Noah had returned from his Grand Tour. For the moment, employment under the government was out of the question. He had left as a good Jeffersonian; he returned as a son of Saint Tammany. On the surface, these were the same thing; beneath, the division had already well begun. Naphtali Phillips, his uncle and benefactor, came once again to his aid.

Phillips was a power in the politics of New York. He had been a journalist from the beginning, having first served on Claypole's *American Advertiser*, one of the important newspapers of Philadelphia. As a youngster of sixteen, and the worthy son of his patriot father, Jonas, he had formed part of the cavalcade that escorted President Washington from Philadelphia to New York, for the inauguration. The Rachel to whom Noah refers in his letters to his uncle was Rachel Hannah, daughter of Moses Mendez Seixas, whom Naphtali had married in 1797. Phillips had been living in New York since the opening year of the new century, and had become proprietor of the *National Advocate*, which he was to own

for a considerable period. He would outlive his nephew—
and his contemporaries, indeed—by many years, not dying
until November 1, 1870, at the age of ninety-eight.[1]

It was Phillips, then, who placed Noah at once in the
editorial chair of *The National Advocate*, which had been
established in 1813 by Tammany Hall under the editorship
of the highly capable Henry Wheaton. Wheaton, an authority on international law, had been appointed one of the
Justices of the Marine Court, New York. In 1816, during
the agitation over Noah's dismissal and rehabilitation, the
ex-diplomat succeeded to Wheaton's position, which for the
next decade he was to occupy with varying fortunes. On
September 8, 1818, in the midst of his troubles with the
government, he was elected a member of the New York
Historical Society, to which he belonged until his resigna-
tion in 1828.

American journalism was not yet out of its black period,
—an orgy of assault, battery, libel, recrimination, accusation,
bribery, scurrility, chicanery, such as makes the succeeding
development of yellow journalism appear by comparison a
Sunday school picnic. Such was, indeed, the tradition of
journalism in our adolescent United States.

Newspapers in those days were dull, unwieldy, tasteless
sheets, supported by advertisers who expected support in
turn. The editors were far more interested in what was
occurring in distant Washington than in what was happening directly under the editorial nose. When Noah succeeded
to the throne—he did develop a habit of assuming royal airs,
and for a while commanded close attention from party leaders
at Albany—there were over three hundred newspapers in the

---

[1] See *AJHS*, vol. xxi, pp. 172–174.

country, most of them weeklies, semi-weeklies or even tri-weeklies. At the close of the War of 1812 New York had seven dailies; the *Advocate* had a circulation of eight hundred. Peddling of papers was in its prenatal stage and would not be born until *The Sun* rose in 1833; the subscriber paid in advance and the journal was delivered to him.

Boston and Philadelphia still led New York in the development of journalism. The gazette, like the national literature itself, had already emerged from theology into politics; journalism in the sense by which we know it today had not yet definitely arisen, and would not arise for ten years or more, when the stress of political revolution in Europe and in America was to alter the complexion of world affairs.

It is easy to become over-virtuous in condemnation of the political career upon which Noah was now embarking. It was even more easy for his enemies to do so, or for him, in the same half-sincere spirit, to condemn his political opponents. Allowing for all exaggeration, Noah's public career —and of how many politicians is this not true?—at times stands in strange contrast to the idealisms of his private life.

What Noah wanted of *The National Advocate* was a living, and power to advance himself in the local, state and national politics. His eye swept the panorama, as it were, alighting now on the shrievalty, now on the contract for the state printing, again upon a foreign post that would make him once again the proud—and redeemed—representative of his nation and of his people.

During these ventures, however, he would, by very force of his lively personality rather than through any conscious purpose, be contributing to the improvement of the New York press. And certainly the press of the city could stand much in the way of improvement over its ship listings, its advertisements, its bickering editorials. Mr. Pray, at first the anonymous author of the *Memoirs* of the elder Bennett, and certainly not to be suspected of undue favoritism for Noah, in after years pointed out Noah, together with William L. Stone of the *Commercial Advertiser* and William Coleman of the *New York Evening Post*, as the gradual introducers of a better style. Of these, wrote Pray, "Mr. Noah was the most original and the most popular."[1]

For this popularity there was, again, a personal reason. Noah was still young,—in the sunny, early thirties. There was gusto in the fellow. Foreign travel, a mildly exotic presence flavored with a discreet touch of Byronism, a gift for repartee, an alertness to the importance of the era, a certain geniality that made him quite as popular with the ladies as with the gentlemen, a fundamental sincerity and earnestness beneath the strata of political protestations, eccentricities of temperament that never threatened the social structure, an eagerness to help struggling authorship, a literal acceptance of the principles announced in the Constitution and in that far more important document, the Declaration of Independence,—these traits were heightened, rather than blurred, by his Jewish origin.

Just as, in the Georgia of Dr. Nunez and his group, there had been no thought to exclude Jews together with Papists,

[1] *Memoirs of James Gordon Bennett And His Times.* By A Journalist. New York, 1855, p. 45.

Other sources touching upon this period, and upon Noah's part in it, are "The Rise of Metropolitan Journalism," in *The American Historical Review*, by Charles H. Levermore, April, 1901, pp. 446–465; *History of American Journalism*, by James Melvin Lee, Boston, 1917; and *Journalism in the United States*, from 1690 to 1872, by Frederic Hudson, New York, 1873, especially Chapter XVIII. These sources must be consulted with caution; they are obscured sometimes by partisanism and at other times by error of fact. In so far as error relates to Noah, I indicate it in the proper place.

not through fondness for the Jew but rather through having overlooked the possibility of Jewish immigration, so in the country of Noah's late youth there were still too few Jews to matter. Noah naturally became one of the first Jews in American politics, and he was shrewd enough to realize the great potentialities of such leadership.

That shrewdness, none the less, was companioned from the first with an idealistic dedication. Side by side with the Quixote in him, mounted on the Rosinante of his dreams, jogged Sancho Panza on the spine of his hardy *burro*. And did not the Manchegan hidalgo promise Master Wide Paunch the governorship of an island? Even the island appears in the tale of Noah, wherein again he is at once the Knight of the Doleful Countenance and the doughty, practical squire. That, however, is as yet hardly a dream.

Tammany had been born under the aegis of an Indian, Tammanend, elevated to the status of sainthood, in scoffing reference to such patrons of Tory organizations as Saint George. In the beginning it had sought, by the incantations of this Indian pseudo-saint, to combat everything English in the colonial and post-colonial life of the United States. Ostensibly, then, it was an anti-monarchistic organization, a libertarian fraternity, first of the hundred-percent, Anglophobiac, anti-Catholic strongholds, forerunner of the Ku Kluxers, old and new.

As for the Jews, yet again they were too few to count. How was St. Tammany to foresee the day when his shrine would be overrun with Irish and Jews? Certainly, before long, owing to its later enemy, De Witt Clinton, the Wigwam was thronged with sons of Erin, and tomahawks gave way not so much to shillalahs as to the raw human fist. As early as 1805 The Society of Tammany, or Columbian Order, had been incorporated as a charitable organization; it is still under the control of the charter that was signed by Thomas Tillotson, Secretary of State, at Albany, on February 24, 1807.

Tammany, anti-English, had been pro-war in 1812. The war, indeed, had recruited new strength to its waning forces. Unpopular as it had been, it seems to have had, upon the nation as a whole, a unifying effect. The Era of Good Feeling had begun.

The West and the Southwest were being opened up. The Union was enriched by Indiana in 1816, and in the three succeeding years, respectively, by Mississippi, Illinois and Alabama. Immigration poured fresh streams of continental vitality into the national currents. The invention of the cotton gin, in 1793, and the new machinery out of England for spinning and weaving, suddenly made cotton raising a profitable industry, increased the value of the Negro slave, and shed upon the fertile fields of the Southwest the light of a new Eldorado.

The era of good feeling, however, was followed almost retributively by a commercial collapse. The years 1819 and 1820 mocked at the two years that had gone before. The United States Bank was impugned . . . Florida, in 1819, was ceded to us by Spain . . . Missouri, next year, was admitted as a slave state, with the proviso that slavery in the Louisiana territory should be prohibited north of 36° 30′ . . . Maine parted company with Massachusetts and came in as an independent state. A civil war was being blueprinted across the map of the union . . .

The reëlection of Monroe in 1820 wiped out the Federal party. Below the Rio Grande the Central and South American dependencies of Spain had, after a decade of epical conflict, shaken off the yoke of the motherland. The Western World, in contradistinction to the East, seemed committed to democracy. In Europe, the Holy Alliance, sensing the end of an era, set forth to save Europe for Monarchy.

When the hand of the Holy Alliance cast its shadow across America, Monroe decided to make clear the attitude of the United States toward foreign aggression not only in the Northern half of our hemisphere but in the Southern as well. In a famous message of December 23, 1823, he elucidated the Monroe Doctrine, wherein, virtually, he cried "Hands Off!" to the Alliance and to Russia. It was, in its crude way, one of the earliest forecasts of what has come to be known as Pan-Americanism. Also, and in far less idealistic fashion, it staked a claim . . . The United States, erasing the shadow of Europe from the map of Spanish and Portuguese America, had begun to cast its own . . . [1]

2. SPREAD EAGLE AND DAVID'S SHIELD

There was, to parallel in a thin but persistent line this graph of the national progress, a Noah doctrine, too. Several doctrines, in fact. For this, leading from the imbroglio of the recall through the Utopian adventure that made of Noah, literally, a king for a day, was the High Noachian Decade . . . Books and pamphlets flow from his ready hand. The penman of Tammany, he is also Tammany's spokesman. He speechifies, he editorializes, and when he is permitted the privilege—often, in fact, when he is not—he pontificates.

---

[1] The Monroe Doctrine, it is but fair to indicate, is not regarded by Spanish America with unmixed approbation. Too, Spanish Americans know that doctrine far better than the North Americans know the so-called Drago Doctrine enunciated in 1902 by Dr. Drago, then foreign minister of the Argentine republic.

He enjoys his position of power, the manifest irradiation of his personality. To be sure, he is editor of *The National Advocate* at the pittance of $1500. a year, subject to annual reappointment, but his columns shall be transformed into a lever by which he will move heaven and earth, remoulding them both to his heart's desire.

His editorials in the official organ of Tammany, when not devoted to orchestrating the political issues of the epoch with special Wigwam effects, ranged not too far afield. He upheld the solid, the homely virtues,—the copybook maxims (often none the worse for their domesticity) of joy, temperance, and repose, which slam the door in the doctor's nose . . .

He preached thus early, this man born of the city and destined never to leave it, the nobility of the farmer, the sound beauties of "back to the land." The first quarter of the nineteenth century was not yet completed; New York, nevertheless, appears already to have been overrun with rustics who fluttered like light-struck moths to the future metropolis.

Noah was vividly, increasingly conscious of the two great factors that shaped his life: our national destiny and the destiny of the Jewish people. He was, as a result of the experience of the War of 1812, for preparedness. He set the American eagle screeching all around the six points of David's Shield. In 1817, appointed by Tammany the official orator for the celebration of the 41st anniversary of American independence before a combined meeting of the Tammany Society or Columbian Order, the Hibernian Provident Society, the Columbian Society, the Union Society of Shipwrights and Caulkers, the Tailors', House Carpenters' and Masons' Benevolent Societies, he was still crowing over the "late war," the justice of our cause, the triumph of our navy and arms.

One of the earliest advocates of Pan-Americanism, he was glorying prospectively in the liberation of the whole Western world "from the sway and control of European powers." This was six years before the enunciation of the Monroe Doctrine; it developed, however, a policy that had been cradled in the farewell message of Washington. "America shall rise," declaimed Noah, using that name to cover the Americas of the South and North, "in all the majesty of freedom, and defy the world."

Envisaging the United States as a haven for the oppressed, he beheld it, naturally, as a temporary home for the Wandering Jew on his long, mystical journey from the Past to the Future in the land of Zion. "Under our political father, the immortal Washington, the most illustrious emigrants have fought valiantly for our liberties. Ireland gave us Montgomery; France, Lafayette; Germany, Steuben and DeKalb; Poland, Kosciusko and Pulaski . . ."

On April 17 of the following year Noah, delivering a discourse at the consecration of the synagogue, the Kahal Kadosh Shearith Israel (the Holy Congregation of the Remnants of Israel), voiced for his fellow-Jews hopes no less optimistic.

Amidst his conventional speech-making on this day Noah had many moments of penetrating insight. Pleading for toleration, for the abolition of bigotry and superstition, he could suddenly touch, as with a beacon of perspicacity shining through the denseness of soulless rhetoric, upon "commercial jealousy, always the real cause of intolerance."

America was Zion *pro tempore*.

"Until the Jews can recover their ancient rights and dominions, and take their ranks among the governments of the earth, this is their chosen country; here they can rest with the persecuted of every clime, secure in person and property, protected from tyranny and oppression, and participating of (sic) equal rights and immunities. Forty years of experience have tested the wisdom of our institutions, and they only will be surrendered with the existence of the nation."

What he counseled for Gentile, he counseled for Jew. He was a firm believer in vocational training as a foil to the literary and moral life. He was for the "attainment of some mechanic art", and for the avoidance of "those crooked paths of traffic, miscalled commerce."

The Jews, originally, had been an agricultural people. Let them return to agriculture,—"the cradle of virtue, and the school of patriotism."

Already, in embryo, the scheme for the colonization of the Jews was in his mind. There were seven million Jews in the world; of these, three thousand were in the United States, and one thousand in New York City. These seven million were "a number greater than at any period of our history, and possessing more wealth, activity, influence, and talents, than any body of people of their number on earth. The signal for breaking the Turkish scepter in Europe will be their emancipation; they will deliver the north of Africa from its oppressors; they will assist to establish civilization in European Turkey, and may revive commerce and the arts in Greece; they will march in triumphant numbers, and possess themselves once more of Syria, and take their rank among the governments of the earth. This is not fancy. I have been too much among them in Europe and Africa—I am too well acquainted with their views and sentiments in Asia, to doubt their intentions. They hold the purse strings, and can wield the sword; they can bring 100,000 men into the field. Let us then hope that the day is not far distant when, from the operation of liberal and enlightened measures, we may look towards that country where our people have established a mild, just, and honourable government, accredited by the world, and admired by all good men."

These were already the words of a new Judge in Israel,— a hope, a promise, and a prospectus . . . Of the value of this speech as an indication of his political importance, Noah was hardly unaware. No sooner was it off the press than the editor of *The National Advocate* sent copies of it to the living ex-presidents of the United States.

His letter to Madison, dated May 6, 1818, was of especial significance. "I regret," it reads in part, "that I have not had the pleasure of seeing you since my return from the Mediterranean. It arose from a belief that my recal (sic) was the result of very unfavourable impressions made on your mind; if these impressions have existed, I do sincerely hope that they have been removed by subsequent explanations, for I wish you to be assured, and I have no object in view in making the assertion, that no injury arose in Barbary to the public service from my religion as relating to myself, on the contrary, my influence and standing abroad was highly creditable & flattering.

"I would wish, not only for the sake of my coreligionaires, but for that of your administration, that if my letter of recal, cannot be erased from the Books of the Department of State, that such explanation may be subjoined, and may prevent any evils arising from the precedent;—for as my accounts are adjusted, & a balance struck in my favour, the objection in that letter, refers solely to my religion, an objection, that I am persuaded you cannot feel, nor authorize others to feel . . ."[1]

[1] In view of the plain intention of Noah's letter, which I copy from a photostatic reproduction of the document made for me in Washington, it is pertinent to reprint the utterly misleading comment that appears in *Writings of James Madison,*

Acknowledgments from Thomas Jefferson, James Madison and John Adams were afterwards printed by Noah in the Appendix to his *Travels*. In Jefferson's letter, sent on May 28, 1818, from Monticello, there was a touch of the simple nobility that characterized this great statesman, so aristocratic in personality for all his high services to the people called common. In Jefferson's sympathy with the Jews there was no condescension; he saw that while "we are free by law, we are not so in practise; public opinion erects itself into an Inquisition, and exercises its office with as much fanaticism as fans the flames of an Auto da fe." Adams, writing from Quincy, Massachusetts, on July 31, avowed that not even Noah outdid him in ideas upon the "right of private judgment and the liberty of conscience, both in religion and philosophy . . . Let the wits joke; the philosophers sneer! It has pleased the Providence of the 'first cause', the universal cause, that Abraham should give religion, not only to Hebrews, but to Christians and Mahometans, the greatest part of the modern civilized world."

What of Madison? For it is undeniable that even to this day the recall of Noah because of his religion is not entirely convincing to Jews of independent mind. There, of course, is the letter transmitted to Noah by Stephen Decatur. On the other hand, the record of Madison from the first is distinguished for his championship, side by side with Jefferson, of religious freedom. It was Madison who, opposing the measure of Patrick Henry (1784) for the subsidizing of the Christian religion in Virginia, prepared a Memorial and

vol. viii, p. 412, edited by Gaillard Hunt, 1908. Noah's letter, according to the editor, "hoped that the impression that his recall from the foreign service was due to irregularities in his accounts might be removed and that it might be attributed to his religion"(!).

Remonstrance against its adoption that finally swung popular opinion into the camp of toleration.

Madison replied from Montpelier, on May 15th, affirming his belief in the freedom of religious opinions. As to Noah's foreign mission, "it cannot but be agreeable to me to learn that your accounts have been closed in a manner so favorable to you. And I know too well the justice and candor of the present executive to doubt that an official preservation will be readily allowed to explanations necessary to protect your character, against the effect of any impressions whenever ascertained to be erroneous. It was certain, that your religious profession was well known at the time you received your commission, and that in itself could not be a motive in your recal."

To complicate the matter, the letter of recall, which Noah was so eager to have erased from the books of the Department of State, has long been missing from the government archives.

No sooner has Noah been exonerated by the administration, and delivered the 1817 Tammany oration celebrating the 41st anniversary of our Independence, than he is found again protecting his character. Life, in this decade, was for Noah a kaleidoscopic shuffling from press-room to green-room, from green-room to court-room.

Noah and Tammany had been, from the first, enemies of that staunch old Federalist, De Witt Clinton. Clinton, nevertheless, had just been elected Governor of New York over the opposition; as chief executive he was empowered to hand out the much-sought graft of the State printing. Regarded as the originator, in his State, of the policy that to the victor belong the spoils, Clinton at once became the target of the most seductive editorial ogling. Even some of the newspapers that had opposed him joined this bid for what Noah denounced—when he could not get it—as "feeding at the public crib". Incensed at this turn-about, Noah campaigned in his columns against the sudden converts.

And now it happened that a letter fell into his hands— how? when? where? why?—addressed to Alden Spooner, the editor of *The Columbian*, by Messrs. Barnam and Nelson of Poughkeepsie, indelicately referring to Mr. Noah as "a wretch" and commenting upon the mooted matter of the State printing. Noah made a copy, sent on the original to the addressee, printed the letter in his *Advocate*, added some caustic comment, and—found himself shortly charged with opening unlawfully the United States mails. Spooner publicly branded him, in *The Columbian*, as The Knight of the Broken Seal, "who converted to his own use property known to be stolen." Counter-suit by Noah, for the publication of a libel. And counter-suit by the government, charging both Noah and Spooner with contempt of court for publishing unkindly articles upon the conduct and judgment of the court.

From the testimony it appeared, among other things, that Noah, like an orthodox Jew, did no business at the newspaper office on Saturdays . . . "Men who merely change ground to share the patronage of a State," he averred, "are past blushing." . . . Spooner, in the alleged libelous article, had referred to him as Major, Massah, Moses, Noah. Thus early his officiousness, his proud and at times obnoxious leadership of his people, was travestied. "The political consequences of this great State," mocked Spooner, "rested on the shoulders of this modern Atlas—a stranger, with no ties of family or property." The aspersion as to property Noah well could ignore. But his family? Shades of Dr. Nunez, of David Mendez Machado, of Jonas Phillips, of Manuel Noah! In his next speech, at the Consecration of the new synagogue for the Remnants of Israel, he remembered these distinguished forbears . . .

A tempest in a tea-pot . . . Much ado about nothing . . . Noah had been found guilty of misdemeanor, but the judge set the verdict aside on the ground that the evidence was all on Noah's side. Spooner went free, through disagreement of the jury, on the charge of libel. Apologies and explanations convinced the court that no contempt had been intended.

Yet the onus of the charge against Noah was kept alive by his political detractors, and we find him as late as 1841, in a letter to Governor Wm. H. Seward of New York, reverting to the trial of 1817 and—now a familiar gesture—defending his honor. It appears that a clerk in Noah's office had found the letter open on the floor—how had it come there, of all places?—and had laid it on his own desk. "Three days afterward he brought the letter to me"—why so long a delay in a matter so palpably important to *The National Advocate* and to Noah?—"which I copied and sent the original back to Spooner and published its contents more in a spirit of pleasantry"—!—"than from any other consideration. *The National Advocate* was the organ of the old Bucktail party at that time and the *Columbian* espoused the cause of De Witt Clinton. D. C. Van Wyck, Dr. Sever and other friends of Mr. Clinton, believing that political capital might be made out of it easily procured an indictment against me, their sheriff selecting a political grand jury for the purpose."

Judge Radcliff himself offered the conjecture that some person might have taken the letter in question from the vessel that brought it to New York and maliciously dropped it in the office. In any case, as Noah insisted almost a quarter of a century later, "it did not leave a stain on my character." This, in view of the offices later held by him, would seem to be quite so.[1] It was by no means, however, the last time that Noah would be seen, on official business, in court. For if this amazing paladin of his nation and his people was a knight *sans peur*, most assuredly he was not always, in the eyes of his political enemies, *sans reproche*.

3. FORESHADOWINGS OF UTOPIA

Always, to Noah's vindications, major or minor, there was a sour aftertaste. And always there would be, in his mind, need of positive accomplishment to eradicate the unpleasantness of the impression. That he had not surrendered entirely his aspirations to distinction in the field of foreign diplomacy, —that, in the midst of his political entanglements and the desire for lucrative posts in the domestic service, he had not forgotten his pledge to a liberated Jewry,—that, for all his prominence in unsavory public squabbles, he retained the respect of his fellow-citizens,—all this appears from his strivings, his successes and his failures of the years in which he sat in the editor's chair of *The National Advocate*.

It should be kept in mind, too, that although Noah had printed a defense of his foreign activities in 1816, as soon as he was back from Tunis, he did not publish his *Travels* until

---

[1] For the data relevant to this trial see *American State Trials*, Edited by John D. Lawson, LL.D., St. Louis, 1914, pp. 671–698; *City Hall* (N. Y.) *Recorder*, 13; 3 *City Hall Recorder*, 27; *AJHS*, "New Matter Relating to Mordecai M. Noah," by G. Herbert Cone. Vol. ii, pp. 131–137. The letter to Gov. Seward referred to in the text is dated New York, February 22, 1841, and is to be found in the collection of the New York Historical Society.

M. M. Noah

NOAH AT 34

From the frontispiece of his "Travels in England, France,
Spain and the Barbary States in the years 1813–14 and 15"
[Published in 1819]

1819. By this time he was a leading editor—noted or notorious, depending upon which political glasses one wore—and had already been exposed to other suspicions.

As early as this he was being set down in contemporary verse by the wits of the town as a fellow who often parted company with truth, but who was, for a' that and a' that, a likeable sort. After all, who is a politico to call another politico a liar? Fitz-Greene Halleck, in his *Fanny*, summed up the attitude neatly:

> To these authentic facts each bucktail swore;
> But Clinton's friends averred, in contradiction,
> They were but fables, told by Mr. Noah,
> Who had a privilege to deal in fiction,
> Because he'd written travels, and a melo—
> Drama; and was, withal, a pleasant fellow.[1]

John Adams and John Quincy Adams did not wear the same spectacles when they looked at this ambitious young Jew. The odors raised by the recall and the investigation were still to be sniffed in Washington. When, some time in 1820, Noah was again urging himself for a foreign appointment, the Secretary of State set down in his diary a not very complimentary notation:

"W. Lee came with a letter from M. M. Noah, editor of the New York Advocate [sic], a Jew, who was once Consul at Tunis, recalled for indiscretions, and who has published a Book of Travels against Mr. Madison and Mr. Monroe." [This is misleading, as the *Travels* consist chiefly of historical, geographical, ethnic and commercial information. Noah's defense, however, certainly has overtones of hostility to the act of the administration.] "He has great projects for colonizing Jews in this country, and wants to be sent as Chargé

---

[1] See *The Political Works of Fitz-Greene Halleck*, New York, 1852, p. 123, *Fanny*. *Fanny* itself was originally published in 1819.

d'affaires to Vienna for the promotion of them. He is an incorrect, and very ignorant, but sprightly writer, and as a partisan editor of a newspaper has considerable power. He argues with great earnestness his merits in supporting the administration, as a title to the President's favor. He is, like all editors of newspapers in this country who have any talent, an author to be let. There is not one of them whose friendship is worth having, nor one whose enmity is not formidable. They are a sort of assassins who sit with loaded blunder-busses at the corner of streets and fire them off for hire or for sport at any passenger they select. They are principally foreigners; but Noah is a native. He is salaried at a low rate by the anti-Clintonian Tammanies at New York to keep up a constant fire against his administration; and Noah pretends that this is serving the General Government, because Clinton is a standing presidential candidate and carries on an insidious war against Mr. Monroe."[1]

The "great projects for colonizing Jews in this country" were already well in progress early in this same year; they must have been formed, indeed, during Noah's stay abroad, as is to be inferred from certain of his statements with regard to the condition of Jews in foreign lands. The legislative records of New York State contain entries indicating that Noah had already applied for a grant of Grand Island, the site of his never materialized colony:

Wednesday, January 19, 1820. "The memorial of Mordecai M. Noah, of New York, praying the State to authorize the sale to him of Grand Island, in the Niagara River, was read and referred to the select committee consisting of Mr. Ulshoeffer, Mr. Hatfield and Mr. Oakley."[2]

---

[1] See *Memoirs of John Quincy Adams*, Comprising Portions of his Diary from 1795 to 1848. Edited by Charles Francis Adams. Philadelphia, 1875.

[2] I quote from *AJHS*, vol. ii, pp. 131–137, article, "New Matter Relating to Mordecai M. Noah," by G. Herbert Cone. Mr. Cone drew his material from the Assembly Journal, 1820.

Monday, January 24, 1820. "Mr. Ulshoeffer from the select committee to whom was referred the memorial of Mordecai M. Noah, of the city of New York, relative to the purchase of Grand Island, reported:

"That the petitioner applies to the State for a grant of the said island, for the purpose of attempting to have the same settled by emigrants of the Jewish religion from Europe; that he not only considers the situation of Grand Island as well adapted for the contemplated purpose, but that the obtaining of the title from the State would be very advantageous in inducing the emigration of capitalists, as well as others.

"The committee did not doubt, but that the recent persecution of the Jews in various parts of Europe, may favor the views of the petitioner, and that the settlement of Grand Island would be a desirable object to this State. It is one of the greatest characteristics of the United States that they offer an asylum to the unfortunate and persecuted of all religious denominations; but to preserve our equal rights, it is essential, as the petitioner states, that we should offer no preference to any sect. Without reference, therefore, to any object of the petitioner, which may be supposed to present a claim for any purpose of religion, but considering that the legislature has repeatedly declared its intention of affording equal protection and enjoyment to all who may inhabit within it, and that it is for the interest of the State to dispose of the said island, there can be no objection, in the opinion of the committee, to the grant thereof to Mr. Noah for value, in the usual way.

"They have accordingly prepared a bill, providing for the survey and sale of said island, agreeably to the prayer of the petitioner, which they have directed their chairman to ask leave to bring in."

"Ordered that leave be given to bring in said bill.

"Mr. Ulshoeffer, according to leave, brought in the said bill entitled 'An act directing the commissioners of the land office to survey and sell Grand Island, in the Niagara River, to Mordecai M. Noah,' which said bill was read the first time, and by unanimous consent was also read the second time and committed to the committee of the house."

Nothing, however, came of Noah's application. Yet, as ever, he rebounded from this failure with hopes undimmed. If not Grand Island, then how, for example, about Newport? In less than a year he is discovered hard at work trumpeting, through the columns of *The National Advocate*—his paper, it would appear, as well as Tammany's!—the virtues of Little Rhode Island as a temporary haven for the European Jew. In the interim he has been disabused of his notions concerning the inherited agriculturalism of Israel.

"The Jews in Europe, however, have expressed to me their doubt as to the disposition of their brethren to clear land, make settlements, and cultivate the soil, so incompatible with their present pursuits, and have rather given the preference to commercial places, where all the necessaries of life, and even luxuries may be purchased; and where immediate and beneficial application may be had for their money and enterprise. In fact there have been some earnest enquiries as to the advantages of manufacturing establishments of cloth, linens, glass, silks, and other articles, which now languish in Germany and France, and which if transferred to this country, it is hoped would yield a better profit, while they afforded the proprietors additional rights and privileges. Accordingly, a more central situation has been examined, and the State of Rhode Island appears to combine the greatest advantages.

"The Town of Newport has a Harbor inferior to none in the Union. The climate is remarkably healthy, expenses of living moderate; it has been the residence of respectable Jewish merchants, and has a very spacious place of worship already erected. The whole state, which is not as large as one county in this state, appears well calculated for manufactures and the charter on subjects of religion is as liberal as could be desired. It follows then, from the most prudent calculations that Rhode Island is at present the most eligible spot for Jewish emigrants, and will, I trust occupy their immediate attention. There is nothing visionary or even difficult in promoting an extensive Jewish emigration to this country. Men everywhere consult their safety and happiness; and when once they are satisfied that their civil and religious liberty will be respected—their health and enterprise preserved and encouraged, they will venture upon an experiment which promises every advantage. I am tired of seeing a nation of seven millions of people, rich and intelligent, wandering about the world, without a home, which they can claim as their own, and looking to the restoration to an ancient country, which one eighth would not inhabit, if they recovered it tomorrow. Where the Jews can be protected by laws which they will have some agency in enacting, and where a laudable ambition will lead to the possession of posts of honor and confidence, and where they can mingle their voice freely in the councils of the nation and have the privilege of taking their place in the field and in the cabinet, I do consider that they will possess every temporal blessing which has been promised them. It is not however perfectly in order, to make a colony of them in this country. It could not be done. They will spread themselves over the Union, and be amalgamated with other citizens. They may be most numerous in places where their interest is best promoted."[1]

This Noah fellow blows hot and cold. Agriculture? Yes—and No. Colony? Yes—and, less than a year later, No. And, as we shall see in a few years, yet Yes again. Such alternation of mood and opinion suggests at once the opportunism of the politician and the instability of a sanguine temperament. There is no more reason, however, to question

---

[1] See the *New Hampshire Gazette*, January 16, 1821, which quotes a current issue of *The National Advocate*.

the fundamental sincerity of Noah's motives than to over-look the practical possibilities—for him—that accompanied such a project. The Knight of the Doleful Countenance and the Squire of the Wide Paunch travel always together . . .

4. FAREWELL—A SHORT FAREWELL —TO POLITICS

There is excellent evidence that Noah, at the very outset of his political career, was so disgusted with his treatment and his prospects that he was ready to abandon it for his early love, the theater. In fact, sometime in 1818, he was making behind the scenes a determined effort to leave not only politics but the state of New York. He had accumulated a quiver of grievances. Here he was, in his prime, a slave to the editorial chair at a meager $1500. He was engaged professionally, as a Tammanyite, in combating Governor Clinton, a gentleman toward whom he felt not the slightest personal animosity. Indeed, he had the highest esteem for Clinton's character. *The Advocate* was being hard pressed by creditors. Messrs. Crolius, Jasper Ward and Hugh Maxwell, when he had applied for the clerkship of the corporation in place of General Morton, had opposed and defeated him.

Opportunity for a welcome change came through a letter from Mr. Gilfert, of the Charleston Theater. According to that manager, the leases of the Charleston, Savannah, Augusta, Norfolk and Richmond theaters were his property. He invited Noah to join him in the project of turning this chain into a profitable venture. For this, as Noah's share in the partnership, $20,000. would be needed, half of which was required at once in cash.

The chance won Noah over. But as a man without funds he would have to raise the money through influential friends. Happening one day to mention the matter to an old acquaintance, Dr. Secor, a director of the newly established Franklin Bank, Noah was pleased to have his good opinion of the investment concurred in. Secor undertook to secure the loan; a day or two later, however, it appeared that he could raise but a quarter of the required sum, so the matter was dropped. A Mr. Graham of New York, furnishing the money, became associated with Gilfert; and that was, so far as Noah was concerned, the end of the story.

Not so far as his political enemies were concerned, however. For, now, in 1821, when Noah was seeking appointment as Sheriff of New York City and County, the tale was suddenly brought to life again, with an interesting commentary by his opponents. Noah had become a worthy target.

By 1820 he had achieved, together with Stephen Allen, virtual leadership of Tammany. The new amendments to the municipal constitution, which Noah was to celebrate with a little theatrical afterpiece that has not come down to us, were yet a few years away. The Council of Appointment —the tree from which were shaken the political plums of the city—came therefore under the power of Allen, the reigning Grand Sachem, Noah, and their following of old Burrites. Golden was removed from the Mayor's office and Allen appointed in his place. The shrievalty was waiting for Noah, and was no doubt regarded as a stepping stone to far more important office. The other offices at the disposal of the Council were prepared to become a composite Wigwam. It was the moment for a strategic counterstroke.

Reviving the affair of the projected loan of 1818, Noah's enemies maintained that it had been a veiled offer to sell himself to the Clintonians. If the entire $10,000. could not be raised, he is alleged to have intimated, $7000. would be sufficient. According to testimony given by Dr. Secor, in a trial of later date whose progress threw this flashback upon the screen of contemporary politics, Noah had suggested to him that he apply to the friends of Governor Clinton for the loan, for which he would give a mortgage of half the leases of the theater as security, repaying the debt with legal interest. Just which friends of Clinton were to be interviewed had been left to Dr. Secor.

Among other inducements said to have been held out by Noah were the chief one that Clinton would get rid, by the retirement of Noah from politics, of his most powerful journalistic opponent. According to the testimony of Henry Post, cashier of the Franklin Bank, Noah, quitting the State, would attack Monroe either from Philadelphia or Charleston, or both.

Incidental testimony in the trial brought out the facts that Noah, at this period (1818), lived at the home of Naphtali Phillips, later keeping house in Church or Chapel street. With Noah lived his sister, Judith, and his father, both dependent upon him.

Out of this accusation, as of so many others before it and after, came nothing that could do more than suggest a suspicion of Noah's strangely complicated motives. Never the black sheep that his accusers sought to make of him, he was never, we may suspect, the white one that he sought to make of himself. It is clear, however, that he held, early or late, few if any profound political, as distinguished from nationalistic and idealistic, convictions.[1]

---

[1] The trial that brought out these data and the various interpretations placed upon them did not take place until Friday, December 12, 1823, before Judge Samuel R. Betts, of the Circuit Court held in the First Judicial District in the Senate of

5. THE SHRIEVALTY AND ANTI-SEMITISM

The attempt to thwart Noah's aspirations to the shrievalty proved unsuccessful. He was appointed in 1822 by Mr. Skinner's council. It is at this point, indeed, that the problem of Jewish influence in Tammany was crystallized, and that the latent anti-Semitism in the municipal life came naturally to a head.

What? A Jew for sheriff? Did not the citizens realize that there were times when a sheriff was called upon to perform a hanging? Who was a Jew, now, that he should be allowed to hang a Christian? To which Noah made the ready reply: Pretty sort of Christian that should require hanging at *anyone's* hands!

However, like so many horrors foreseen, this one did not eventuate. Instead, Noah shortly involved himself in another piece of quixotry, this time a too-too-Christian kindness for which there was not lacking, from Christians, most unchristian condemnation.

By an irony that the hard-pressed Noah may have appreciated, there were, under his charge, many prisoners whose only crime was their inability to meet their debts. New York, a hundred and more years ago, was subject to recurrent epidemics; it happened, in the year 1822, that the yellow fever returned with peculiar virulence, and that, as might

New York, at City Hall, New York City. A fairly full account of the action is to be found in *Report of the Trial of An Action On The Cases brought by Silvanus Miller, Esq., late Surrogate of the City and County of New York against Mordecai M. Noah, Esq., editor of The National Advocate.* By L. H. Clarke, New York, 1823.

Noah, on February 1, 1823, wrote to the *Albany Argus* a letter in which Miller thought himself to be libeled; hence, finally, the action. No verdict was agreed upon, although the jury stayed out all night. The case was dropped.

have been expected under the circumstances, it appeared in the Debtors' Jail, then situated in Ludlow Street at City Hall Park.

Noah was too kind-hearted to watch the pest extend its ravages to the helpless prisoners. Thoughtlessly, so far as his own responsibilities were concerned, he threw open the gates and released the threatened unfortunates. For, as it appears, he and the sureties upon his bond as sheriff were answerable for the combined financial obligations of every debtor thus liberated. Later, a bill was introduced into the New York legislature to reimburse him for the debt with which he had thus saddled himself; it was defeated, however.

The reverend clergy of Gotham not only denounced the opening of the jail doors but represented to the municipal fathers that God had sent the plague to the community for having named a Jew as sheriff. Nothing was mentioned about the filthy streets of the city, or the impure water supplied by a private corporation. Nor was it deemed necessary to explain why, in previous years, though no Jew sat in the sheriff's office, the cholera and yellow fever had raged through their courses. *Cherchez le juif* . . . It was an ancient cry, and must have sounded acridly in the ears of the gentleman who had protested, in Tunis, that the United States was not a Christian nation . . . It was during this visitation, incidentally, that the wife of Naphtali Phillips, Noah's aunt Rachel, succumbed to the pest.

Again, then, the letter of the law abandoned in favor of the humane spirit. Again, by Noah, an overriding of his instructions, a resultant clash with the authorities, and a demand for vindication. It is seemingly one of the compulsions of Noah's character, founded upon impatience with legalistic restraint, upon a heart that is forever running away with a head.[1]

The loss, if loss there was—for our sources of information here are not of the highest credibility—was never made good to Noah by the State, and it is reported that Noah required of his children never to advance any claim for the money thus disbursed by their father.

If Noah was to succeed himself as Sheriff it would have to be by popular election, as the office, between his assumption of its duties and the serving of his term, had become elective. The regular Tammany appointment, however, had to be won if Wigwam support was to be assured. With the aggravation of factional rivalry came increased unscrupulousness of methods. Noah this time faced, from his opponents, a frank fire of anti-Semitism.

The contest for the shrievalty was a backwash from the maneuvering that was in progress for the presidential campaign. Tammany was so evidently unconquerable that Governor Clinton refused to stand for reëlection, while the Federalists refused even to go through the motions of nominating candidates for Congress and the Legislature. On October 30, the nominating committee of the Wigwam duly reported Noah's name as reappointee for Sheriff; Benjamin Romaine, however, moved to substitute Peter H. Wendover.

Behind Noah's reappointment was the hand of Martin Van Buren, leader of the New York Tammany group.

---

[1] Mr. Wolf, in the unreliable account to which I have several times referred, speaks of Noah paying out "over two hundred thousand dollars on this account, which completely impoverished him." The figure, in relation to Noah's finances, is fantastic. Noah returned from Tunis a poor man; he was receiving, as editor of *The National Advocate*, $1500. a year; it is unlikely that in his entire career he ever earned two hundred thousand dollars, let alone having it in his possession all at once.

Noah, indeed, was looked upon as the chief of Van Buren's editorial corps. He had cast his eyes upon the office of State printer, which was held at the time by Cantine. He had expected, to judge by his correspondence, to get the perquisite for the asking. "I am not so certain that I can be defeated—but if so, I am willing to hazard a defeat, reserving to myself the right of spreading the facts before the world, and exhibiting the system of peddling away the patronage of the State."

Noah, it turned out, was defeated. It was to silence his recriminations that Van Buren had thrown in his weight in favor of reappointment to the shrievalty.

"Two factors," records Gustavus Meyers, the historian of Tammany Hall, "were at work here; one was religious prejudice against Noah . . .; the other, and greater, was the struggle between the partisans of Andrew Jackson, John Quincy Adams and William H. Crawford to get control of Tammany Hall, as a necessary preliminary to the efforts of each for the nomination for president. Romaine was an Adams supporter and could easily have nominated a ticket independent of Tammany Hall, but it would have lacked 'regularity', and hence popular support. A row ensued; and while Noah's party rushed out of Tammany Hall claiming the 'regular' nomination, the other faction, by the light of a solitary candle, passed resolutions denouncing Noah and claiming that Wendover was the 'regular' nominee.

"Each of the candidates placed himself before the people, declaring that a majority of the nominating committee favored him as a 'regular'. The leaders of the organization inclined to Noah, as one of its heads, but Wendover skillfully appealed to anti-Semitic bigotry and gathered a large following. The Sachems dared not interfere between them, and consequently each had a room in Tammany Hall, where his tickets were distributed and his agents made their headquarters. Noah was defeated at the polls; but his defeat did not impair his influence in Tammany Hall."[1]

Noah did not strengthen himself by the dictatorial manner in which he made demands, or by the habit he had of considering as traitors to the party—publishing them, too, as such —all who did not see eye to eye with him in matters of local and national policy. Thus, when Mr. Charles King's *American*, the other Republican-Democratic paper of the city, came forth in ardent support of the candidacy of John Quincy Adams for the presidency of the United States, Noah pledged his *Advocate* to the then Secretary of the Treasury, William H. Crawford. Whoever was not for Crawford was *Advocate*-ly stigmatized as a traitor to truth, goodness, beauty and Democracy.

All Washington had been eagerly perusing the *Advocate* to see what Noah was having to say about the Presidency. When he came out for Crawford, it was taken for granted, and rightly, that he spoke for "the little magician," Van Buren.

Just as Noah's defeat for the State printership had caused Van Buren to procure for him the nomination for the shrievalty, so his defeat for the shrievalty won for him, from Van Buren, as balm for his wounded pride, election as Grand Sachem of Tammany. The titles, and even the instruments, of power he possessed. Inside the Wigwam, however, he possessed powerful enemies, too, and friends with whom the inevitable break was one day to come. Among these enemies was Ulshoeffer, who had helped spoil Noah's plans for the office of State printer, though he had been nominated for the office by the Democratic legislature. Ulshoeffer, making a

---

[1] See Gustavus Meyers, *History of Tammany Hall*, New York, 1901, pp. 72, 73 and passim.

secret inquiry at the time, wondered whether Noah was really authorized to say, as he did in his columns, "that all who are not his friends had better stay at home and not offer their names at Albany this winter."[1]

It was probably at this epoch that Noah's break with Van Buren really began. Van Buren's attitude toward him seems, especially in view of letters that came to light well after the period, to have been dictated by expediency rather than any more fundamental quality. Noah was a man to be feared, and therefore to be placated. He was, after all, a very popular editor, and a fellow with a skillful, trenchant pen.

Noah, on the other hand, had a proper sense of his own political importance as a journalist. He felt that he was entitled to advancement, and that he was not receiving reward in proportion to the practical services that he contributed. From the realistic standpoint of politics—and Noah was dealing, of course, with politicians engaged in very practical activities—the editor of the *Advocate* was quite within reason.[2]

---

[1] See Dennis Tilden Lynch, *An Epoch and a Man: Martin Van Buren*, especially Chapter XXVII.

[2] That Noah's mind was not occupied exclusively by politics at this time—or, for that matter, at any other time—is revealed by a longish item in the N. Y. *Evening Post* of January 29, 1824. See Phelps Stokes, *Iconography of Manhattan Island*, p. 1636.

Noah, in a letter to the Mayor of New York, writes:

"A new invention for boring the earth for pure water has been in successful operation in England for the last three years. In a late journey through one of the southern states, I saw one of the machines in operation and became at once convinced that a similar apparatus would facilitate us in ascertaining beyond any doubt the quality of water on this island.

"I have great pleasure in acquainting you, and thro' you the Common Council that I have not only furnished myself with the necessary drawings of the machinery, but have made several improvements on them . . ."

(Hereupon follows a long column with details of his plan).

6. "Major Bombastes Furioso" . . .

The withdrawal of Noah from the editorship of *The National Advocate*, upon the eve of his Ararat project, is one of the many tales in his career revolving upon financial difficulties and the oft-repeated defense of his integrity.

Upon Noah's defeat for the shrievalty Phillips had offered nephew Noah a half-interest in the newspaper, for $4000. The ex-sheriff, being virtually penniless, set about making loans of $1000. through friends: Stephen Price, Henry Eckford, Thomas Gibbon and two unnamed acquaintances of Price. Noah agreed to repay the loans during the next three years. Upon returning, in January, 1824, from a visit to Charleston, Noah learned that his partner, Phillips, was financially at bay, with almost $10,000. in debts confronting him. This was a serious impasse for the *Advocate*. As the Tammany organ was threatened with extinction, Noah interviewed two of the Wigwam leaders, Jonathan Thompson and John Targee, asking them to intercede with Eckford, a man of means, to save the paper. Eckford agreed to join Thompson and Targee, on condition that Phillips be retired with a bonus, as it were, of $1000. yearly for the following three years. This, by way of recognition of his services to the party. Noah was to go on as editor, at an annual salary of $1000.—a reduction of $500. Noah was further allowed until January 16 so to settle his affairs that he would be able to resume ownership of the *Advocate*. Eckford made one other stipulation: he was to place a young man in the office as bookkeeper and treasurer.

It turned out very soon that Eckford's plan was to capture the newspaper and the influence that it wielded. When Thompson and Targee, aware at last of Eckford's scheme, offered to buy him out, he refused. Further, he stigmatized Noah as a turncoat who was deserting Tammany and going over to their arch-enemy, Clinton. He had his man Friday censor Noah's editorials, rewriting them as he pleased. When, as the last straw, Eckford placed Judge Van Ness in the *Advocate* office, gradually making him the virtual editor, Noah was compelled by self-respect to resign.

There was to be an epilogue to this tale. Noah, of whom it was later said that he would have liked to edit every paper in the city,—of whom, indeed, it has been noticed, from certain passages in his *Travels*, that he considered himself sufficiently able to sit in the Presidential chair of the nation, —had one infallible remedy for journalistic trial and defeat: invariably he founded another newspaper.

The split with Eckford was very soon to cost that scheming fellow dear, and he would be sent to disgrace by the very editor whom he had ousted from the first *Advocate*. For New York was soon in the midst of a journalistic battle of various *Advocates*. Noah was determined, in founding a new paper, to retain the name of the old. When he established his own *National Advocate*, Eckford and Snowden (Snowden was the latest editor of the original *Advocate*) enjoined him from using the name. He altered the title now to *Noah's New York National Advocate*, was again enjoined, and this time chose the name, *The New York Enquirer*.[1] From a political, internal dissension, the fight gradually grew into a battle of classes, with Noah, suddenly emerging as a muckraker, in the rôle of St. George against the dragon of Wall Street business interests.

---

[1] *A Statement of Facts Relating to the Conduct of Henry Eckford, As Connected With The National Advocate*. By M. M. Noah. New York, 1824.

This episode, however, in which Noah triumphed over the forces of evil, was to culminate after the fiasco of Ararat in 1825. The fury of Noah's attack, indeed, may have gathered animus from that colossal disappointment. Meantime the artistry of the man, and his social appetites, were being fed by a success on the stage and in the green-room that paralleled his never-complete vindications in the halls of justice. He was still the Major Bombastes Furioso, the "most puissant Bombastes," that the *Evening Post* had called him in 1821. On January 17 of that year William Coleman had printed the letter by Silvanus Miller that was to eventuate, after much ink-slinging, in the abortive trial of December, 1823.

VII

FOOTLIGHTS

1. DRAMATURGE D'OCCASION

As a leading editor, a prominent politician, a paunchy orator—by now his sideburns had disappeared—a figure much in the public eye and ear, with a number of books to his credit, not to speak of a couple of plays, Noah was bound to take a leading rôle in the theatrical life of the day. His superabundant energy overflowed into every available channel.

The ten years between 1820 and 1830 were not only a decade in which his powers and hopes reached their zenith, gradually to subside into an echo of their original music, but for our playhouses they were a busy transition. Against a shifting background of foreign taste and talent, against moral fervors, native values were emerging. As late as 1824, President Dwight of Yale College could be writing that "to indulge a taste for playgoing means nothing more nor less than the loss of the most valuable treasure, the immortal soul. If man be determined at so great a price to indulge the gratifications of his unhallowed desires, and yield obedience to the precepts of false morality, he is the murderer of his own soul!"[1]

---

[1] Quoted by Mary Caroline Crawford, in *The Romance of the American Theatre*, page 24, Boston, 1925.

The cities in which the playhouse flourished—Charleston, Washington, Baltimore, New York, Philadelphia—were comfortably populated with such cheerful suicides as these. Philadelphia, of old the intellectual center of the nation, was slowly yielding its theatrical leadership, which included control of the Baltimore showhouses. As the country grew out of the stagecoach era, as Fulton's folly became the improved steamboat, and Clinton's Big Ditch emerged as the Erie Canal, as turnpikes increased in number, as a proletarian class arose with a modicum of leisure,—as the interior of the playhouse itself advanced from candlelight and smoky spermaceti lamps to the new wonder of gas, conditions were conspiring to make New York the amusement focus of the nation.

The Keans, Charles Mathews, the elder Booth, Macready, the Kembles, Conway, Cooke,—these English stars landed first in New York and were there appreciated before they traveled over the circuit. It was they, rather than the play, that people flocked to see. The actor, not the drama, was the thing. Our Forrests, when they at last arose to rival these importations, and to foster a native product, were decried by all but such patriots as Bryant, Halleck, Legget and Noah. It was an arduous life, but with rewards proportionately great.

Native drama, from the very beginning, had begged suffrage from the upper classes, whose upperness, so far as the arts were concerned, consisted chiefly in a spiritual allegiance to England. Tyler had invoked theatrical patriotism; so had Barker; so would Noah and later dramatists invoke it.

Our theaters were ill-ventilated fire-traps. Imagination, however, once the curtain had risen from behind the glamor of the oil lights, wrought its familiar miracle. That the ranters of the day should have captivated their audiences attests yet again the ever-willing surrender of the playgoer's fancy. Plays, as crude as the acting and the scenery and the theaters, reeked of blood and reverberated with thunder. It was our histrionic, our dramaturgic, adolescence,—a prolonged transition from a prolonged infancy, as sober, as humorless as the awkward age. Small wonder that soon the burlesque, the minstrel show, the travesty and the conscienceless pun, would flourish as an antidote begotten by the very miasma of our "serious" stage.

Of this transitional period Noah was an important part; one of the most recent of our historians of American drama goes so far as to suggest, indeed, that his plays "deserved more recognition than they received."[1] They seem to have received plenty—from their author, in any case. And, to judge from the printed comment and controversy of the time, from his contemporaries, too.

Price and Simpson, managers of the Park Theater, which queened it for so long over the other Gotham houses, were friends of the Tammany editor. This made it as easy for Noah to live behind the scenes as in front of the footlights. To be sure, writing in 1832 to Dunlap, the first historian of our native stage, our versatile Noah abounded in modest demurrers. His plays, he protested, had been written *ad captandum*, or, as who should say, on the wing. He was a mere amateur, "a sort of volunteer supernumerary", a dramatic writer "by particular desire, and for this night only," as was printed on the play-bills. His "line", he avowed, had been "in the more rugged paths of politics, a line in

---

[1] *A History of the American Drama.* From The Beginning to the Civil War. By Arthur Hobson Quinn, New York, 1923, p. 198.

which there is more fact than poetry, more feeling than fiction; in which, to be sure, there are 'exits and entrances' —where the 'prompter's whistle' is constantly heard in the voice of the people, but which, in our popular government, almost disqualifies us for the more soft and agreeable translation to the lofty conceptions of tragedy, the pure diction of genteel comedy, or the wit, gaiety and humor of broad farce."

The disclaimer is polite—and unconvincing. In his politics Noah was theatrical; in his theatricals, political. These doings are all of a piece. When John Searle, to celebrate the occasion of Charles Mathews' first appearance at the Park Theater (in the farce, *Monsieur Tonson*), painted a picture of the interior, assigning to Noah a prominent position among the play-lovers, he but antedated on canvas the perspective of history. At the dinner given in honor of Kean, closing his first visit to America, in December of 1820, who was it that rose to deliver the toast, if not the ubiquitous Mordecai?

The first of Noah's plays for the Park Theater was produced on June 21, 1819, and was printed shortly thereafter. It was a patriotic-historic evocation entitled *She Would Be A Soldier, or The Plains of Chippewa.*[1] The play was repeated on Monday, July 5th, in appropriate observance of the star-spangled holiday.

Noah, as fond of writing prefaces as any Shaw, took occasion, after explaining that his *bagatelle* was written in a few days, to discuss the chances of the native theatrical product. This he did, all things considered, with a rare equanimity.

[1] See the very important *Annals of The New York Stage*, by George D. C. Odell. New York, 1927, vol. II, p. 535. The play is reprinted in Montrose J. Moses' *Representative Plays By American Dramatists.*

For the casts and other details of Noah's dramas, see Appendix I, "Addenda to Noah's Plays."

"Writing plays," he avowed, "is not my 'vocation'; and even if the mania was to seize me I should have to contend with powerful obstacles, and very stubborn prejudices; to be sure, these in time might be removed, but I have no idea of being the first to descend into the arena, and become a gladiator for the American Drama. These prejudices against native productions, however they may be deplored as impugning native genius, are nevertheless very natural. An American audience, I have no doubt, would be highly pleased with an American play, if the performance afforded as much gratification as a good English one; but they pay their money to be pleased, and if we cannot afford pleasure, we have no prescriptive right to ask for approbation . . .

"Mr. Dunlap, of this city, has written volumes of plays, and written well, 'excellent well,' but he made nothing; nay, he hardly obtained that civic wreath which he fairly earned. Barker, of Philadelphia, whose muse is the most delicate and enticing, has hung up his harp, which, I dare say, is covered with dust and cobwebs; and even Harby, of Charleston, whose talents are of the finest order, and who is a bold yet chaste poet, gained but little profit and applause from his labours. We must not expect, therefore, more encouragement for the American Drama than may be sufficient to urge us on. We will succeed in time, as well as the English, because we have the same language, and equal intellect; but there must be system and discipline in writing plays—a knowledge of stage effect—of sound, cadences, fitness of time and place, interest of plot, spirit of delineation, nature, poetry, and a hundred *et ceteras*, which are required, to constitute a good dramatic poet, who cannot, in this country, and while occupied in other pursuits, spring up over night like asparagus, or be watered and put in the sun, like a geranium in a flower pot.

". . . New plays, in this country, are generally performed, for the first time, as anonymous productions: I did not withhold my name from this, because I knew that my friends would go and see it performed, with the hope of being pleased, and my opponents would go with other motives, so that between the two parties a good house would be the result. This was actually the case, and two performances produced nearly $2,400; I hope this may encourage Americans of more talent to attempt something.

"National plays should be encouraged. They have done everything for the British nation, and can do much for us; they keep alive the recollection of important events, by representing them in a manner at once natural and alluring. We have a fine scope, and abundant materials to work with, and a noble country to justify the attempt. The Battle of Chippewa was selected, because it was the most neat and spirited battle fought during the late war, and I wish I was able to do it more justice."

Our drama, long before Noah, had conjured forth its gladiators. Despite the resolution of the Continental Congress, on October 20, 1774, which discountenanced "all kinds of gaming, cock-fighting, exhibitions of shews, plays, and other expensive diversions and entertainments," there was a plenty of topical drama. Largely, as in the case of the impassioned dramatic activity that followed upon the establishment of the Union of Socialist Soviet Republics, and for a similar reason, this drama was discussive and propagandistic. Far more passionate than logical, it sprang momentarily to artistic life, impelled by the heat of its passions. But for a moment only.

The evolution of a national form into which to transmute the new mines of national material could hardly have occurred to our few playwrights; had it done so, it would have appeared as the very height of aesthetic, academic affectation. Just as, at first, making for ourselves national songs, for the words proclaiming our independence of the enemy we borrowed the very tunes of that enemy,—just as Francis Key, but a few years before, had fitted his patriotic words to an old English drinking tune,—so in our stumbling efforts toward a native drama we laid, cuckoo-like, our eggs in foreign nests. English, French, German pieces lay ready for adaptation. Why should managers risk money on problematic homespun talent when approved material was to be had, across the water, for the asking?

Historians and biographers were in little better case than native dramatists. Writing, several years after the zenith of his dramatic career, to a gentleman who proposed to prepare a biography of Bolívar, Noah took the opportunity to comment that "In Europe where there are men of fortune & men of leisure every book sells & every author is rewarded." (Slightly exaggerated, *n'est-ce pas?*) "In our country we want literary population, & wealth to patronise literary labours."[1]

Recording the first production of Noah's first melodrama to deal with a native theme, Mr. Odell finds it "strange to relate" that the piece was "admittedly American in subject-matter and authorship." Many an American had resorted to anonymity so as to avoid the prejudice against American compositions. Others had pretended English origin. "Only the editorial influence of the author," continues Mr. Odell, "could have affected so unusual a result."

Of the play itself, distinguishing between historic importance and dramatic worth, little need be said. It is a thrice-told tale of a heroine who, fleeing a detested suitor, dons

---

[1] From a manuscript letter dated New York, July 29, 1828, in the Harvard College Library Collection.

male disguise and follows her lover to the American camp, there to find him apparently unfaithful. Attempting to communicate with her adored Lenox, Christine, owing to her incriminating silence, is about to be executed as a spy. Of course Lenox rescues her for a happier fate.

The battle of Chippewa, which was still fresh in the minds of all patriots, had taken place on July 5, 1814, under the direction of the victorious Generals, Jacob Brown and Winfield Scott. Those who have tested Noah's report by the records find that his description of the encounter is fairly accurate. It is more than likely that contemporary spectators found it rather amusing to have Lenox, in the course of the play—as Professor Quinn reminds us—relate to General Brown the details of the battle that Brown himself had directed.

2. A SIEGE, A CONFLAGRATION, A NEW THEATER

Mr. Noah, in his letter of 1832 addressed to Dunlap, is neither a complete historian of his theatrical activities, nor a trustworthy one. "My last appearance as a dramatic writer," he wrote in that document, "was in another national piece called 'The Siege of Tripoli', which the managers persuaded me to bring out for my own benefit, being my first attempt to derive any profit from dramatic efforts. The piece was elegantly got up—the house crowded with beauty and fashion—everything went off in the happiest manner; when, a short time after the audience retired, the Park Theater was discovered to be on fire, and in a short time was a heap of ruins. This conflagration burnt out all my dramatic fire and energy, since when I have been, as you well know, peaceable employed in settling the affairs of the nations, and mildly engaged in the political differences and disagreements which are so fruitful in our great state."

It is not strange that the career of Noah should be so strewn with dubious dates, events and outcomes, if the man himself, only ten years after the height of his theatrical activities, should confuse the chronology of his plays. *The Siege of Tripoli* does not appear to have been printed. Had Noah troubled, however, to glance back over the files of his own *National Advocate*, or to have recalled the date of the famous fire that razed the first Park Theater, he would have established the proper order of the piece. *The Siege of Tripoli*, far from being his last play, was the third to be given at the Park.

On March 16, 1820, was presented *The Wandering Boys, or The Castle of Olival*. This was none other than an adaptation, by an English hand, of Noah's youthful melodrama, *Paul and Alexis*, written for Mrs. Young and produced in Charleston just before he left for his duties as Consul to Tunis.

On May 15 the management of the Park Theater offered the final novelty of the season, *The Siege of Tripoli*.

By the custom of the day, the proceeds of the third performance, which in this case occurred on the 24th, went to the author of the piece. The play, which seems to have been a success, went off as usual. About one or two o'clock that morning the theater was discovered to be in flames, beyond saving. Fortunately, the treasurer of the company had taken the receipts of the evening with him. Noah's profits were four hundred dollars; he forgot to tell Dunlap, among other things, that he at once turned over this sum to the members of the company who seemed most to need it. Between the burning of the old Park and the erection of the New the managers occupied the theater on Anthony Street, in which they were installed, without costumes or scenery, on May 29. On July 4, 1820, Noah's *Siege of Tripoli* was repeated . . . Under the name *Yusef Caramalli* it would be welcomed in Philadelphia on January 25, 1822.

Yusef Caramalli, or The Siege of Tripoli, was generally received as a good omen for the eventual emergence and success of the native drama. Like its predecessor, it was in great measure a tribute to the prowess of new America. It was, moreover, founded upon the studies and experiences of Noah during his consulship at Tunis. Nor are we to be surprised if dungeons, incarcerations and stout-hearted heroines play an oratorical rôle, before a background boasting a maximum of photographic realism.

The Pasha of Tripoli is at war with both Spain and the United States. He captures an American vessel, on board which are Gonzales and his bride-to-be, Rosabel. The Pasha is smitten with the woman's beauty; she, fearing the effects of a monarch's rivalry (although this Pasha, Yusef, appears to be humane and understanding) conceals her betrothal to Gonzales. Gonzales, however, of a violently jealous nature, unable to endure the Pasha's attentions to Rosabel, plots to seize a vessel and escape with his betrothed. Also, in order to test her feelings, he suggests that she assassinate Yusef. Upon her refusal he attempts suicide, only to be saved by the Pasha, who thus learns the true state of affairs. Secretly he determines to set them at liberty.

Harry Montfort, American Lieutenant and captive of the frigate *Philadelphia*, is another who has yielded to Rosabel's charms; he keeps his secret, even from her. The Pasha is ready to restore her to her lover, but Gonzeles, jealous beyond reason, considers this generosity as proof that Rosabel has been unfaithful. He throws her into the sea and escapes in a vessel. Rosabel is rescued by Montfort. When later events return Gonzales to the Pasha's hands, Yusef imprisons the fanatical lover, who, even when Rosabel visits him in his cell, refuses to believe in her innocence, glories in his assaults and regrets only that they should have proved unsuccessful. Inducing the Pasha to allow her to pass judgment upon the unworthy wretch, she exiles him to a nearby island, and gives her hand to the heroic Lieutenant.

This ingenuous action occurs against such historic scenes as the burning of the *Philadelphia* by Decatur; the victory of Eaton at Derne; the Pasha's suit for peace with the United States. The scene painter Robbins prepared a specially advertised scene representing the harbor of Tripoli, the Pasha's Castle, the Consul's House and other landmarks, taken from a photograph by Mr. Earle. The papers reported that Commodore Chauncey permitted a number of the "gallant tars of the Washington to volunteer on the occasion, and Major Smith, the Commandant of the Marines" was equally generous with a detachment of his men. The result was a display of soldiers and sailors almost filling the stage and bringing down the house with music of fife and drum and the martial tramp of feet.

Cries of "Author! Author!" rang through the theater. When Mr. Simpson succeeded in reaching Noah, however, the dramatist declined to take his bow, and begged to be excused . . . Miss Johnson's benefit on the opening night amounted to the tidy sum of $1200. As another unidentified newspaper remarked, "These national plays are well calculated to keep alive the memory of national services. It will not be long before we shall have an *American* drama, if they are equally as (sic) well encouraged."[1]

Noah, it appears, was associated in the minds of producer and public as a national-holiday author. A familiar figure at the old Park, a personage during the Anthony Street interim, he returned with the new Park Theater to public favor. In *Marion, or The Hero Of Lake George*, he sought to repeat the success of *She Must Be A Soldier*. The two are, in every genetic sense, companion pieces. As the earlier had drawn upon the War of 1812, the later used as point of inspiration the Battle of Saratoga in the Revolution. The motif of the woman who, in order to save her lover, disguises herself as a man, had fascinated Noah since he had borrowed so heavily from the French for his maiden-effort, *The Fortress of Sorrento*. It was repeated in the drama of Chippewa; it is repeated again in the melodrama of Marion.

Marion, or The Hero of Lake George was disclosed to New York's first-nighters on the evening of November 25, 1821, Evacuation Day, at the New Theater, which had opened its doors on Saturday, September 1st of that year. Familiar talents graced the bill of what Mr. Odell describes as "this important native work".

The melodrama, from the historian's—and even the producer's—standpoint, appears to possess a factitious importance. Odell[2] is not the only commentator to have discovered in its excited simplicity a cinematic character,—a certain skill with the elements of suspense and melodramatic danger, an "ample knowledge of stage effect derived from two decades

[1] The clippings on which these notations are based are to be found in the huge Theatrical Collection of Harvard College.
[2] *Annals of the New York Stage*, vol. iii, pp. 16, 17, 30.

of blood and thunder." He lauds it as "one of the best pieces of its kind," and discovers, in its printed version, additional proof that side flats with doors, far from having been introduced to the stage by Mme. Vestris, in her production of *London Assurance* (1841), were well known to the American stage of 1821.[1]

The play is an orgy of noble sentiments and deeds, in which the Romeo-Juliet motif is applied to the theme of the Revolution,—in which Emma's Tory brother, Beverly, captivated by her rebel husband, Marion, can confess that "We almost like the treason because we love the traitor," thus preparing us for his mother's capitulation, and his own, to the cause of the revolutionists and to the marriage of their Emma to Marion.

Its quality, as drama, may be savored in the close of Act I, when Marion, about to be taken by the Britishers, harangues the crowd:

In the name of liberty, obey him not. Friends! Countrymen! would you surrender to a cruel death, a soldier who fights for freedom? Would you give to those merciless men a citizen, who voluntarily has sacrificed his fortune, his health, his comfort, that your homes and your firesides may be tranquil and happy? The rising glory of our country, its rapid march to freedom, the sacred struggle, and the claims of posterity, cry aloud against the sinful act. No! let foreign mercenaries find no succour among a brave people fighting for independence.

Or at the opening of Act II, in which Marion, imprisoned, salutes the daybreak:

Day dawns, and the lively bugles re-echoing through the forest arouse the slumbering soldier, while the bright beams

[1] See Appendix I.

of the rising sun will soon be reflected from the polished musquets and glittering sabres. How cheering, how animating; yet to me how painful. Confined again to the gloomy walls of a dungeon, and in the power of a cruel enemy, hope has almost forsaken me. Let me not despair—though *my* life be sacrificed, yet there are stout hearts and iron nerves still left to do our cause full justice. My wife! my dear Emma! how will you bear this separation—how reconcile yourself to your Marion's death? Oh let me not doubt her fortitude. She will bear it like the wife of a soldier. Like one who loves her husband dearly, but whose glory is yet dearer to her. (*Noise of bolts and bars without.*) So! here comes the persecutor to close the final scene.

3. NOAH VS. COLEMAN

For reasons as excellent as they were amusing, Noah dedicated the printed copy of Marion,[1] "without permission", to his rival, the editor of the *Evening Post*. That worthy physician-littérateur, William Coleman, had given himself the pleasure of abusing the piece without taking the trouble to witness it. More, he proclaimed publicly his absence from the performance.

"On Monday," he had written to his *Post*, "a new play called Marion was presented at our theatre, written by the renowned editor of the *Advocate* (God bless us!) who with his usual modesty, and more than his usual gallantry, recommended that the soldiery should occupy the dress boxes, and drive the ladies up stairs to second tier. I was not present (I had been once before at the christening of one of his brats) but reports unite in declaring it was the most wretched stuff

[1] *Marion, or, The Hero of Lake George.* A Drama in Three Acts. New York, (January) 1822.

that ever insulted an audience. He tells us, this morning, since nobody else will tell it for him, that there were about 2436 persons present. It is probable that there may have been that number; for, it would be strange, indeed, if there could not have been found as many in this city, soldiers and all, who would accept of a ticket on a holiday night. The crowd on a first night can be no test, but let him give it out again, and if he does not hear the second part of the same air which was played at the second presentation of the Battle of Chippewa, he may bless his stars for his good luck. That's all."

It was far from all. The records reveal Coleman's malice. He himself, after the première of *The Siege of Tripoli*, had sung an altogether different air. In the *Post* of May 16, 1820—as Noah took care to remind him, with reprint, in the Dedication to *Marion*—he had complimented the playwright for his generosity in offering the piece to Miss Johnson; had reported that the piece had met "with a greater degree of success than we ever recollect to have attended an original piece on our stage." Noah, observed Coleman, had been very happy "in the local allusions with which the piece abounds, and which were enjoyed with a keen relish by the audience. When the curtain fell, there arose a great outcry for the author, from all parts of the house, and the pit stood up, determined that he should appear. Nothing could be heard but author, author, author, &c. &c. We conclude this hasty notice by expressing the hope, that this piece may be productive of profit, as well as honour, to its ingenious author."

The date of Coleman's paragraph upon Noah's *Siege of Tripoli* is important to the political and judiciary history of these gentlemen. It will be recalled[1] that although Noah's alleged offer to sell himself out to Clinton, at a fee of between $7000. and $10,000., had occurred during 1818, the original accusatory innuendo of Silvanus Miller did not appear in the columns of Coleman's *Evening Post* until January, 1821. Here was Coleman himself, *as late as May 16, 1820*, praising Noah unreservedly. This lends added weight to Noah's insistence that the charge was injected into municipal affairs for the express purpose of spoiling his chances of obtaining the shrievalty. If the charges were true, those who made them were guilty of withholding action for almost three years, and in a sense became partners in a conspiracy of silence.

It is interesting to observe that even in 1822 the Revolutionary War and the War of 1812 were still being fought.

"The world," orated Noah to the dedicatee-*malgré-lui* of his play, "has attributed your opposition, to certain motives which I do not think exist. They say that our political differences have produced a personal excitement on your part, which breaks out in flashes against anything that I may chance to write . . . In confidence, let me whisper my suspicions in your ear:—I fear that you never cordially approved the principles of our revolutionary war. I do not find fault with you; this is a free country, and men have a legitimate right to maintain their opinions; but I certainly doubt the policy of enforcing this opinion at this late day, and likewise very much question your prudence in pushing your hostility so furiously against the country during the late war.

"Believe me, my dear Doctor, whatever hopes Great Britain may have formerly indulged of recovering the sovereignty of this great empire, such hopes no longer prevail in the cabinet of St. James . . . Examine, for a moment, the situation of this country. We have twenty-four states in the confederacy, each sovereign and independent—a vast extent

---

[1] See previous chapter.

of territory—a strongly fortified seaboard—a very respectable and efficient naval force—upwards of a million of men capable of bearing arms—and many thousand pieces of artillery. What hopes of conquest, therefore, can a foreign power indulge, separated from us by a world of waters?

"If you are satisfied of this, it is time for you to submit;—to be reconciled to the country, and read the history of our revolutionary war . . .

"In consequence of our independence as a nation, you now enjoy the *otium cum dignitate*—a fine house, handsomely furnished, your equipage, your musical coteries, your comfortable game of chess, your 'rum jelly'. You can sit by your crackling fire, dressed in your silk morning gown, velvet cap, and green morocco slippers—surrounded in your old age —I was going to say by friends—at least, by a sensible family of handsome children—your table well supplied, and your wine of the best Nabob quality . . . Instead of being the humble vassal of a sovereign, you are one of the sovereign people yourself; you are part proprietor of a free press; you may abuse the country; you may ridicule its strength; make merry with the institutions; you may sneer at the barbarism of the people; at their unfashionable integrity, and prudish morality; nay, you may even abuse my plays, but this you can do without hindrance or control, and there is no person who dare make you afraid;—why not be friends then with the country—why be the last to acknowledge its independence? . . . As I intend to dramatize certain other events of that period, promise me not to abuse them as you have done this poor ricketty bantling, whom you have thus dragged prematurely to the light, and I shall forever acknowledge myself to be, Dear Doctor, most seriously and reverentially,

"Your true admirer and friend, to command,

THE AUTHOR."

Infelicitous as a critic, Coleman was equally unfortunate as a prophet. For the success of *Marion* was, for those days, so salient as to draw special comment from one of the most recent historians of our drama. Mr. Quinn, indeed, uses it as proof that, for all the virtuous complaints of the native playwright, the public was generous with its patronage. Wood's Diary records the receipts for the performances of this period. Such English favorites as *Fazio* and *The School for Scandal*, and the Shakespearean repertory, had been playing to houses averaging $200. to $300. The Noah piece, on a rainy night, took in $435; the following night, with clear weather, brought in $811.50.[1]

Marion, in fact, was popular for many years; it was given at the Broadway Theater on July 8, 1848. And surely the shades of Noah, as garrulous in Elysium as ever he was on this earth, but lately had reason to leer in the direction of Coleman's ghost. For, on April 22, 1932, as the first of three performances commemorating the bicentennial of George Washington's birth, the students of Columbia University presented at the Mc Millin Academic Theater *Marion, or The Hero of Lake George* . . .

4. Print—and Realism—vs. Performance

To maintain his reputation as waver of the flag and as patriot-in-chief to the management of the Park, Noah prepared a theatrical celebration for March 4, 1822. The city had been provided with a new constitution; the theater had illuminated its front, and for this night, in addition to the dramatized version of Cooper's *Spy*, which had been presented for the first time three evenings before, offered *Oh, Yes! or, The New Constitution*, "by a Gentleman of this City."

[1] Quinn, op. cit., p. 152.

The piece was not printed; what it was like we may guess from the program, from which it appears that Cowell, Kent, Mrs. Holman, Reed, Woodhull and Phillips were in the cast. There were scenic views of City Hall, of Tammany Hall as seen from the middle of the Park; there was a procession of Standard Bearers, with "the number of the majorities of the different wards of the city", and in conclusion a ballet dance by Juliet Durang.

Evidently the New Constitution was to Tammany's taste, for the view of the Hall on the stage of the Park showed it illuminated in honor of the day. It was this Constitution, by the way, that had made the office of sheriff elective; perhaps, when Noah lost the shrievalty he changed his title to *Oh, No!*

Within three and a half months Noah, the paladin of oppressed peoples, was ready with a new play, inspired by the struggle of Greece for Liberty. The realism of *The Siege of Tripoli* had set the old Park afire. *The Grecian Captive*, which opened on the evening of June 17, 1822, was to meet with events less startling but, in their way, hardly less memorable.

The program omitted two of the chief characters,—an elephant and a camel, procured, in a passion for more realism and for local color, from a nearby menagerie. "At great expense to the management," no doubt. And thereby hangs the tale . . . or, part of it.

The Grecian Captive, or The Fall of Athens was written by Noah for his friend, though relation, the actor Aaron Phillips. Phillips, as Noah told Dunlap, wanted "something to bring a house", whereupon our paladin seized upon the contemporary excitement, not overlooking its ideological reference to our own achievement of independence. He stretched a point and wrote the *pièce d'occasion* in blank verse. He stretched another, and whether through his own desire or that of the evening's beneficiary, had printed copies of the piece distributed gratis to the thousand patrons as they entered the showhouse. It would have been bad enough thus to tempt an audience into distraction from the actors on the stage; but the fact that the play was in blank verse made it all the easier for the reader-spectators to catch the actors, who had so hurriedly prepared their rôles, in marked deviations from the text. It was not only the fluttering of the pages as, with one accord, the public frequently turned the leaves of the duodecimo pamphlet,[1] that disturbed the performers into forgetfulness. Indeed, even the elephant and the camel shied at the crackling of paper. No. The dramatis personae were not letter perfect in the first place.

Why should they have been, as one of the chief comedians was to ask twenty-two years after? The play was for one night only. Cowell, with a generation passed between the night of the play and his recording of it, could still recall vividly his consternation at the sight and sound of those playbooks being thumbed as the piece progressed. "I am not easily embarrassed. If I had not been the principal victim in the whole business—for I was on the stage nearly the whole of the piece—I could have enjoyed the anxiety of the audience endeavoring to find out where we were. You might see them thumbing over the leaves, one after another, and then turn them all back, listen an instant, and then listen again. Another appeals to his neighbor, and he shakes his head in despair. I was assured very seriously by a young

---

[1] *The Grecian Captive, or The Fall of Athens.* By M. M. Noah. As Performed at the New York (sic) Theatre. Published by E. M. Murden, Circulating Library and Dramatic Repository. No. 4 Chambers-Street.

critic, the next day, that I had *actually sometimes cut out a whole page at a time*. But I could not laugh at it, and considered the arrangement a rudeness on the part of Mr. Phillips. At nearly the close of a long and laborious season, a whole company has cheerfully, for the sake of serving him, undertaken to *get through* with a composition that the author himself could never wish should see daylight; and though Phillips knew that not a soul could learn more than the action, he, for the sake of a few dollars, lets an audience into a secret which, for their own sake, as well as ours, they had better not have known."

Noah, trying to soothe the irate Cowell, acknowledged on the spot that it had been bad taste to distribute the books of the play. He confessed, too, that the language "was very hard to learn." Cowell, unappeased, stuttered back, "So is Peter Piper picked a peck of pickled peppers, but it's trash for all that!" Alas, worse was yet to come. All that Noah vouchsafes to us in his reminiscence of the piece is that the elephant, a huge fellow, so rocked the castle on his back, the Grecian general nearly lost his balance. Miss Johnson's adventures on camel-back he spares us. Cowell, relentlessly, tells the whole story, and with a gusto undimmed by two decades. It was Phillips, as Alexander, who came on in the last scene, *"wiggling* on the back of a real elephant." Unfortunately, the noble representative of the Proboscidea was not house-broken, and, in Cowell's dainty euphemism, introduced into the action "an unexpected hydraulic experiment . . . to the great astonishment and discomfiture of the musicians". Amid the shouts of the audience the performance came to a most undignified close.

The next day, in the *Advocate*, Noah with Christian forgiveness overlooked the share that Cowell and his associates had

had in damning the piece with an indifferent and unconscientious performance. He even excused the actors, and attributed the fiasco to his imprudence in permitting the books to be given away.[1]

In any case, Noah, anticipating history, had in his play restored Athens to Greece.

As with more than one of Noah's plays, *The Grecian Captive* refers back, in all likelihood, to the same French melodrama that John Howard Payne used for his *Ali Pacha, or The Signet Ring*. This may be one of the reasons why Payne's play had been attributed to Noah. The tale of the captive beauty and her restoration to the arms of love is trite; the blank verse of Noah is as stilted as his prose. The animating cause of the action, however, as almost always in Noah, is the spirit of liberation. The characters are virtually Americans, and Greece itself is described in terms but slightly altered from the famous line of the then virginal Star-Spangled Banner.

Kiminski, at the end, delivers the glorious message against a pageant of universal heroes that begins with Homer and parades right down to Washington, Bolívar and Lafayette:

Kim. Behold a glorious termination to all our painful struggles! Greece is free! The land of the great, the home of the brave. The queen of the Arts has broken the bonds of tyranny and slavery—and a glorious day succeeds to a long night of peril and calamity—Now to merit freedom by the establishment of just laws—a free and benevolent spirit to all.

The curious, in quest of side-lights upon the civic and theatrical situations in the New York of 1823, may turn for

---

[1] *See Thirty Years Passed Among The Players In England And America* . . . Theatrical Life of Joe Cowell, Comedian. Written By Himself, New York, 1844. Part 2, American. Chapter III.

acrid comment upon Noah and his fellow-playwrights to the jaundiced pages of a tiny volume by Samuel B. Judah. This lawyer, playwright and rhymester, in his corrosive medley, turned scorpion-like upon the city and almost every one of its celebrities. In his hobbling pentameters he saw, at times, with the keen sight of hatred. His *Gotham And The Gothamites*, however, was promptly suppressed and he himself—as soon as he was pulled forth from his anonymity—sent to prison. He was released because of ill health.[1]

5. SLOW CURTAIN

The Grecian Captive is the last of Noah's plays to have come down to us in the printed text. At least two more, at long intervals, were produced at the Park Theater. On September 8, 1824, in honor of Lafayette's visit to the famous playhouse, Noah resumed his rôle of patriotico-artistic reception committee and playwright-laureate, offering in homage his *Siege of Yorktown*. What that play was like—it followed the performance of *Laugh When You Can*—we may only conjecture. At most, a patriotic after-piece.

The list of Noah's plays may be, as here recounted, complete; it is not, however, authenticated beyond question, and surely we get the least assistance from Noah himself and his contemporaries. Thus Hudson, in his not unfailingly reliable history of our journalism, attributes to him *Ali Pacha, or The Signet Ring*, which belongs to John Howard Payne; the *Siege of Dalmatia*, which seems to be an error for *Damascus*, and was written by John Hughes; the ballet, *Natalie*, and a tragedy, *Ambition*, of which the latter was not produced until long after Noah had died.

[1] See Appendix I.

It is to Rees that we owe the attribution of *Oh, Yes, or The New Constitution*, to Noah, as also that of an undiscoverable piece entitled *The Grand Canal*. He tells us, too, that the Major's following, as represented by the editor of *The Mirror*, looked forward to the promise of a play by their favorite to be entitled *Seven Years In The Life Of A Politician*.[1] A pity that Noah never found the time to fulfill this promise, suggesting so many possibilities for timely disclosures, criticism of contemporary personalities and principles, and autobiographical data.

Noah compares not at all ill with the playwrights of his day. That, to be sure, is a negative compliment. Dramatic taste was still at a low ebb, and even when fine words were used they referred to mediocre performance. Crudity was the rule in dramaturgic conception and in production, nor is it unlikely that if we were to witness the acting of his time we should be less pleased than were our ancestors with the strutting, declamatory methods of the oil and gaslight epoch. A stage we had; drama, not yet.

Noah is an ancestor of all such as, in our theater, wave stoutly the American flag. His latest descendant is the George M. Cohan of the musical comedies. Our paladin had begun that waving in real life long before his first American piece was produced in New York. From his contemporaries he learned much; he was a generous borrower of ideas and plots, from France especially. Yet, into his plays, for all their self-helpings from pieces melodramatic, Gothic, and piratical, he managed to inject not only the recent realities of national existence but scenes and sentiments from his own uncommon

---

[1] See *The Dramatic Authors of America*. By James Rees. Philadelphia, 1845, p. 109–111.

experiences . . . For this reason the plays, with all their rhodomontade, their fustian, their star-spangled-banality, their hollow thunder, remain a part of Noah's biography and part, as well, of the biography of our nation.

Noah's greatest play, planned during all these years on a veritably cosmic scale, was fast approaching production. It was given in a single performance, with an entire city as stage. Its cast was regimental. Its author was all but Jehovan. And the fiasco reverberated through the continents.

THE CORNERSTONE OF NOAH'S PROJECTED HAVEN FOR THE JEWS

It now reposes in the rooms of the Buffalo Historical Society.

VIII

EMBARKATION FOR UTOPIA

1. PAGEANT OF PARADOX

A T daybreak of September 15, 1825, the inhabitants of the
frontier village of Buffalo were startled out of their slumber by a loud detonation booming from the front of the Court House and reverberating across the Lake. Dawn was coming up like thunder. Cannon, in many-mouthed celebration, were to roar before that historic day was done. Shortly, excited communicants in Masonic and military array, accompanied by throngs of exalted civilians, would be streaming in from the general direction of New York City, to swell beyond comfort the normal population of twenty-five hundred. Sleepy Buffalo had suddenly acquired a place upon the map. Today, in the fiftieth year of American independence, was to be founded a republic within the republic,—a haven of religious freedom within the haven of political liberty. A new, if self-appointed, redeemer had arisen in Zion.

By ten o'clock the military and Masonic companies had lined up before the Masonic Lodge. Within an hour the procession, led by Grand Marshal Colonel Potter on a prancing steed, was moving. The tramp of soldiery, of national, state and municipal officers, advanced to the spot where the corner stone of a new Canaan was to be laid. Behind the band and the vanguard filed stewards, apprentices and representatives of their associated crafts, master masons, senior and junior deacons, senior and junior wardens, masters and past-masters of Lodges, members of the reverend clergy, more stewards bearing the symbolic corn, wine and oil, and a principal architect, with square, level and plumb, flanked on either side by a Globe, and backed by a Bible. There must have been, too, in this paradoxical pageantry, a sprinkling of the Chosen People for whom this new Promised Land, this Ararat, had been chosen . . .

And now all eyes were fixed upon a portly gentleman of forty, proudly erect of carriage, florid of face, keen of eye, sandy-haired over fleshy cheeks and an eagle's beak, who strode just ahead of the rear guard of Royal Arch Masons and Knights Templar. Over his black costume, majestically austere, were thrown rich judicial robes of crimson silk, trimmed with the purity of ermine. From his thickish neck depended a medal of gold glistening from high embossments.

It was a striking rig-out, and he himself, with a practiced theatrical eye, had designed it. More: he had designed his ephemeral eminence and its grandiose title. This was the prime mover of the day unto which would be more than sufficient the evil and good thereof. This was he who, for his redemptorist activities, had by Palestine been named Prince of the House of David . . . "I, Mordecai Manuel Noah, Citizen of the United States of America, late Consul of the said States for the City and Kingdom of Tunis, High Sheriff of New York, Counsellor at Law, and, by the grace of God [and printer's ink!] Governor and Judge of Israel."

Through the blare of the band under this sunny sky the striding Prince beholds an apocalyptic vision. The Jews, rightful possessors of Palestine, are slaves in their own territory. In the Holy Land (outside of Jerusalem, Hebron and Tiberias, where there are but several hundred families, comprising three of the most ancient congregations in the world) dwell some hundred thousand of these Dispossessed of history. Suddenly, at the signal of his proclamation, the Disinherited of the nations arise beneath their burdens, and begin, across continents, across oceans, a March to Freedom. From *Erez Yisrael* they come, from the shores of the Mediterranean . . . From the few hundreds in Samaria they come . . . From Crimea and the Ukraine, from the ten thousand in Cochin China, black Jews and white . . . From the coasts of Malabar and Coremandel, from the heart of India . . . From the million and a half in the dominions of the Ottoman Porte and the Barbary States, from the hundred thousand in Constantinople and Saloniki, from Cairo and Ispahan and from beyond the Euphrates . . . Now in straggling knots, now in regiments, tramping sturdily, inaudibly, here beside their redeemer . . .

God moves in ways mysterious His wonders to perform. For whither, of all places, should our Messiah and his pageant be directing their steps, if not to the one spot in Buffalo where a Jewish Messiah would be only less welcome than the Prince of Darkness, or the Pope of the Holy Roman Catholic Church? To the modest frame structure, then but five years old, under whose tiny four-pointed tower was housed the St. Paul's Episcopal Church . . . And where should the corner stone of the nascent Utopia be reposing if not—in four-square defiance of all anathema—upon the very communion table of St. Paul's?

Underneath a Hebrew inscription from Deuteronomy, 6.4,

שמע ישראל ה' אלהינו ה' אחד,

which every pious Jew prays in the face of danger and before delivering himself up to sleep or to death, was engraved upon the face of the stone, which is still to be seen in the Buffalo Historical Museum, the legend:

ARARAT
A City of Refuge for the Jews
Founded by MORDECAI MANUEL NOAH
in the month of Tizri Sept. 1825 &
in the Fiftieth Year of American Independence

Reaching the door to the church, the troops, like the waters of the Red Sea, divided to make way for the entrance of the procession into the aisles. The band struck up the Grand March from *Judas Maccabeus*. No sooner had these strains died out than within, from the pipes of the new Hall and Erben organ installed but ten days earlier, at an expense of $430., poured forth a *Jubilate*. There was a flutter of femininity in the red-cushioned seats as the Reverend Addison Searle began, in emphatic tones, the reading of the Morning Service. The choir, to the tune of Old Hundredth, intoned "Before Jehovah's Awful Throne". There was the morning prayer, followed by lessons, respectively, from Jeremiah 31 and Zephaniah 3.8. There were special Psalms for the occasion, 97, 98, 99, 100, and 127, the last recited in verse. Antecommunion service, a Psalm in the original Hebrew, Benediction . . . and the religious observance was over.

Mr. Mordecai Manuel Noah, however, had just begun. That which had preceded had been but a theatrical setting for his Messianic maneuvers. Luck, too, had been with him.

The blueprint of Ararat had been mapped out not against the lanes of Buffalo but across the wilderness of Grand Island, a body of some 17,381 acres, lying in the Niagara River, County of Erie, State of New York, about eight miles long, six miles across at the greatest breadth and, at the time of this embarkation, densely grown with timber. Noah, amid the metaphysics of his crowded plans, had little time for such practicalities as geography. Curiosity, if not adherence, attracted to the frontier village throngs far in excess of the boating facilities to Grand Island. It was necessary to find quickly a spot that should serve as symbolical proxy for the founding of the Jewish Intra-nation.

Noah knew but two souls in Buffalo,—Isaac S. Smith, whom he had met in Africa, during the exciting consular days at Tunis, and the Reverend Mr. Addison Searle, who, in those selfsame days, had been a United States chaplain on a government ship cruising the Mediterranean waters. It was through Mr. Smith that the corner stone of Ararat had been procured from the sandstone quarries at Cleveland, Ohio; the inscription, prepared by Noah, was cut by Seth Chapin of Buffalo. And it was through the cordiality of Searle that the tiny stronghold of Episcopalianism was thrown open to Hebrew endeavor.

The Reverend Mr. Searle had entered upon his new duties on March 30 of that year, and there is every reason to believe that if he had not been rector on September 15, 1825, there would have been no dedicatory services in St. Paul's. As it turned out, Noah's latitudinarian friend-in-need was censured for this unwonted display of toleration and for having taken part in the play.[1]

For a play it was, since nothing that was Noah could ever free itself entirely from histrionism. Against the background of the hymns and lessons and services of this kaleidoscopic morning the self-appointed Judge in Israel arose to deliver a meandering discourse, strangely, yet humanly, compounded of religiosity, theology, politics, patriotism, ethnology, delusions of grandeur and . . . real estate.

2. HANDS ACROSS THE CREEDS

This was, declared the Patriarch—and Grand Sachem of Tammany Hall—a Jewish Declaration of Independence.

Magniloquently he reaffirmed the Chosen-ness of his People, and the reëstablishment of the Hebrew government. The nations of the old and new world, he said, "including the children of Africa, have had their rights acknowledged and their governments recognized. The oldest of nations, powerful in numbers and great in resources, remains isolated, without a home, country, or government . . . In calling the Jews together under the protection of the American Constitution and laws and governed by our happy and salutary institutions, it is proper for me to state that this asylum is temporary and provisionary. The Jews never should and never will relinquish the just hope of regaining possession of their ancient heritage, and events in the neighborhood of Palestine indicate an extraordinary change of affairs."

---

[1] For information about the edifice in which the foundation ceremonies took place, consult *History of St. Paul's Church*, Buffalo, N. Y., 1817–1903, by Charles W. Evans (d. 1889) and Continued from 1889 to 1903 by Alice M. Evans Bartlett and G. Hunter Bartlett.

Greece was almost independent of the Ottoman Porte.
Turkey was weakening. Russia was about to march against
Constantinople. Egypt was encouraging commerce and agriculture. The Turks, driven beyond the Bosphorus, might
leave the land of Canaan open to its rightful owners.

For this reorganization of the Jews, Noah, after swiftly
reviewing the various systems by which they had governed
themselves, decided upon the latest,—that of Judges presided
over by the non-hereditary office of Chief Magistrate. Wherefore, having elected himself to that distinction, he justified
his choice.

"Born in a free country, and educated in liberal principles,
familiar with all the duties of government, having enjoyed
the confidence of my fellow citizens in various public trusts,
ardently attached to the principles of our holy faith, and
having devoted years of labor and study to ameliorate the
condition of the Jews, with an unsullied conscience and a
firm reliance on Almighty God, I offer myself as an humble
instrument of his divine will, and solicit the confidence and
protection of our beloved brethren throughout the world.
If there be any person possessing greater facilities and a more
ardent zeal in attempting to restore the Jews to their rights
as a sovereign and independent people, to such will I cheerfully surrender the trust . . .

"Firm of purpose, when the object is public good, I allow
no difficulties to check my progress. Urged to its consideration by strong and irresistible impulse, the project has always
presented itself to me in the most cheering light, in the most
alluring colors; and if the attempt shall result in ameliorating
the condition of the Jews, and shall create a generous and
liberal feeling towards them and open to them the avenues
of science, learning, fame, honor and happiness, who shall

say that I have failed? I ask the trial—and will abide the result."

Hereupon, Noah proceeded to orate a condensed history of the Jews in Europe, from the moment that they settled in England with Julius Caesar down to the very shores of Grand Island, *anno Domini* 1825. It was not an unaffecting summary, based upon something deeper than the chronology of cruelty and misunderstanding with which Noah, from long study and frequent speech-making, was so familiar; it was a dignified, if conservative, emotional epitome.

For Noah, declaiming there in booming prose, at the rector's desk in the high pulpit, to the pews and the full gallery around three sides of the little church, hope smiled down from the heavens. For his hearers, too. It was the Jubilee of the republic. The United States was still something new under God's sun. Optimism was not only a personal idiosyncrasy; it was a national mood.

"Why?" he asked, under the roof of a church into whose liturgy was still written the curse against his own people,— "Why should Christians persecute Jews? Sprung from a common stock, and connected by human ties which should be binding;—if those ties are empty and evanescent, where is the warrant for this intolerance?—not in the religion which they profess; that teaches mildness, charity and good will to all . . . The Jews and Christians are only known by their hostility towards each other. This hostility neither religion recognizes . . . Times have undergone an important change —we all begin to feel that we are formed of the same materials, subject to the same frailties, destined to the same death, and hoping for the same immortality.—Here, then, in this free and happy country, distinctions in religion are unknown; here we enjoy liberty without licentiousness, and land without oppression."

Land . . . Before the Jews had been a nation they had been an agricultural people, and it was again the ambition of Noah to reëstablish the Jews upon the soil. He waxed lyrical, proclaiming agriculture the natural and noble pursuit of man. The State of New York, with its six million acres of cultivated land, suddenly blossomed into a quasi-Sicilian landscape brushed by the stylus of Theocritus.

Between one sentence and another the prophecy becomes a prospectus, and Theocritus is shortly holding out to Jewish capital the inducements of profitable investments in grist-mills, saw-mills, oil mills, fulling mills, carding machines, cotton and woolen factories, iron foundries, trip hammers, distilleries, tanneries, asheries, breweries and numerous *etceteras*. Grand Island, seat of the New Jerusalem, and surrounded by water-power, flashes forth as an ideal site for the erection of . . . industrial plants.

3. "IT IS MY WILL"—
AND THE INDIANS ARE JEWS

Noah had already sent forth to the world his "Proclamation to the Jews". Not a little of his discourse, indeed, was a paraphrase of that ambitious, unsuspecting document. It was in this noble—and practical—pronunciamento that he had dubbed himself Governor and Judge of Israel, and had outlined, against the background of Grand Island, an international polity. His Ararat was not for Jews alone; he invited "my beloved people throughout the world, in common with those of every religious denomination." He renewed, in the name of the Lord, the government of the Jewish nation, and

197

enjoined it "upon all our pious and venerable Rabbis, our Priesdents and Elders of Synagogues, Chiefs of Colleges, and brethren in authority throughout the world, to circulate and make known this my proclamation, and give to it full publicity, credence and effect."

He ordered — *"It is my will"* — that a census of Jews throughout the world be taken.

He *permitted* to remain those Jews who preferred to remain where they were, but asked them to encourage the emigration of the young.

He enjoined all Jews who happened at the time to be in "military employment of the different sovereigns of Europe" to "keep in the ranks until further orders, and conduct themselves with bravery and fidelity." *Until further orders!*

He *commanded* that, in the impending wars between Greece and Turkey, the Jews observe strict neutrality.

He *abolished forever* polygamy among the Jews. At this word, the Asiatic and African Jews, presumably, were to lay aside their superfluous—*if* superfluous—wives and return meekly to double, instead of triple or quadruple, blessedness.

Prayers "shall forever be said in the Hebrew language"; Noah, however, affably permitted the delivery of discourses on the principles of the Jewish faith in the language of the country.

The wide orbit of his invitation to Utopia, circumscribing Jews of all climes and colors, included among these colors none other than Lo, the American Indian,—"in all probability, the descendants of the lost tribes of Israel, which were carried captive by the King of Assyria." Noah desired finally to reunite them "with their brethren the chosen people."

The theory that the American Indian is of Semitic descent is an outcropping of the greater theory concerning the Lost Tribes of Israel. The minor theory originated contemporaneously with the study of the Indian by the earliest explorers of this continent,—gentry, on the whole, too well versed in the literal contents of the Bible and, in the data of ethnology, too ill. To them, correspondence of custom (whether imaginary or real) spelt identity of origin. Noah's researches, of course, were nothing more brow-furrowing than the perusal of books long ago refuted.[1]

It was not so many years before the issuance of this proclamation that the Governor and Judge of Israel, in his speech of 1817, had looked down upon the Indian as "the savage of the wilderness, whose repast is blood, and whose mercy is death." What had caused this *volte-face*? The theory that the ancient Jews had cultural relations with the Red Man is now considered obsolete and enlists no support among ethnological experts. Yet contemporary investigators, while maintaining a scientific objectivity, suggest, without endorsing it, a persistence of the notion. Thus, Mr. Walter Hart Blumenthal writes: "Although recurrent announcements that Phoenician inscriptions have been found as petroglyphs on the Amazon may be baseless, and indeed most of the allegations advanced as 'arguments', groundless, yet there are phases of the problem that invite serious investigation. Moreover, it is not beyond the bounds of probability that indications will be discovered of ancient cultural affiliations which had their roots in the primitive Semitic area, almost certainly among the racial

[1] For a rapid survey of the Lost Tribes theory as applied to the American Indian see *The Lost Tribes Theory*, Suggestions Toward Rewriting Hebrew History, by Allen H. Godbey, Ph.D., Durham (North Carolina), 1930, Chapter I. Professor Godbey also gives valuable collateral references.

strains centered of old on the Mediterranean and the Nile, —if not within the historic vista, at least among their precursors. In other words, there are ramifications of the outworn and crude Ten Tribe theory still within the purview of scholarship . . . "[1]

I doubt that Noah, once having accepted the theory that the American Indians were the descendants of the lost tribes of Israel, ever abandoned it. As late as twelve years after the building of Ararat upon a foundation of oratory he was delivering, before the Mercantile Library Association, Clinton Hall, New York, and handing over to the printer, a Discourse on the subject. Once again, beginning with the authority of Menasseh Ben Israel, who in 1650 had published in Amsterdam his *Mikveh Israel* (The Hope of Israel), based upon the contemporary belief that the lost tribes had been found in Red America, and quoting with an appearance of vast ethnological learning, from Lopez de Gomara, Erecella (he means Ercilla), the Abbé Clavigero, De Vega, Du Pratz, Bartram and whom not else, Noah reaffirms the Semitic origin of our aborigines.[2]

The Semitico-Indian theory appeared more convincing in Noah's day than in our own. Nor, in the light of that earlier day, need Noah have been such a fool or fanatic as he may appear in the perspective of history. As he was not the first or the last to be lured by the mirage of Utopia, so in his

---

[1] See *In Old America*, Random Chapters on the Early Aborigines. By Walter Hart Blumenthal. With a Foreword by George Alexander Kohut. New York. 1931. Introduction, p. vii.

[2] See *Discourse on The Evidences of The American Indians Being The Descendants of the Lost Tribes of Israel*. By M. M. Noah. New York. James Van Norden. 27 Pine St., 1837. The discourse was translated into German in 1838.

For Menasseh Ben Israel's notions upon the subject, consult *The Life of Menasseh Ben Israel*, by Cecil Roth, Philadelphia, 1934, pp. 176–224.

facile ethnological research he erred in respectable company
His stretching forth of the brotherly hand may have been
dictated, too, not only by a poetic gullibility, but by a very
practical consideration. When he invited the Indians to
Ararat-by-the-Niagara together with all the *other* Jews of
the world it may well have been because there were tribes
of them as close by as Tonawanda, and a conciliatory gesture
was good policy.

Proceeding from Indians to the practical considerations
of financing Utopia, Noah invented a poll tax, to consist of
three shekels in silver, per annum, or one Spanish dollar,
which "is hereby levied upon each Jew throughout the world,
to be collected by the Treasurers of the different congregations, for the purpose of defraying the various expenses of
re-organizing the government, of aiding emigrants in the
purchase of agricultural implements, providing for their
immediate wants and comforts, and assisting their families
in making their first settlements; together with such free-will
offerings as may be generously made in the furtherance of
the laudable objects connected with the restoration of the
people and the glory of the Jewish nation. A Judge of Israel
shall be chosen once in every four years by the Consistory at
Paris, at which time proxies from every congregation shall
be received."

The Proclamation concluded with a summons to the Jewish
intelligentsia of Europe, and a prayer for universal peace.

"I do hereby name as Commissioners, the most learned
and pious Abraham de Cologna, Knight of the Iron Crown
of Lombardy, Grand Rabbi of the Jews, and President of
the Consistory at Paris; likewise the Grand Rabbi Andrade
of Bordeaux; and also our learned and esteemed Grand Rabbis
of the German and Portugal Jews, in London, Rabbis

Herschell and Mendola; together with the Honorable Aaron
Nunez Cardoza, of Gibraltar, Abraham Busnac, of Leghorn,
Benjamin Gradis, of Bordeaux, Dr. E. Gans and Professor
Zunz, of Berlin, and Dr. Leo Woolf of Hamburgh; to aid
and assist in carrying into effect the provisions of this my
proclamation, with powers to appoint the necessary agents
in the several parts of the world, and to establish Emigration
societies, in order that the Jews may be concentrated and
capacitated to act as a distinct body, having at the head of
each kingdom or republic such presiding officers as I shall
upon their recommendation appoint. Instructions to these
my Commissioners shall be forthwith transmitted; and a
more enlarged and general view of plan, motives and objects
will be detailed in the address to the nation. The Consistory
at Paris is hereby authorized and empowered to name three
discreet persons of competent abilities, to visit the United
States, and make such report to the nation as the actual
condition of this country shall warrant.

"I do appoint Roshodes Adar, February 7th, 1826, to be
observed with suitable demonstrations as a day of Thanksgiving to the Lord God of Israel, for the manifold blessings
and signal protection which He has deigned to extend to
his people, and in order that on that great occasion our
prayers may be offered for the continuance of his divine
mercy and the fulfillment of all the promises and pledges
made to the race of Jacob.

"I recommend peace and union among us; charity and
good-will to all; toleration and liberality to our brethren of
every religious denomination, enjoined by the mild and just
precepts of our holy religion; honor and good faith in the
fulfillment of all our contracts; together with temperance,
economy and industry in our habits.

"I humbly intreat to be remembered in your prayers; and,
lastly and most earnestly, I do enjoin you to 'Keep the charge
of the Lord thy God, to walk in his ways, to keep his statutes
and his commandments and his judgments and his testi-

monies, as it is written in the laws of Moses, that thou mayest prosper in all thou doest, and whithersoever thou turnest thyself.' "

The Proclamation was signed by Noah's friend, A. B. Seixas, Secretary pro tem., and given at Buffalo as of the second day of Tizri, in the year of the World, 5596, corresponding with the fifteenth day of September, 1825, and in the fiftieth year of American Independence.[1]

The day had been greeted with gunpowder; it ended with music, cannonade and libation. The ceremonies over, a salute of twenty-four guns was fired by the artillery. The band burst into a medley of popular airs, after which the procession returned to the Masonic Lodge. Here disbanding, Masons and military, ready now no doubt for the real business of the day, repaired to the Eagle Tavern.

And Noah? For the local newspaper, *The Buffalo Patriot*, he prepared a full account of the solemn ceremonies. To it, later, he added a plan of the proposed City, and a further appeal to his brethren in Europe. Without so much as setting foot upon the City of his dreams—it is questionable, indeed, whether he ever trod the soil of Grand Island, before this day or after—he returned to New York, to the secular cares, to the world of harsh factuality.

It was all over . . . Already . . . A still, though not a noiseless, birth . . . To paraphrase the greatest of poets, the baseless fabric of Noah's vision, like an insubstantial pageant, faded and left but a rock behind—a decaying corner

---

[1] In many places September 2nd is given as the date of the founding of Ararat. This may be owing to confusion with the "second day of Tizri." It has been pointed out that Noah selected September 15th because it was the first available date after the opening of the current Hebrew New Year.

stone that would haunt the unredeemed redeemer. The
mockery of Europe and America would heat his ears, then
silence, the mockery of mockery . . . Nobody had heeded
the call of the latter-day savior. No flood descended from
the heavens to submerge the iniquity and the indifference of
the nations. Noah's Ark, grounded upon a barren Ararat,
was left high, dry and empty.

It was a sardonic apotheosis,—a cenotaph of hope and
reputation. Noah had been the orator at a funeral.[1]

4. VALUES—SPIRITUAL AND REAL ESTATE

Noah having been at once Quixote and Sancho, it is sometimes difficult to say whether his Grand Island scheme was
predominantly an ardent ideal or a cold investment . . .
Ararat and Barataria . . .

There is concrete evidence that, however high-minded our
paladin may have been about his City of Refuge, he was
not blind to the possibilities of Ararat as a venture in real
estate. Land booms were already old phenomena in the
United States. Grand Island had been purchased by the
State of New York in 1815, and was shortly infested by
squatters. It became the haunt of timber-pirates and out-
laws in general, constituting a sort of no man's country. The
State is said to have paid to the Seneca Indians $11,000. for
the territory,—a price more fair at least than the $24. for
which the isle of Manhattan was purchased from the red man.

[1] The chief source of information about the ceremonies attending the foundation
of Ararat is an account written by Lewis F. Allen, and read by him at a meeting
of the Buffalo Historical Society on March 5, 1866. It appeared, originally, in
Thomas' *Buffalo City Directory* for 1867, pp. 25–37; it was reprinted in vol. 1 of
the Society's publications, 1879, and again reprinted in vol. 25, 1921, pp. 113–144.
It is to be found most easily as reprinted in *AJHS*, vol. VIII, pp. 98–118.

A year before the Noachian débâcle the State had surveyed the island, which was dense with timber and notable as a hunting and fishing ground. Whether any of Noah's money went into the purchase of the 2550 acres that was made by his friend, Samuel Leggett, is not certain. Surely, however, Noah hoped, with the success of his enterprise, to acquire gradually the ownership of the entire island. The 2550 acres were in two lots, one at the head of the island, the other at the center, opposite Tonawanda and, what is more important, at the entrance of the Erie canal into the Niagara River. Noah, as an anti-Clintonian, had opposed the crowning achievement of Clinton's career. He was not averse, however, to profiting from the immense volume of new business that would be opened by the inauguration of the Erie Canal. He sat now, indeed, upon the Canal celebration committee. Buffalo lacked the capital to compete with the cities that Noah planned to establish at strategical positions on the island.

His reasoning, as a commercial organizer, seemed so sound that other capitalists were led to speculate in Island lots; notably, John B. Yates and Archibald McIntyre, who had purchased from the State the system of lotteries by which, in those days, colleges and churches were often financed. Among other purchasers were Levi Beardsley, James O'Morse and Alvan Stewart, who acquired a considerable portion of the Island. Beardsley has related[1] that, having been offered a handsome advance on their purchase, they wrote for advice to Noah. Noah advised them "by no means to sell at present, as he had no doubt of the success of his project, which would greatly enhance the value of our lands."

[1] See his *Reminiscences*, New York, 1852, pp. 156–157.

As late as October 5, 1825, Noah was writing to Alvan Stewart, "We have not as yet been able to fix upon any definitive plans relative to Grand Island, waiting to see the effect produced in Europe. Although I think the land worth more than 50 per cent advance on the purchase, I am sure it will bring more yet . . ."[1]

Grand Island, alas, was to prove as fruitless temporally as spiritually. Whether as an investment of the soul or of the national currency, it was equally a failure. Before the new year was very old, Noah would know only too well "the effect produced in Europe."

5. AFTERMATH

It is interesting that though the futility, the vanity, the self-seeking of Noah's "Ararat" have not been forgotten, his position in the history of Jewish self-determination is on the whole a highly honored one. The intention has been taken for the achievement. He emerges as an eccentric, surely, but none the less as an important pioneer in the story of Zionistic endeavor. If his descendants in the struggle for a Jewish homeland cannot honor his head, they do all honor to his heart.

This was, with one or two exceptions, the charitable attitude even of those contemporaries who were in high positions to pass upon his megalomaniac sentimentality. The very deputies upon whom he called to assist him, in one way or another betrayed his unsolicited faith. Eduard Gans, who, together with Dr. Leopold Zunz, had, as recently as January 1, 1822, written to him so sincerely, so hopefully from Europe,

[1] The original of this letter is in the private collection of Leon Hühner, Esq.

abandoned his Jewishness and adopted Christianity in the very year of Noah's "Ararat."

The letter had told how eagerly the Jews of Europe looked to the United States as an ark of freedom, and asked for particulars concerning the Jews of the country, State by State.[1] Curiously enough, Noah did not make the document public until October 4, 1825, when, in answer to the storm of hostile and ridiculing criticism called forth by his Messianic scheme, he printed it in *The Albany Daily Advertiser*. He published it, he averred, "to exhibit an evidence of the fact that, although the Jews in the United States were not prepared for emigration . . . yet those abroad . . . have been alive to the project and in expectation of events which have taken place." Still more curiously, and to show how closely hand in hand went Noah's idealism and his hopes for profitable real-estate returns, his letter to Alvan Stewart, already quoted, was written on the very next day after the Zunz document was printed, with Noah's protestations, in *The Albany Advertiser*.

Zunz's defection was as a premonitory symbol. In the *Journal des Débats*, Abraham de Cologna, Chief Rabbi of Paris, rejecting Noah's invitation, administered the rebuke pious. This in itself was a *coup de grace*.

The letter to the journalistic spokesman of the French government was translated into a number of tongues and was widely reprinted in Europe and in the United States.

"Sir—The wisdom and love of truth which distinguish your journal, and the well merited reputation it enjoys in France and in foreign countries, induce me to hope that your politeness will grant me a place in your next number for some

---

[1] The full text of this letter, with interesting annotations, is to be found in *AJHS*, vol. xx, pp. 147–149.

observations which I address to the public in interests of
reason and truth.

"The French and English papers have lately announced
the singular project of a Mr. Noah, who calls himself the
founder of the city Ararat, in the United States of North
America. Certainly if Mr. Noah was, as he is supposed to be,
the proprietor or occupier of a great extent of uncultivated
land, and confined himself to the engagement of men without fortunes to run the risk of colonizing with him, promising
them at the same time mountains of gold, nobody would
think of disputing his right to follow the fashion of sending
forth projects; but Mr. Noah aspires to play a much more
elevated character. He dreams of a heavenly mission; he
talks prophetically; he styles himself a judge over Israel;
he gives orders to all the Israelites in the world; he levies
the tax upon all Hebrew heads. In his exaltation he even
goes so far as to make the central Jewish consistory of France
his Chargé d'affaires, and he honours the President of this
body with the noble rank of 'Commissioner of Emigration.'
The whole is excellent; but two trifles are wanting; first, the
well authenticated proof of the mission and authority of
Mr. Noah. 2ndly, the prophetic text which points out a
marsh in North America as the spot for re-assembling the
scattered remains of Israel.

"To speak seriously, it is right at once to inform Mr. Noah,
that the venerable Messrs. Herschell and Mendola, Chief
Rabbis at London, and myself, thank him, but positively
refuse the appointments he has been pleased to confer upon
us. We declare that according to our dogmas, God alone
knows the epoch of the Israelitish restoration, that he alone
will make it known to the whole universe by signs entirely
unequivocal, and that every attempt on our part to re-
assemble with any politico-national design is forbidden, as
an act of high treason against the Divine Majesty. Mr. Noah
has doubtless forgotten that the Israelites, faithful to the
principles of their belief, are too much attached to the countries where they dwell, and devoted to the Governments

under which they enjoy liberty and protection, not to treat as a mere jest the chimerical consulate of a pseudo-restorer.

"As however justice requires some consideration to the absent, we should be sorry to refuse him the title of a visionary of good intentions.

"Accept, Mr. Editor, the assurance of the distinguished and respectful sentiments with which I remain your most humble servant,

The Grand Rabbi. DE COLOGNA."

To this Noah made a weak reply. He was happy to be considered at least a visionary of good intentions . . . "The result of the experiment," he maintained, "will show something of practical utility, or I am mistaken in the character of this country and its institutions. At all events, this opposition to an incipient stage will do good; it will excite curiosity and promote inquiry, which is all I ask at present."[1]

If De Cologna and Herschell were content to find Noah, at worst, guilty of blasphemy, Andrade, the Chief Rabbi of Bordeaux, declared him a plain charlatan. So did Judah Jeitteles, the leader of the Jewish Enlightenment (*Haskalah*) in Austria. In the pages of the journal, *Bikkure Ha'Ittim*, he translated the details of Noah's call unto the nations, and subjected it to blistering ridicule.

It is to be questioned whether Noah's proclamation was allowed to appear in any of the papers of Poland and Russia. The police headquarters of Vienna scented, in the Grand Island scheme, a disguised revolutionary plot aiming at the overthrow of the Hapsburg monarchy. So that, as Gelber reports, the copies of the proclamation were withheld. Russia, for like reasons, enforced a like suppression; a condensed

---

[1] As quoted in *Niles' Register*, January 21, 1825, pp. 350–351. A copy, in English, of the letter from the Grand Rabbi, Abraham de Cologna, appears also in this issue.

notice of Noah's call, however, did appear in the *Moscow Telegraph*.

The English, German and Austrian press were less hindered; the results among their readers were, however, equally academic.

Since the truth grows in the mouths of honest men, it appears that some of the foreign papers promoted Major Noah to the office of Mayor of New York City. The *Berliner Nachrichten von Staats-und Gelehrtensachen* and the *Vossische Zeitung*, early in November, printed accounts of Ararat that could easily have been more spiced with sarcasm. The *Wiener Allgemeine Zeitung* went so far as to announce that news of the restoration of the Jewish nation had been withheld by the New York press through fear that "the Stock Exchange would be thrown into a panic upon finding itself suddenly threatened by the loss of so many people and so much capital."[1]

---

[1] I find this tid-bit in *Zur Vorgeschichte Des Zionismus. Judenstaatsprojekte in den Jahren* 1695–1845. By Dr. M. M. Gelber, Vienna, 1927, p. 289, note 51. Dr. Gelber's chapter on Noah, pp. 62–84, together with the notes thereto appertaining, form the best account of the repercussion of the Utopian plan among the Jews of the world.

Other reports are to be read in *Die Welt* for January 31, 1902, in which Dr. Heinrich Loewe (pp. 8–10) gives a resumé of clippings from various European news papers. Dr. M. Kayserling, in *Allgemeine Zeitung des Judentums*, 1898 (pp. 101–103), in the course of a brief paper on "Ein Judenstaat-Gründer," which contains the errors of biographical detail that are to be found in all contemporary accounts of Noah, has references to the foreign reception of the Grand Island plan.

The matter of the press-reception of Noah's project, owing to the difficulties in gaining access to files of domestic and foreign papers of the period, is still more hazy than it should be. Though there is no doubt as to what happened—or, rather, did not happen—it would make an interesting monograph if some competent person would compile a digest of the comments that greeted the call to Ararat when it was sent forth from the Ark of Grand Island.

In the current ridicule of Noah, even Heinrich Heine participated. The humorist, in a letter dated April 23, 1826, addressed to Moses Moser—First Vice Secretary of the *Verein fuer Kultur und Wissenschaft der Juden*, of which Gans and Zunz were, respectively, President and Vice President, and which, by their letter of January 1, 1822, had notified Noah of his election to the association—pretended to have seen Gans and Noah in a dream. Noah, it appeared, had performed the miracle of silencing Gans (*"Gans war, oh Wunder! stumm wie ein Fisch."*) That Gabriel Riesser was interested in Noah's project is evident from a letter sent to him by his father on January 24, 1826, antedating by many years the verdict of Jewish posterity. "It seems to me that this man took as his model not the Prophets, but rather the Patriarchs . . . As petty or ridiculous as the matter may appear at present, need and time and circumstance may cause our descendants to judge it altogether differently . . ."[1]

The ridicule, like the flood that had sustained the original Noah through the forty days of cosmic cleansing, at last abated. The perspective of history has washed away much of the fanaticism inherent in his project and has left, among the historians of Zionism, the image of a worthy pioneer.

Raisin discovers in Noah the "first real Zionist," and one who was by no means a fanatic. Noah's Zionism was political, and it was his destiny to have come two or three generations before his time. He was a precursor of the newer Zionism, of Herzl, Pinsker, Hess and Smolenskin. "While the Zionism of the leaders from Hess onward was more or less the result of oppression and persecution from without, Noah's Zionism was an inner recognition that there would be no place for

[1] For the Heine and Riesser references see Gelber, op. cit., pp. 288–289.

Israel . . . unless the Jew returned to the land of his ancestors." Noah, indeed, on the score of his later pronouncements, delivered almost twenty years after the fiasco of Ararat, becomes in Raisin's eyes a great prophet of Israel sounding forth a great prophecy.[1]

Gelber, a quarter of a century after Raisin, ratifies in its essentials this judgement.[2] He agrees with Raisin that Noah never presented a clear picture of the projected State. "Nevertheless, he is certainly the first Jewish initiator of the Jewish State idea in the nineteenth century," and a forerunner of Theodor Herzl by more than fifty years.

In the story of Zionism, indeed, Noah is more than this. He is, as Dr. Abram Lipsky called him,[3] the "first American Zionist". He is, as Gelber recognizes, "surely the first one actually to have undertaken the realisation of a Jewish State."

Gottheil, though he sees the grotesquerie of Noah's project, insists that it was "built upon principles which have found acceptance in later days. He saw clearly the need for the Jews of some segregation, of a return to the cultivation of the soil, that though only a certain number of Jews could be benefited by a segregation, the whole Jewish race would profit by it, that it was necessary to cultivate the land,— and, finally, that his scheme provided only for a half way house to Palestine . . ."[4]

---

[1] See *Mordecai Manuel Noah*, Zionist, Author and Statesman. By the Rev. Max Raisin, B.A. Warsaw, 1905. (In Hebrew)

[2] Op. cit., Ch. VIII.

[3] See *The Maccabean*, December, 1908. "The First American Zionist." By Abram Lipsky, Ph.D.

[4] *Zionism*, by Richard J. H. Gottheil, Philadelphia, 1914, pp. 38–39.

So, too, Kallen, who, finding the Utopia of Noah "over-laid a little with elements of mountebankery and melodrama . . . damned from the outset by its charlatanic character", nevertheless perceives at its core "good sense and sound statesmanship."[1]

As Noah had used the heroes of his nation to lend heroism and dignity to his plays, so he in turn, because of Ararat chiefly, became a character in Jewish fiction and drama. It was Zangwill who, in 1899, first brought him into fiction, making of him, in the tale "Noah's Ark", one of *They That Walk In Darkness*. Harry Sackler, in his Yiddish play, *Major Noah*, turns the gentleman of Ararat into the material of a comedy. The honeymooners of Howells' *Their Wedding Journey* still sigh over him, and make the mistake —still made—of believing that Noah laid his foundation-stone on the Island itself. Alfred H. Lewis's novel, *Peggy O'Neal*, appearing four years after Zangwill's tale, romanticizes the American Jewish paladin with all the license of a fictioneer. . . . The man, clearly, has passed into American legend . . .

It was not only as a figure for fiction that Noah impressed Zangwill. In a speech delivered before the London University Society, on December 16, 1916, commemorating the 25th anniversary of Pinsker's death, the great writer did not hesitate to associate with the names of Pinsker and Herzl that of the American Jewish pioneer. This time, it appeared, Noah was one of those that walk in the Light.

"Pinsker's 'Auto-Emancipation,' published in 1881," said Zangwill, was a "brilliant anticipation of much later history

---

[1] *Zionism And World Politics*, by Horace M. Kallen, Ph.D., New York, 1921, pp. 41–42.

and literature, and its brilliance was not that of flowers or of jewels but of fire . . . It was a great book. Yet Herzl, when he wrote his 'Judenstaat', in 1895, had probably never heard of it . . . I said that Pinsker was the father of Auto-Emancipation. But it is a wise child that knows his own father, and I, too, had never seen this book till years after the Ito was established. Before Pinsker, there had been the American Sephardi, Mordecai Manuel Noah, who, in 1825, not only planned a great Jewish colony on an island in the State of New York, but actually bought land for it, and issued an invitation to the ghettos of Europe to flock to his Ararat, and even held the Dedication Service—as readers of my story, 'Noah's Ark', may remember. How comes it that a Russian like Pinsker, an Austrian like Herzl, an American like Noah, and an Englishman like myself, are still putting forth the same solution of the Jewish problem? Is it plagiarism? Not at all. Herzl, Pinsker, Noah, were in sublime unconsciousness of one another. It is because there is what the advertisements call 'a felt want', and this want prompts everywhere the same suggestion for meeting it. The bulk of our troubles springing from our lack of a common land or even of a majority anywhere, it is a natural suggestion that we should reëstablish ourselves upon a normal, national basis.

"The interesting fact remains that Herzl's Congress, called for Territorialism, ended in the adoption of Palestine as its goal,—that Pinsker's Congress, called for Territorialism, ended in a society to aid Palestine immigrants, and that even Noah's institution, 'Ararat', was replaced by a rallying call to Zion."[1]

It is curious to discover the relation of Noah's foundered enterprise to the temper of his times. Ever since human

[1] See A. B. Makover's pamphlet, *Mordecai Manuel Noah*, p. 83.

groups became conscious of their gregariousness and of their common interests, they have been looking back, or forward —psychologically these directions are the same—to a paradise lost or a paradise regained. Cities of God, Utopias, phalansteries, farms, colonies—these are but different names for man's optimism in the face of religious and social dissension. Even in this respect, Noah was immediately in advance of his day. A full quarter of a century after Noah's Folly, Emerson was writing from Boston, "We are a little wild here with numberless projects of social reform; not a leading man but has a draft of a new community in his waistcoat pocket." Noah's colonizing illness, then, older far than Plato, was pandemic.

IX

"THE GREAT MOGUL"...

1. The Eckford-Barker Scandal

Thus it turned out that the great event toward the end of 1825 was not the founding of a Utopian island but the opening of the Erie Canal. News traveled slowly in the first quarter of the nineteenth century, and many a hopeful Jew first learned of Noah's promised land long after the new Moses was devoutly praying that the world—and he—would forget the unfulfilled Canaan. The corner stone of Ararat, symbol of the ill-starred venture, for a while haunted Noah's thoughts; he wished it well out of the way,—this Jacob's pillow that brought no dreams of heaven.

Yet the man bounded back from disappointment and failure with a resilience, even an optimism, that never diminished. He was now past forty. The major lines of his life had been laid; the closing third of his career would, with the exception of his late marriage, follow the familiar pattern. The mud of politics would bespatter him; black printer's ink would catch him in its viscous flood; his enemies would mire him in scandal and innuendo, and he would be a target for the rising animus of anti-Semitism. It was a less decorous day than our own, and Noah was very much a man of his day. Through it all, however, he emerges as an acknowledged leader of his people, a remembered contributor to civic integrity and progress, a friend to the poor citizen, to the aspiring writer, a wit of the town, a ready paragrapher,—one of our first "columnists," indeed,—a notable personality of the New York that flourished between the time of opening of the Erie Canal and the first definite intimations of the Civil War.

The journalistic quarrels that had begun when Noah was virtually forced off the original *Advocate* had never ceased. Now they were resumed with a bitterness born, perhaps, of the Grand Island fiasco.

Since 1824, as a result of the quarrel of the various *Advocates*, Noah had launched upon a determined exposure of his enemies, Henry Eckford and Jacob Barker. The trial of Eckford, Barker and Matthew L. Davis proved to be one of the high lights of Gotham's criminal records. The indictment of the Grand Jury, dated September 15, 1826, charged these eminent sons of Tammany, together with Mark Spencer, William P. Rathbone, Thomas Vermilyea and a lesser fry, with a long list of financial frauds.[1]

At the first trial, the jury disagreed. At the second, the men arraigned were convicted. But this time Tammany dis-

---

[1] These included the following victims and amounts: The Mechanics' Fire Insurance Company: 1000 shares of its own capital stock; 1000 shares of United States Bank Stock; and $50,000. The Fulton Bank: 2000 shares of its own capital stock; and $50,000. The Tradesman's Bank: 2000 shares of its own capital stock; and $50,000. The Morris Canal and Banking Company: ditto. The Life and Fire Insurance Company: 2000 shares of its own capital stock.

The group, moreover, was charged with fraudulently obtaining 1000 promissory notes amounting to almost $100 each, belonging to the Fulton Bank, and with executing the same fraud upon the other banks already named, as well as obtaining, by fraud, from Henry Barclay, George Barclay, and others, the sum of $50,000.

agreed,—with the verdict and the administration of justice. Though one of its own Grand Sachems, Major Noah himself, had been instrumental in bringing these malefactors to task, the Wigwam was determined to stand by its own. And stand it did. When the public had vented its first passion of revulsion against the bank raiders, a new trial was granted to Davis and powerful political influence secured for him an acquittal. The money that Barker had robbed, despite his second conviction, purchased him immunity. He never served a day. As for Eckford, he frankly fled to the far East, dying in Syria. Not too long afterward, a gentleman named Swartwout, who provided a noun for the dictionary of financial misdoing, was to develop, for similar reasons, a similar interest in the Orient. Barker, who published a pamphlet maintaining his innocence and charging a "frame-up", moved to the South and lived on until ninety.

To be sure, someone had to be punished—"take the rap," we call it, at the hour—for the theft of these several millions. So a quartet of distinctly minor thieves felt the tender lash of Tammany. Mowatt and Hyatt received a sentence of two years apiece; the Lambert brothers each got a year.

Noah had merely twisted the Tiger's tail.[1] Yet, allowing for any private satisfaction he may have felt in revenging himself upon his enemies, he had performed a great civic service. His exposure was considered one of the great journalistic exploits of the day.

It was a critical moment in Noah's career. Jacksonian democracy was on the verge of triumph . . . Jackson was a name that was to play a major rôle in the public policies and

---

[1] See for brief accounts of the trial, and other references, Gustavus Myers, *History of Tammany Hall*, pp. 83–85; *Memoirs of James Gordon Bennett And His Times* (Pray), pp. 71–73.

the private life of the Major. Outside was the fighting Andrew Jackson, whom Tammany, hot upon the inauguration of John Quincy Adams, had picked as the next President of the United States. On May 12, 1825, he had been toasted as the hero of New Orleans and the successor to "Old Man Eloquent". Inside was a young Jewess, daughter of Daniel Jackson; sister of Solomon H. Jackson, who edited the first American-Jewish magazine to be published in this country, *The Jew* . . . Rebecca Esther Jackson was the name of the girl . . . Major Noah's side was successful with both Jackson campaigns. He married Rebecca in New York on the evening of November 28, 1827, the Rev. M. Hart officiating. The hero of New Orleans was to be the "people's choice" in 1829.

2. SINFONIA DOMESTICA

On December 10, 1827, an eager grandmother wrote from London a long letter arduously composed, to a granddaughter who had already been married in New York City. She began,

"My dear Rebeca

"I reciv'd your letter dated November 14th whare in you in forme me of your going to be married we ware agreeable surpris d indeed quite astonise'd as you never gave us the least hint in any of your former letters I suppose it is quite a sudden change I hope and trust in god it will be a good one . . . my dear Rebeca frome your observation that Mr. Noah being few (five?) years older than your self it is quite proper I wish you may spend your years as happy as I have with your dr grandfather who is now 93 years old . . . I am shure your dear fathar and mother would not have agreed to your having Mr. Noah if they had not aprove'd of him

. . . you say the Major talks of coming to England what a gratification it would be to us to see you Both . . . Regard to Mr. Noah wishing him every happyness in this world and may you both in goy [enjoy] maney year helth togather tell him I have not the pleasure of knowing him but I knowd his fathar and grandfathar I hope I shall have the pleasure of knowing him . . .

There followed, on the third sheet (foolscap size, unruled) a short letter to Mrs. Aaron's daughter, Marey (sic), in which the alert old woman expressed again her surprise at Rebecca's marriage. "Your fathar and myself would have liked to have been present beeing our firthst grandchild we had a good cry however that was Imposable we give Mr. Jackson and you much Joy and may you live to see your youngest marrid." Not to be outdone, Uncle David Aaron Phillips, after the letter was folded over twice, penned his own sentiments to Rebecca, continuing them from one fold to the other. "Allow me to congratulate you," he said, "on your marridge and likewise let me ad that I think you have made a very good choice and I dont know any man you could have bestow'd you hand better. he (The Major) is a man of good sense and understanding and in every respect a gentleman. and I hope he will bestow all his good qualification on you and make you a good partner. as you say he is a few years in advance. it is better to be the old man Darling than the young ones Drugg [drudge]. Make my best and kind love to your husband (*who I suppose is by this time*) and except the same yourself and Believe me to remain your Truly Affectionate Uncle . . ."[1]

It has come down that, at the moment before his marriage, Noah was president of a noted bachelors' club of Gotham. Was it the Bread And Cheese, of which he is supposed to

---

[1] The manuscript letter from which these excerpts are drawn forms part of my Noah collection.

have been one of the founders? Yet, surely, Noah was not
—to risk a bull—wedded to bachelorhood. His ideal of
woman he had formed during his coming-of-age in the
Phillips household. It was, as afterward expanded in his
domestic essays written for the *National Advocate*, a generally old-fashioned ideal. Noah had had plenty to say about
bachelors, too,—of elderly fellows who, though no enemy to
matrimony, had put off the day of marriage so long "that it
now presents an awful aspect", terrifying them as the field
of battle does the acknowledged coward. Noah disliked old
bachelors; that is why, perhaps, he married before it was
too late. Romance? Yes. But say, too, the spectacle of
unhemmed handkerchiefs, ill-tended clothes, cravats awry,
rent ruffles and heels worn through.

Thus we may find him proclaiming, in the *Advocate* of
December 16, 1819:

"That a race of old bachelors are a burden to society—
are fit objects for animadversion, for satire, nay, even for
special taxation—I never for a moment doubted. I do not
mean your old bachelors who, like myself have neither talents
nor attractions sufficiently powerful to engage the affections
of a young lady—they are to be pitied—but I mean your
venerable dandies, men having the means to marry without
the inclination, men who remain single all their days from
the vanity of supposing that they can obtain any woman
from the mere asking her."

The London letter from the bride's grandmother bears
witness either to a white deception on the part of Rebecca
Jackson, or to a grandmotherly euphemism. The Major
was much more than a "few" or "five" years his wife's senior,
though he was hardly aged enough to make of his wife, even
had he wished to, an "old man's drugg." Noah, at the time

of his marriage, was in his forty-third year; his wife, in her seventeenth. It was still a day of early marriage—for women —and of large families. And for all Noah's contemporary fulminations against the unhygienic constriction of the corset, and the wasp-like waists that were the visible result, Rebecca Jackson, on the evidence of her portrait, was possessed of the hour-glass figure up to then tabooed by her husband . . . It was a delicate form of retribution. Men speak too much nonsense about women; and women, about each other.

There was another pleasant aspect to this marriage. It represented a union of the Portuguese-Jew (the Sephardic branch) with the Ashkenazi (the Jew of German or Polish origin). Though Major Noah was much occupied, and on occasion exercised, over matters of religious import, he was hardly a passionate devotee. As the offspring, on the maternal side, of Sephardim, born in a city that could boast, at the time, of a single synagogue, which observed the Sephardic ritual, he had been and would remain identified with the Congregation Shearith Israel. His name, however, is found among the signers of the call, in 1825, for the establishment of the B'Nai Jeshurun,—New York's second synagogue, and the first to observe the ritual of the German Jews. So is that of Daniel Jackson, father of Mrs. Rebecca Esther Noah. It may well be, then, that Noah's interest in the new synagogue was heightened by his devotion to Jackson's daughter.

Noah's home, at the corner of Broadway and Franklin Street, across the way from the residence of William Waldorf Astor, was a port of call for poor immigrant Jews. Ararat, the City of Jews, had failed as a territory; in Noah's heart it persisted as an ideal of communal living. His purse was open to coreligionist and Gentile alike. To the immigrant in search of a living the first step was usually the peddler's

REBECCA JACKSON NOAH

From a portrait by Jarvis, now in possession of the Congregation
Shearith Israel, New York City.

route. The wanderings of the Middle Ages were now repeated over the virgin soil of the United States. It was Noah who, by paying for the contents of the peddler's pack, started many a struggling Jew on the road of self-support, dignity, and even prosperity.

Noah's position as the leading Jewish publicist of the quarter century between the establishment of the B'Nai Jeshurun and the time of his death is strongly attested by his concurrent representative activities in behalf of both the Sephardic and the Ashkenazic congregations. Though Noah was not a member of the B'Nai Jeshurun, he was regarded, to the end, as a "constant friend, patron, counsellor and guide," and his "name was always cherished."[1]

He delivered the address of the Thanksgiving Service of the Congregation, in 1826, at Washington Hall; the Elm St. Synagogue would not be ready for occupancy until next year. On September 15, 1827, less than three months after the consecration of the new Synagogue (on June 29), Noah delivered a Sabbath morning oration in the new edifice. It was he, too, who was the principal speaker at the celebration of the first anniversary. Noah, in a word, was virtually the spokesman of New York Jewry, which, at the time, consisted of some thousand souls. Clearly then, the project of Ararat had not injured his standing.

Rebecca Jackson, from the scanty evidence available, was in almost every respect the ideal wife that her husband, as a bachelor, had been hymning in the public prints. She was gifted in domesticity; she had both wit and humor; she could sprinkle her letters with foreign phrases; she appears to have brought with her a modest competence, which she and her

[1] See *A Century of Judaism In New York*. B'Nai Jeshurun Congregation, 1825–1925. By Israel Goldstein, M.A., D.H.L. New York, 1930, p. 90.

husband managed with varying success. All in all, the marriage seemed to endow Noah with a new lease of life, at the very moment that the diplomat, politician, orator, editor and publicist had become a prey to yet another disillusionment.[1]

3. JACKSON AND JOURNALISM— THE UNITED STATES BANK

The triumph of Andrew Jackson in the election of 1828 seemed to confirm the good luck that marriage had brought. For the office of Surveyor of the Port of New York was part of the spoils to fall, eventually, to the rehabilitated Major.

Not without much anguish of soul, however, and of print. A change was coming over politics and, therefore, over journalism. Of this change Noah was a part, and his efforts seem to have been pointed consistently toward conservatism. It had become for him increasingly important to find and hold a political job. If this is kept in mind, it is a simple matter to understand the inconsistencies for which he was more and more becoming conspicuous. This explanation is not necessarily a condemnation of the man; it merely confirms a state of affairs that is inseparable from politics, and a state of

[1] With respect to the portraits of Noah and his wife, Dr De Sola Pool wrote to me, on April 17, 1931, that "The pictures of Noah and his wife were done by Jarvis, one of the best American portrait painters of his day. Both are in good condition. When Hermann Struck was over here some time ago, he washed them both. Noah himself appears to me to be somewhat idealized. He has light brown eyes and a fine English pink complexion. There is something Byronesque, as of a demi-god defying the lightning, in his pose. Mrs. Noah is a gracious lady with sleek and modest black hair, gaily tinted cheeks, dark eyes, water claret dress, and with a wasp-like, violently corseted waist. The pictures belong to my congregation." (i. e., Shearith Israel, New York.)

mind that characterized, in his own days, as it does in ours, politicians far more prominent than Noah ever managed to become.

With Noah on his *Enquirer* was an ambitious young man named James Gordon Bennett, who was developing ideas and a manner very much his own. He had been chosen by Noah to replace W. G. Graham, who, up to the time of his death in another of the stupid duels that still disfigured American public life, had been associate editor on *The Enquirer*. Bennett, on the *Enquirer*, really inaugurated those letters from Washington that began a new era in American journalism. He was a good Tammany man at the time. It was Bennett who, as one stormy petrel to another, shortly thereafter suggested to the irascible Webb, editor of the rival *Enquirer*, a merger with the *Courier*.

Meantime, Noah was having plenty of trouble, public and private. His mind was still on another incumbency of the sheriff's office, which at this period paid $10,000. a year. On October 2, 1828, he sent to Van Buren a confidential letter in which he protested against the failure of the spoils system to operate—in his favor. "I am not without apprehension that the valuable offices will be carried off by persons having no political claims . . . My name has been mentioned very generally as a candidate for Sheriff and is generally well received. Personally I have no feeling & no wishes on the subject, but the time has arrived when it is necessary for the republican party to do something for their paper which they can do at this moment as the regular ticket will succeed by a great majority.

"With the exception of the short & unprofitable period in which I held the Sheriff's office the party has not contributed one Dollar for the support of the paper & has left me alone unaided without Capital or friends to fight their battles and gain their victories for *ten years* while many who have done but little for the cause are retiring with full pockets. It is extremely difficult to carry on a political paper in a commercial community at an expense of $25,000 per annum without aid from the party & this can come in a more agreeable shape than subscriptions and contributions."[1]

Toward the end of June, of this same year, Noah had been publicly assaulted by E. J. Roberts, a former partner of his upon the *Enquirer*. Roberts had been outraged by one of Noah's paragraphs, and had decided to take the law—and a thick cowhide whip—into his own hands. As the editor and playwright was entering the Park Theater one Friday evening he was confronted by the lash; there was an impromptu wrestling match, and by the time the police arrived Noah was underneath, shoulders almost to the mat. He sustained a bad gash in the face. For a moment, during the excitement, it was thought that the theater was again on fire, and an alarm was given. On July 14, Roberts was found guilty, in the Court of Sessions, of assault and battery.

Less than a week later, on July 19, James G. Brooks, formerly the editor of the *Minerva*, a literary paper, and now on *The Courier* with James Watson Webb, covered the walls of the city—it was another custom of the day, an attenuated form of the duel—with a signed poster: "I publish M. M. Noah of the *Enquirer* as a coward." Nothing happened. It was part of the routine of journalism in the late 1820's. Shifts in policy made new alignments. Soon such erstwhile enemies as Webb and Noah, brought together by Bennett,

[1] See *AJHS*, vol. xxii, pp. 81–82.

would be united in a "holy" war against their uniter,—a war consecrated, when all the high-sounding protestations are dismissed, to the Great God Circulation.

De Witt Clinton, foe of Tammany bred in its lair, had died in the governorship, on February 11, 1828. According to Myers, Tammany nominations, now looked upon as equivalent to election, were during this period at the disposal of a small clique of which Noah was the head.[1] This does not seem to fit in with Noah's complaints to Van Buren, or with his unsatisfied ambition to regain the shrievalty.

The Noahs had celebrated the election of Jackson with the birth of their first-born, Manuel Mordecai, on December 23, 1828. Noah, once again riding the illusive crests of political hope, was in Washington before the President-elect arrived for the inauguration. He stopped, as usual, at Gadsby's,— the hostelry formerly owned by the father of that Peggy Eaton (née O'Neal) who was to be thrust, by Jackson's enemies, into the suspicion of playing a wry-mouthed Aspasia to this home-spun Pericles . . .

Noah, still on good terms with Jackson, would forget his strictures upon feminine propriety and rush gallantly to the defense of the aspersed Peggy.

He understood, he wrote in his paper, "the allusions to DuBarry, and so does the public . . . The person . . . *infamously* compared to a Pompadour or a DuBarry, has never mingled in public affairs (oh, no!) or attempted to control the measures of the Administration. An object of envy and jealousy among a certain class of scandalous *coteries* of Washington, she has resented with becoming indignation,

[1] *History of Tammany Hall*, p. 89.

the attempts to defame her reputation for political purpose and to destroy her domestic comfort, and the character of her offspring. The woman thus compared to the vile Pompadour is an *American female* . . . a wife and a mother . . . the wife of an amiable and estimable man, of honorable, sensitive and high minded feelings . . . the mother of several young children . . . a woman of excellent heart . . . devoid of pride or ostentation . . . a friend of the poor and comfortless, mingling her tears with her charities to the afflicted . . . Such a woman is selected by the enemies of the present Administration . . . dragged before the public . . . slandered and vilified, to sustain an unholy war against patriotism and fidelity . . . If the wife of any member of the Cabinet dare have an opinion, or express that opinion on public affairs, she is to be surrounded by spies, denounced to the public and compared to the infamous courtesans of the time of Louis XIV. and XV. We blush for the degeneracy of the age, for our own countrymen, for honor, chivalry, and sentiment."[1]

Wherever Noah went, thoughts of his home, his wife and his children, accompanied him nostalgically. Always people were to ask eagerly for his wife; why had he not brought her along? Always there would be a new infant to keep her at home, or the rigors of travel in those days of steamboat and stagecoach . . . "My friend Duff Green", writes Noah to his wife from a seat in the House of Representatives, "has been elected Printer to Congress & in the evening I went to drink Champaigne with him & found a vast concourse of members and senators who were rejoiced to see me. Gen.

[1] See *Peggy Eaton*, by Queena Pollock, p. 146.

Jackson arrived this morning so that I had a few hours start of him & have held two or three levees. How all this may end, my love, I cannot say. I have many friends who wish me well & I have no doubt will say all that can be said for one—for our comfort and prosperity I am anxious that something should be done for me, but if I fail I hope by industry and economy to be always able to live respectably & independently and if we are not rich we will at least be contented, for with your prudence & good sense I am sure we will be able to make both ends meet. I am now writing at the reporters' desks in this splendid (sic) and am surrounded with ladies as the Senate shortly will come in to count the electoral votes—which is an interesting ceremony . . . I am glad that you hired a careful person. Don't have any intemperate servant about you . . ."[1]

Noah was in fine fettle. Fortune, for the moment, seemed to be smiling upon him. He had come to Washington together with a score of other editors, all seeking the reward of their journalistic support. This visit to the capitol en masse had been christened "the irruption of the Goths". Someone suggested that Noah should lead the advance upon President Jackson, but he at once declined. "I am too fat and in too good condition. If Old Hickory sees me, he will think that editors require no office. I'd better not lead. Our deputation must be headed by our worst-looking—the lean, the halt, the blind." Upon which Major Noah placed Blair, Kendall and Hill at the head of the deputation.

"Nothing but rumours about the New Cabinet," says another letter. "Everybody asks me what I want. I tell them anything worth accepting, but I cannot say what that

<hr/>

[1] Letters quoted in this chapter, unless otherwise credited, belong to my private collection and have not heretofore been made public.

will be. I shall not be forgotten by my friends & must rest content with their assurances for the present."

The assurances, however, solidified into fact. When Jackson made Samuel Swartwout Collector of the Port of New York, he maneuvered Noah into the office of the Surveyor. The Senate, at first, rejected by a vote of 25 to 23 the nomination of the New York editor.

Noah was a target of ridicule for the anti-Jackson senators. Through him they aimed at the President. Bowers, the historian of this period, speaks of the "bigoted members of the Senate", who rejected Noah "with much hilarity." Under the circumstances there must have been a certain amount of anti-Semitism mixed with the political rancor. Nor would Noah's outstanding efforts to secure Jackson's election have endeared him to the twenty-five who voted against his appointment.

Noah, moreover, was but one of a group of editors who had fallen under the senatorial displeasure. Linked with him were Major Henry Lee, James B. Gardner, Moses Dawson, Amos Kendall and Isaac Hill. Lee, having been rejected unanimously, was out of the running. President Jackson, however, had his mind—and it was an obstinate mind!—made up on Noah.[1]

He came to his rescue by representing to the Senators that they had been misinformed as to certain facts. This time there was a tie, but Calhoun came to the rescue with the deciding vote.[2]

---

[1] See Claude G. Bowers, *The Party Battles of the Jackson Period*, pp. 39, 82 86, 203.

[2] Thus it was, according to Bowers. According to another account, it was Van Buren who ensured Noah's appointment to the Surveyorship, as solace for his failure to procure again the shrievalty, the year before. "I sorely regret the loss

The logical upward step was into the office of the Collector, and there is reason to believe that during Swartwout's occupancy, which was to end in a major scandal that would not leave Noah's name unassailed, Noah conceived the hope of becoming his successor.

But alas for the bedfellows of politics! Long before Swartwout was exposed in 1837 Noah was on the outs with Webb, with Jackson, with Bennett, with Van Buren, and his much maligned reputation was involved in yet another bank scandal. This time the institution was the United States Bank itself, the pet abomination of the President of the United States. Just what took place it is difficult, in the face of contradictory statements, to determine with unimpeachable accuracy. Was Noah, in this instance, as he was alleged in many others to be, a politico-journalistic schemer soliciting ill-disguised bribes? Or was he, as so often before, a more or less innocent bystander, victimized by circumstantial evidence? Or, yet again, something of each?

The Courier and Enquirer, up to November, 1829, had not been especially distinguished for hostility to the United States Bank. Bennett recalled that Noah, on the old *Enquirer*, had always expressed himself in favor of a modified re-charter of the Bank; Noah, indeed, though believing that the Bank had originally been chartered without authority from the Constitution, believed also that it could act as a "salutary check

of Noah's election," wrote Van Buren to Jesse Hoyt, on November 8, 1828, "as well on his own account, as on account of the cost his election has been to the party; but one point is gained, viz: he must be satisfied that his friends have, with their eyes open, sustained a great struggle, and run much hazard on his account. I hope there will yet be some way found of doing something for him."

See William MacKenzie, *The Life And Times of Martin Van Buren*, Boston, 1846, pp. 201–205.

upon the improvident issues of state banks." One day in November, 1829, alleges Bennett, going to Noah's office— that of Surveyor of the Port—he found him reading a letter that he had just received from Amos Kendall. The letter informed Noah that Jackson, in his message of the following month, to be delivered at the opening of Congress, would proceed against the United States Bank. That day, Kendall's letter was sent to the newspaper office to be published next morning as an editorial. "This was the first savage attack on the United States Bank, whose charter was to expire in 1836, in the columns of the *Courier and Enquirer*." From this day on, Webb, Courier and Noah consistently attacked the re-charter of the Bank and its excessive power over the States.

Some time in the Spring of 1831, however, Bennett alleges to have discovered, from a conversation with Silas E. Burroughs, that negotiations were under way between Burroughs and Noah to change the attitude of the newspaper. Noah was to purchase half the interest of the *Courier and Enquirer*, and Mr. Tylee was to go out. The transaction effected, surely enough the newspaper performed a political turnabout and was thereafter committed to the perpetuation of the Bank . . . Such about-facings were new neither to this newspaper nor to the journalism of the day. On June 26, 1831, Fenimore Cooper had written from Paris, to J. S. Skinner of Baltimore, editor of the *American Turf Register and Sporting Magazine*, ". . . the worst tergiversations of Noah's journal are light compared to those of The Times . . ."[1]

Bennett, on the score of the dubious, inconsistent morals involved in the volte-face, "never did entertain the opinion

---

[1] See *American Literature*, vol. I, May, 1929, for an article by Robert E. Spiller, on "Fenimore Cooper, Critic of His Times," containing new letters from Rome and Paris, 1830–1831.

that Mr. Webb was so much to blame at all . . . as Noah . . .
The Courier and Enquirer was in some financial difficulty at
the period the war was made on the Bank, and Mr. Noah,
when he saw the breeches pocket of Mr. Biddle open, entered
it immediately, and presented the chief exemplar of inconsistency and tergiversation."[1]

The worst construction that has been put upon the case,
which was the subject of a widely-followed Congressional
investigation, is this: Webb and Noah had borrowed, directly
and indirectly, $50,000. from the Bank; Mayor Bowne was
their sponsor to the head of the United States Bank, Nicholas
Biddle. A miniature jungle of Tammany tigers was on the
payroll of the Bank: Churchill C. Cambreleng, Giulian C.
Verplanck, Stephen Allen, Peter Sharpe, Ogden Edwards,
William H. Ireland, John Morss. The Bank had called *The
Courier and Enquirer* to time. And the newspaper that had
charged the Bank "with furnishing capital and thought at
the same moment,"—"with buying men and votes as cattle
in the market,"—"with corrupting the servants of the people,"
and "withering, as by a subtle poison, the liberty of the Press
. . . pointing to its golden vaults as the weapons that will
execute its behests, whenever it shall be necessary to carry
them into execution," now stood pilloried itself as a prosti-
tuted power. Ironically enough, it was Noah who, by the
editor of the *Albany Argus*, had once been accused of writing
these vehement words. Not Noah but Bennett had penned
them,—Bennett who was frequently the author of most of
what appeared in *The Courier and Enquirer*. Bennett, who
happened to be in Washington at the time of the exposure

[1] See *Memoirs of James Gordon Bennett and His Times*. (Pray). Especially
pp. 71, 110–112, 129, 147–150.

of his paper, professed to be as much astonished at the tale of the $50,000. as anybody else in the world.

In the course of the Congressional investigation,[1] among the assets of the Bank was discovered a note signed by Noah. Noah's astonishment at this discovery seems to have been as great as Bennett's. The money for which this note was given, testified Noah, was not received from the Bank at all. It was accepted from a private individual, "as a loan pressed upon him of unemployed funds."[2] Daly, a critic of Noah who was as well disposed toward him as Bennett was ill disposed, conjectured that the note was brought to the bank by some one into whose possession it had passed, "and the bank gave the money upon it to get Noah's influence, or to silence his opposition."

The more critical of these misadventures always meant for Noah the foundation of another newspaper. Off with the old, on with the new . . . One result of the scandal, then, was that Noah sold out his share of *The Courier and Enquirer* to Webb.

Daly has suggested another reason for Noah's having come out against the Jackson administration. Jackson's removal of the government funds from the United States Bank, and his redeposit of this money in the "pet" State banks, were creating a national sensation. New York especially was affected. "There was the attraction", suggests Daly, "to a politician like Noah, of the formation of a powerful political party in opposition to the administration, which the 'Whig' party rapidly became, to the building up of which he could largely contribute by the establishment of a journal of his

---

[1] See *The First Session of the Twenty-Second Congress*, vol. IV, reports numbered 460 to 463, Washington, 1831.

[2] See Daly. *Settlement of Jews in North America.* Continuation in 1893.

own." Such a newspaper could also serve another purpose: to feed Noah's revenge upon Van Buren, who was in line for the Presidency. Van Buren's vote, to be sure, may have ensured the office of Surveyor of the Port to Noah. Political honeymoons, however, are soon over. Van Buren, early in 1831, was being suspected of plotting the removal of Noah from this self-same office. For the rest of their respective lives Van Buren and Noah remained enemies.

On Thursday, August 23, 1832, Mr. Philip Hone entered the following note in his now famous Diary: "The *Courier and Enquirer* has shown signs of disaffection lately to the Jackson Party, of which it has heretofore been the unscrupulous organ. This morning it struck the Jackson flag and substituted the words, 'Principles, not men', for the names of Jackson, Van Buren, and March, which had been at the head of its columns. M. M. Noah advertises his withdrawal from the concern, in the vain hope of retaining the office of Surveyor of the Port. This renunciation will not, however, save him. In the meantime the surviving partner, James Watson Webb, not having the fear of either the before-mentioned potentates before his eyes, comes out this morning with his manifesto, a paper of four columns, exceedingly well written, in a style and language firm and dignified, and throws off the Jackson livery. The Bank veto is the principal ostensible reason for his defection. Other faults of the President are incidentally mentioned, but he has so often defended and justified them that it would hardly do to handle them too roughly at first."

Noah now proceeded to have a falling-out with President Jackson. He had expected to be advanced to the Collectorship of the Port. This failing, he resigned the office of Surveyor.

The new paper was named *The Evening Star*; it was established in association with Thomas Gill, who had been business manager of *The Evening Post*. No sooner had the *Star* begun to shine than the "holy" war of American journalism was on.

4. "The Holy War"—Synagogue Reform

New York, in 1833, had seven morning papers and four that appeared in the evening. The population of the city was a quarter of a million. Columbia College boasted an enrollment of one hundred. The leaders of metropolitan intellectuality were Irving, Cooper, Bryant, Halleck, N. P. Willis and George P. Morris. Webb was in the ascendancy as editor. Suddenly, on this scene, *The Sun* arose,—the first important penny newspaper in the country; within a few years a dozen imitators would enter the field, attempting to capitalize upon the new economy. For a short while Noah tried to companion his *Evening Star* with a *Morning Star*; it soon disappeared from the journalistic firmament. Not so Bennett's *Herald*. Bennett, serving under Webb and Noah, had developed ideas and methods of his own. He was dissatisfied with the stylistic and typographical dullness of the news sheets. He had a nose for scandal, a pen for its exploitation. And soon he had arrayed against him the entire forces of New York journalism, envious of his rapid success and determined to cast him, by fair means or foul, beyond the pale.

The names that Park Benjamin called Bennett in *The Signal*, or that Noah called him in *The Evening Star*, or Webb in *The Courier and Enquirer*, would make a pretty little manual of vituperation. Among the epithets were "pestilential scoundrel," "loathsome and leprous slanderer and libeller," "infamous Scotchman," "black-hearted," "venal wretch" (Benjamin); "moral pestilence", "moral leprosy," "ribald vehicle," "insidious poison," "lowest species of scurrility" (Webb); "common bandit," "humbug," "depraved appetite," "licentious" (Noah).

Within this decade the population of the country rose from nearly 13,000,000 to over 17,000,000. There were 852 newspapers in the nation, with a combined annual circulation of over 68,000,000. By 1840 there would be almost double the number of newspapers, with a combined annual circulation of 196,000,000,—representing, as against a population increase of 32% a circulation increase of 176%.

The Sun introduced the steam-press to American journalism. It placed newsboys for the first time upon the street; hitherto the papers had been sold over the counter, or delivered to subscribers. The telegraph would not be perfected until 1844; news-gathering, however, was performing a mighty accelerando, employing carrier-pigeons, horse-expresses from Washington, express-trains and news-boats (clipper ships, steam-vessels, rowboats, to meet incoming ships). This was the tempo of a new age.

Yet as late as 1835 the New York *Sun* salutes "Major Noah, the Grand Mogul of the Editorial Tribe." It is Noah's apogee in the journalistic ascent. To be sure, there is irony in this Sunny illumination. Has not the same newspaper been indicating that "*The Evening Star* of yesterday comes out in favor of the French lottery, gambling, and phrenology for ladies? Is the man crazy?" Yet the historian of *The Sun* records that Noah was the most popular playwright of his day in America, and that his *Star* was "a good paper, and the *Sun's* quarrels with it were not serious."[1]

As grand mogul of the city's journalistic tribe, and as the acknowledged spokesman of the growing Jewish community of New York, Noah naturally swung between the sacred and the secular. He was thus selected, in the midst of this war of print, to make the chief address of the day when, on January 13, 1834, the new synagogue of the Shearith Israel, built on Crosby Street, was consecrated. It was a notable occasion, and received extended comment in the Gentile press.[2]

Noah spoke for an hour. Though he enjoined upon his hearers a strict observance of their religious institutions, it was characteristic of him that he should, in the selfsame address, make important departures from that strictness. Thus he commented upon the "burdensome nature of some of the ceremonies", founded upon the traditions of the Elders and the Rabbins, in which he hoped for some amelioration of the code; and mentioned that a set of Jews had arisen in Germany "who already had effected such improvements in their synagogue worship." He suggested that services be

---

[1] See *The Story of The Sun*, by Frank M. O'Brien, New York, 1918, to which I am indebted for the figures and some of the details in the paragraphs preceding. Much matter of collateral interest is to be found in Allan Nevin's *The Evening Post*, New York, 1922.

Among the numerous statements of dubious veracity given wide currency in the obituaries of Noah, is a much-repeated one that Noah, later in his journalistic life, was associated with Beach on the New York *Sun*. Mr. O'Brien, in answer to an inquiry, assures me (in a letter dated April 16, 1931) that "Major Noah was never on *The Sun*."

[2] See, for extracts from the newspapers of that day, as well as for a description of the services, *AJHS*, vol. xxi, "Historical Sketch by Naphtali Phillips," pp. 172–228, and especially pp. 198–208.

conducted in the language of the country, and praised the tolerance of his own nation and age. He paid tribute to the noble women of Israel. He advocated public discourses in which, particularly for the benefit of the rising generation, the doctrines and ceremonies of the synagogue would be expounded. Finally, he urged strongly upon the congregation the introduction of music into the service, "pronouncing it a singular fact that a people so distinguished in early times for their music should for a long time have wholly renounced it."

The speech virtually aligned Noah with the Reform Movement that had begun almost a quarter of a century before in Germany. It was not to acquire strength in the United States until Noah had passed away. He foresaw the event, however, and thus became, in addition to his status as pioneer in Zionism, a pioneer in ritualistic reform.

His Zionism, uppermost in his mind, provided the real finale of the discourse published in 1837 on "The Evidences of The American Indians Being The Descendants of the Lost Tribes of Israel". It was delivered before the Mercantile Library Association, in Clinton Hall.[1]

Noah, after listing his "proofs" of the consanguinity that linked the Red man and the Hebrews, plunged into a fervent peroration:

"Firmly as I believe the American Indian to have been descended from the tribes of Israel, and that our continent is full of the most extraordinary vestiges of antiquity, there is one point, a religious as well as a historical point, in which you may possibly continue to doubt, amidst almost convincing evidences.

[1] It was published, with the title as given above, by James Van Norden, 27 Pine Street, New York. See Chapter VIII, pp. 227–230.

"If these are the remnants of the nine and a half tribes which were carried into Assyria, and if we are to believe in all the promises of the restoration, and the fulfilment of the prophecies, respecting the final advent of the Jewish nation, what is to become of these our red brethren, whom we are driving before us so rapidly, that a century more will find them lingering on the borders of the Pacific ocean?

"Possibly, the restoration may be near enough to include even a portion of these interesting people. Our learned Rabbis have always deemed it sinful to compute the period of the restoration; they believe that when the sins of the nation were atoned for, the miracle of their redemption would be manifested. My faith does not rest wholly in miracles— Providence disposes of events, human agency must carry them out. That benign and supreme power which the children of Israel had never forsaken, has protected the chosen people amidst the most appalling dangers, has saved them from the uplifted sword of the Egyptians, the Assyrians, the Medes, the Persians, the Greeks and the Romans, and while the most powerful nations of antiquity have crumbled to pieces, we have been preserved, united and unbroken, the same now as we were in the days of the patriarchs—brought from darkness to light, from the early and rude periods of learning to the bright reality of civilization, of arts, of education and of science.

"The Jewish people must now do something for themselves; they must move onward to the accomplishment of that great event long foretold—long promised—long expected; and when they DO move, that mighty power which has for thousands of years rebuked the proscription and intolerance shown to the Jews, by a benign protection of the *whole* nation, will still cover them with his invincible standard.

"My belief is, that Syria will revert to the Jewish nation by *purchase*, and that the facility exhibited in the accumulation of wealth, has been a providential and peculiar gift to enable them, at a proper time, to re-occupy their ancient possessions by the purse-string instead of the sword.

"We live in a remarkable age, and political events are producing extraordinary changes among the nations of the earth.

"Russia with its gigantic power continues to press hard on Turkey. The Pacha of Egypt, taking advantage of the improvements and inventions of men of genius, is extending his territory and influence to the straits of Babelmandel on the Red Sea, and to the borders of the Russian empire; and the combined force of Russia, Turkey, Persia and Egypt, seriously threaten the safety of British possessions in the East Indies. An intermediate and balancing power is required to check this thirst of conquest and territorial possession, and to keep in check the advances of Russia in Turkey and Persia, and the ambition and love of conquest of Egypt. This can be done by restoring Syria to its rightful owners, not by revolution or blood, but as I have said, by the purchase of that territory from the Pacha of Egypt, for a sum of money too tempting in its amount for him to refuse, in the present reduced state of his coffers. Twelve or thirteen millions of dollars have been spoken of in reference to the cession of that interesting territory, a sum of no consideration to the Jews, for the good will and peaceable possession of a land, which to them is above all price. Under the co-operation and protection of England and France, this re-occupation of Syria within its old territorial limits, is at once reasonable and practicable.

"By opening the ports of Damascus, Tripoli, Joppa, Acre, &c., the whole of the commerce of Turkey, Egypt, and the Mediterranean will be in the hands of those, who even now in part, control the commerce of Europe. From the Danube, the Dniester, the Ukraine, Wallachia and Moldavia, the best of agriculturalists would revive the former fertility of Palestine. Manufacturers from Germany and Holland; an army of experience and bravery from France and Italy; ingenuity, intelligence, activity, energy and enterprise from all parts of the world, would, under a just, a tolerant and a liberal government, present a formidable barrier to the encroachments of surrounding powers, and be a bulwark to the interests of England and France, as well as the rising liberties of Greece.

"Once again unfurl the standard of Judah on Mount Zion, the four corners of the earth will give up the chosen people as the sea will give up its dead, at the sound of the last trumpet. Let the cry be Jerusalem, as it was in the days of the Saracen and the lion-hearted Richard of England, and the rags and wretchedness which have for eighteen centuries enveloped the persons of the Jews, crushed as they were by persecution and injustice, will fall to the earth; and they will stand forth, the richest, the most powerful, the most intelligent nation on the face of the globe, with incalculable wealth, and holding in pledge the crowns and sceptres of kings. Placed in possession of their ancient heritage by and with the consent and co-operation of their Christian brethren, establishing a government of peace and good will on earth, it may then be said, behold the fulfilment of prediction and prophecy: behold the chosen and favorite people of the Almighty God, who in defense of His unity and omnipotence, have been the outcast and proscribed of all nations, and who for thousands of years have patiently endured the severest of human sufferings, in the hope of that great advent of which they have never despaired; and then when taking their rank once more among the nations of the earth, with the good wishes and affectionate regards of the great family of mankind, they may by their tolerance, their good faith, their charity and enlarged liberal views, merit what has been said in their behalf by inspired writers, 'Blessed are they who bless Israel!' "

The Evening Star had been conceived in an atmosphere of political disgruntlement.

In July, 1838, we find its sharp-tongued editor paying his disrespects to Martin Van Buren in a characteristic diatribe:

"You may remember when in 1817 we ran up the Bucktail flag we had but eighteen men with us in the Legislature, and with only three presses in the State, we opposed Dewitt Clinton, on the grounds that he had opposed the war, and run against James Madison for the Presidency, and in three years we carried the State. Where was Martin Van Buren at that time? With the democracy—with the War party— with the Madisonians? No such thing. He was hanging on the skirts of Mr. Clinton: and here let me remind you that hanging on the skirts of eminent men has been the peculiar feature and secret of Mr. Van Buren's advancement. He was elected to the Senate as a Clintonian; he moved in the Convention to have Clinton's nomination as Governor made unanimous; he hung closely to his skirts until he saw the current setting against him, when he dropped off and tacked himself to the skirts of Tompkins, and when Tompkins retired, he got hold of the skirts of Roger Skinner, Perley Keyes and Silas Wright, and clambered into the Senate of the Un. States much to the annoyance of that disinterested politician, Col. Samuel Young. In the Senate he held on to the skirts of Rufus King, until he got introduced into 'good society.' He then took hold of the skirts of Crawford, and when poor Crawford lost the election of President, and John Quincy Adams succeeded he made two or three grabs at his skirts, but Adams wore a spencer and Van Buren missed his hold, and he settled down quietly in the Senate looking round to see whom he could next ride, like the old man in the story of Sinbad the sailor. At length when it was reduced to a certainty that Andrew Jackson would succeed, he creeped by degrees near him, for the old Chief was afraid of Van Buren, and finally he succeeded in getting him by the button, and in this way got into the Cabinet; he then caught hold of the skirts of Eaton, Kendall and Blair, and finally, through their intercessions and efforts, he crawled into the old General's breeches pocket and he made him his successor."[1]

[1] See MacKenzie, op. cit., on Van Buren, p. 198.

In 1840 *The Evening Star* made the definite presidential stride from the Wigwam to the Whigs. For this pronounced turn-about-face Noah had a simple, self-defensive explanation.

"The cry of turncoat", remembered Samuel Lockwood, writing about Noah some seventeen years after the Jewish spokesman had died, "was not soon quelled. Accosted by one who met him in the street just after the transaction, the following dialogue is said to have taken place:

" 'Major Noah, what the deuce is in the wind?'

" 'What do you mean, sir?'

" 'I mean to ask, are Democracy and Whiggery the same, as you have left one and gone to the other?'

" 'Bless you, my good friend, no!—as wide apart as the East is from the West!'

" 'Then how comes it that you went over to the opposite party?'

" 'My dear sir, it is the party which has changed, not *I*! The truth is, I found to my surprise that the *principles* had gone over to the other side; and as I could not honorably desert my principles, or suffer them to desert me, I had in all conscience to go over too!' "[1]

The about-face of Noah would not be his last. Far from betokening an inconsistency rooted in his character, however, it was but a personal reflection of a condition that was prevalent in contemporary affairs. It was, in simple fact, part of the strange bed-fellowship made by politics. Discussing this self-same presidential campaign of 1840, Professor and Mrs. Beard write that General Harrison's campaign managers offered him to the country simply "as a man of

[1] See *Lippincott's Magazine*, vol. 1; 1868, pp. 665–670, article on "Major M. M. Noah," by Samuel Lockwood.

the people while they attacked Van Buren as an eastern aristocrat. In this fashion the tables were reversed: the old party of Tiberius Gracchus was trying to elect a patrician from New York, whereas the party of the rich and well-born was trying to elevate a Cincinnatus straight from the furrow."[1]

The truth is that Noah was sinking into a more or less graceful decline, attended by the usual honors and not unaccompanied by the customary insinuations of his political and journalistic enemies. As the pendulum came to a standstill it wavered across the same course: newspaper, theater, book, oration, courtroom, home . . .

In 1840 he wrote an Introduction to, and published, *The Book of Jasher*, presenting, in 254 double-column pages, these "divinely authenticated annals of the Hebrews."[2] Far more

---

[1] *The Rise of American Civilization*, New York, 1927; 1930, vol. I, p. 576.

[2] *The Book of Jasher, Referred To In Joshua and Second Samuel, Faithfully Translated From The Original Into English*. Salt Lake City, Published by J. H. Parry & Company. The edition I consulted was published in 1887. The translator is not named. The first edition of this book, in Hebrew, appeared in Venice, 1625. It was Noah's edition that Rebecca Gratz had in mind when she wrote to Maria Gist Gratz, on August 27, 1840, "I should like to have made one of your summer party—to have seen your namesake nieces, and heard your observations on the book of Jashar, that extravagant chronicle of bible characters—there is a portion of it very agreeable to me—but so many improbable histories and some impossible exploits entirely destroy its credibility, and one cannot but wonder that the author or his translator, could expect it would ever pass for the veritable book of Jashar referred to in the Scriptures. An intelligent hebrew Scholar, raised my expectations so high, in favor of it before it appeared that I confess I was sadly disappointed, when I found it impossible, as I proceeded in the work, to class it with anything better than an old romance—It was very affecting to hear Abraham & Isaac conversing on the sacrifice, as they journeyed to Mount Moriah, and to find that Jacob shared the fortitude and faith that supported them—but the introduction of Satan, and his malignant effect on the life of Jacob is shocking—particularly as the next event recorded in Scripture history is the death of Sarah—it is true she had reached a good old age and in the course of nature, might be called on to resign her life, and happily too, for as a wife & mother she was blessed, and triumphant, but we

245

important, it was Noah who delivered the principal address, on August 19, 1840, at the synagogue of the B'Nai Jeshurun, protesting against the foul recrudescence of the Passover-blood myth.

It was in this busy year, too, that he wrote the dramatic piece, *Natalie*, for the dancer, Céleste.[1]

The Damascus Libel of 1840 was a blow to the Jews of America no less than to those of Europe. The murder of Father Thomas, superior of the Franciscan convent in the Turkish city, was turned by his brother monks into an excuse for a raid upon the Jews. Father Thomas, they alleged, raising an ancient cry that has not yet been stilled, had been slain for purposes of the Jewish ritual. By the application of torture they elicited a "confession" from a Jewish barber. The French consul used the press of his country to broadcast his venomous allegations to the rest of the world. Official France seemed to be in league against the maligned race, despite all that Crémieux could do. Lord Palmerston, in England, raised his voice in protest; the Christian clergy, as in the United States, came to the assistance of the Jews. President Van Buren, through Secretary of State John Forsyth, urged our consul at Alexandria and our minister at Constantinople to use their good offices to

would rather think she had gone down peacefully to "the place appointed for all living," than to be killed by sudden joy—and the fallen angel the agent. Those who would take the bible history as the foundation of these works should be careful never to violate the spirit and influence of the Sacred book, nor assign motives for events not borne out by its authority—The beautiful history of Joseph too is spoiled in this book—and Moses suffers so many adventures, that we scarcely recognize him as the plain man 'meek' & 'slow of speech' as he records himself to be—but enough of this." (See *Letters of Rebecca Gratz*, edited by David Philipson, Philadelphia, 1929, pp. 280–282.)

[1] See, for details, Appendix I, "Addenda To Noah's Plays."

allay the persecution, "the bare recital of which caused a shudder throughout the civilized world."

Father Thomas had been slain on February 5. American Jews held meetings of protest in New York, on August 19, and in Philadelphia on August 27. A representative assembly of Jews in London resolved to send to the East a deputation consisting of Montefiore, Crémieux and Solomon Munk. Despite official French obstruction, "a collective note from nine other European consuls forced Mehemet Ali to order the release of those Jewish martyrs who had not succumbed to death (September 6). In October, Damascus and all of Syria were freed from the dominion of Mehemet Ali; shortly afterwards Syria was restored to Turkey. Montefiore and Crémieux were received in audience by the Sultan Abdul-Mejid . . . who graciously issued a firman pronouncing ritual murder a base libel on the Jewish people and confirming the inviolability of Jewish persons and property in the Ottoman empire. The united action of the Jews far and wide which the dastardly affair provoked served as a proof that, with all their divisions, political, cultural, and religious, the Jews had a common bond which nothing could destroy."[1]

It was Joseph Jacobs who beheld, in the emotional upheaval over the Damascus affair, the emergence of a New Israel from its latent consciousness. Wiernik, too, regarded

[1] *A History of the Jewish People*, by Max L. Margolis and Alexander Marx, Philadelphia, 1927, pp. 651–653.

See also *A Century of Judaism in New York*. By Israel Goldstein, M.A., D.H.L., New York, 1930, pp. 64–73. Rabbi Goldstein's account of his synagogue, the B'Nai Jeshurun, contains copies of the letters addressed by New York Jewry to President Van Buren, the reply from Secretary of State, John Forsyth, and a copy of the letter addressed by Forsyth to United States Consul John Glidden at Alexandria.

See also *AJHS*, v. VIII, pp. 143–144.

the international episode as "the first time that the Jews of
the United States interested themselves and enlisted the
interest of the Government in the cause of the suffering Jews
in another part of the world, and thus participated in that
consolidation of the Jewish public spirit which resulted from
the memorable occurrence."[1]

Certainly Noah, as an individual, and as one of the first
Jews to occupy conspicuous public office in the United States,
had from the beginning given evidence of this international
consciousness. What is more, he had linked it always with
the general idea of toleration for all, thus rising above special
pleading for his own people. Once again, then, we discover
Noah in the rôle of a pioneer whose ideals are based not only
upon the arguments of theory, but upon the tenets of practical application and upon actual experience in the different
continents of the world.

The Evening Star was dimming. It had done its share in
assuring the election of Harrison to the Presidency. Shortly
thereafter, Gill died. Noah, who never had any great business ability, was altogether at a loss without his highly
efficient partner; it was Gill alone who had managed to maintain the standing of the paper against pressing competition.
With his death, that of *The Evening Star* was decreed. Noah
sold out to one of his evening rivals, *The Commercial Advertiser*.

There was balm for this wound in the appointment of
Noah by Governor Seward to a position on the New York
bench . . . On May 8, 1841, we discover Philip Hone, the
noted Diarist, entering one of his last items about Noah, and
employing an unusual, but not unfamiliar, middle name for

[1] Goldstein, op. cit., p. 66.

that gentleman. "Mordecai Manasseh Noah, an Israelite, former editor of the *Star*, sheriff under the Regency, surveyor of the port under Jackson, I believe, a disciple of Tammany for many a long year, but of late a conservative inclining to Whiggism, has been appointed an associate justice of the Court of Sessions in the city, and has entered upon the duties of his office. This appointment, which stuck some time in the Senate, was finally confirmed without a division, notwithstanding Charles King of the *American* protested against it *totis viribus*. He protested that Noah knew no more about law than he did about the Gospel, which he seemed to think of some little importance in the qualifications of a judge . . ."

It was, in a veiled manner, the cry of "Jew!" that had been raised against Noah as a candidate for the shrievalty. And, if a Jew should not be placed in a position that might mean his hanging a Christian, neither should he—was the implication of King, an old journalistic rival of Noah—sit in judgment over Christians. There were persons who never achieved full conviction of Noah's legal knowledge. There was no doubt, however, that his heart was in the right place.

Daly, in contradistinction to Noah's enemies, was of the opinion that the appointee was well qualified to fill this office. Noah had studied law in his pre-consular days at Charleston. A general knowledge of commercial law was not beyond his abilities. "The office of a criminal judge, moreover, is one that requires in a greater degree than any other judicial station, the tempering of justice with mercy . . ."

Mr. Bennett of *The New York Herald*, however, did not believe that mercy mixed well with printers' ink. Noah's appointment was the signal for an unceasing barrage of scurrility, misrepresentation and caricature, from which undignified references to Noah's religion were rarely absent.

Bennett still remembered the "holy war"; other data he seems to have forgotten.[1] Noah himself entered no complaint; it was a juror who instituted the proceedings that brought Bennett to book for libels, respectively, against Judges Noah and Lynch. In fact, when the case was called, Noah addressed the court, avowing that, so far as he was concerned, the prosecution might be dropped. The attack on him, he explained, was the continuation of an old quarrel in which he had been, to a considerable extent, the aggressor. The Judge denied consent. As there was no defense, the jury brought in a verdict of guilty.

5. SLAVERY—CIVIC PROJECTS— RESTORATION OF THE JEWS—FINIS

Noah did not remain upon the bench long. His labors as associate judge, indeed, appear in the perspective of his later life as an interlude between the inevitable journalistic ventures.

According to Wolf, Noah resigned his judgeship "because he felt himself incompetent to sit upon the trial for forgery of a certain member of Congress whom he had known from boyhood. He had known the parents of the prisoner, good old Quakers, and the idea of having to sentence the son to

---

[1] Daly, op. cit., in his Continuation in 1893, gives currency to an unsubstantiated story that is first encountered, I believe, in an article written by Robert P. Noah for *The Reformer & Jewish Times*, November 15, 1878. According to the last paragraph of this article, the *New York Herald* was founded by Bennett "upon the sum of $100, which the Major lent him. The amount was returned by Mr. Bennett nearly twenty years after." I can find no proof of this statement. "Twenty years after" would be upon the eve of Noah's death, which the *Herald* was the only important newspaper to ignore. The tale, perhaps, is founded upon a loan made by Noah to Bennett in their days upon the *Courier*. When the *Herald* was established, Noah was a rival of Bennett's, editing the *Star*.

the penitentiary in case of conviction was so abhorrent to his kindly nature that he preferred to resign from the bench. The unfortunate man was subsequently convicted and sentenced, and died in the Sing Sing penitentiary."

It reads very much like a gesture that Noah was well capable of making—and meaning . . . In 1842, the year in which Noah was elected to the leadership of the Hebrew Benevolent Society, he was also appointed by President Tyler (through Paul R. George) editor of the official Whig organ, *The Union*. The paper failed almost immediately. It lasted just long enough, however, to involve its editor in a very unpleasant controversy with the arrow-tongued Horace Greeley, who, it is to be suspected, had much the better of the argument, even in the eyes of many Jews. The quarrel, based like so many contemporary quarrels upon political hostility, called forth a stirring rejoinder from Greeley.

Noah, it seems, had accused Greeley of breakfasting with two Negroes at a boarding house on Barclay Street. Just why this should appear reprehensible to a Jew who had spent his active life in asking—say, rather, in demanding, and justly—tolerance for his race, it is not easy to understand, except on the basis of Southern (Charleston) prejudice and political animus. Had not Noah, a quarter of a century before, in his book of *Travels*, bespoken for the Blacks of our South, "a greater equality of rights"?[1] Political heat, apparently, had melted away some of his finer impulses. Greeley's reply, discounting for its pardonable malice, rang with robust reprimand.

[1] See page 86, on which I quote his printed opinion of that time.

251

"We choose our own company in all things", he wrote, "and that of our own race, but cherish little of that spirit which for eighteen centuries has held the kindred of M. M. Noah accursed of God and man, outlawed and outcast, and unfit to be the associates of Christians and Musselmen, or even self-respecting Pagans. Where there are thousands who would not eat with a Negro, there are (or lately were) tens of thousands who would not eat with a Jew. We leave to such renegades as the Judge of Israel"—Ararat, one sees, was still fresh in some memories—"the stirring up of prejudices and the prating of 'usages of society', which over half the world make him an abhorrence, as they not long since would have done here . . . That he is a knave, we think much to his discredit, however unfortunate it may be for that luckless people."[1]

It is said that Noah was palpably hit by Greeley's rejoinder. And well he might be. A few years later, while we were at war with Mexico, Noah made clear his attitude toward the Negro question, abolition, and related considerations.[2] Inveighing against the Wilmot Proviso—"uncalled for and unconstitutional"—he upheld slavery.

"On the subject of abolition," he wrote, in the midst of a passionate diatribe against Van Buren, "I feel that I am as familiar with its history, rise and progress, and have watched all its movements, from the dreadful massacre at St. Domingo, down to the attempt to jeopardize the success of our arms in Mexico, by engrafting the Wilmot Proviso on the Three Million Bill, as any citizen in the Union. In every paper that I have conducted, I have defended the South against fanatics, and what was worse than fanatics, political abolitionists, and

---

[1] *The Life of Horace Greeley,* by James Parton. Boston, 1889, p. 189.
[2] See *A Letter to the Southern Democratic Members of the Convention.* New York, 1848.

claim to know something of their movements. Their whole objects and intentions from the commencement, have been to use the slavery question as an instrument to cripple, if not destroy the political influence of the South . . . They know that slave labor is excluded from those territories [i. e. above 36° 30', the line of the Missouri Compromise] by soil and climate—they know, therefore, that the Wilmot Proviso is out of time and place, that it is uncalled for and unconstitutional. Wherefore do they urge it in every position, in every stage of their proceedings? Because they know it is a fire-brand which they imagine can be profitably wielded against the South, and they seize upon the occasion when our country is engaged in foreign war . . . "

It is not, as Northerners see it today, an enlightened view. Noah, through his early associations in Charleston, had naturally developed certain attitudes of the slave-owning Southerners. Yet it is in this selfsame address that he anticipates, by more than fifteen years, the essential approach of Lincoln. "I entertain," declared Noah, "no sectional views. I go for the Union, and the whole Union!"[1]

---

[1] It may be significant that in 1845 Noah reprinted the *Essays of Howard on Domestic Economy*, which had appeared originally in 1820. These were pseudonymous essays that had previously been published between October, 1818, and June 3, 1820, in the *New York National Advocate*.

According to an obituary notice in *The Atlas*, March 30, 1851, the papers by "Howard" were the "joint labor of himself (Noah) and Mr. William Graham," who was slain in a duel at Hoboken because one of the articles was supposed to contain personal allusions to the family of Edward Livingston.

The essays were republished as *Gleanings From a Gathered Harvest*. Now, the gleanings are reprinted almost verbatim from the *Essays of Howard*, omitting, however, the final paper of that collection, which was on slave ships and slavery.

In addition to minor alterations and the deletion of a sentence or two here and there, Noah has added titles to the sections, such as "Fashionable Follies," "Master and Man," and "The Refectory."

This attitude, it is likely, had been inherited by Noah from his days as an ardent Jacksonian. Jackson, during the period of the fight with Calhoun over nullification, had made clear his stand for the national unity at all costs. It was in 1830 that Jackson had directed at Calhoun, during a Jefferson dinner, the famous toast, "Our Federal Union—it must and shall be preserved."[1]

Far more important than Noah's controversy with Greeley, or the journalistic and political conflicts that he was waging immediately before and after 1844, is the speech he delivered at the Tabernacle on October 28 and December 2 of that year. It has become famous, in the history of American Zionism, as the "Discourse on the Restoration of the Jews." It was, in truth, something more than an oratorical exercise in the stereotyped manner. Damascus was only four years behind. The need for Jewish solidarity, for restoration, was in Noah's eyes greater than ever, and the opportunity commensurately great.[2]

Prefacing his speech, he wrote: "I confidently believe in the restoration of the Jews, and in the coming of the Messiah; and believing that political events are daily assuming a shape which may finally lead to that great event, I consider it a

---

The Preface to *Gleanings*, however, is entirely misleading. It makes no reference to a previous appearance of the essays. It even says, "so this is the first attempt, which, if well received, I may be induced to follow it up with something more substantial, more worthy perhaps of public approval."

[1] *The Rise of American Civilization*, by Charles and Mary Beard, vol. I, pp. 560–561.

[2] *The Discourse on the Restoration of the Jews* was printed, in pamphlet form, at least twice. Harper & Brothers published it in 1845, with a map of the land of Israel. In Baltimore it was republished, early in the 1900's, by D. S. Blondheim, who wrote an introductory note. The latter edition carries a footnote indicating that "this article is reprinted from *The Maccabean* of April, 1905."

duty to call upon the free people of this country to aid us in any efforts which, in our present position, it may be deemed prudent to adopt . . ."

The United States, once considered by him a temporary Zion,—a port of call, as it were, on the voyage to the eternal haven,—now appeared as the great Jewish Hope. It was "the only country which has given civil and religious rights to the Jews equal with the other sects; the only country which has not persecuted them," and therefore it "shall present to the Lord his chosen and down-trodden people, and pave the way for the restoration to Zion. Let me therefore impress upon your minds the important fact, that the liberty and independence of the Jewish nation may grow out of a single effort which this nation may make in their behalf. That effort is to procure for them a permission to purchase and hold land in security and peace; their titles and possessions confirmed; their fields and flocks undisturbed. They want only protection, and the work is accomplished. The Turkish government cannot be insensible to the fact that clouds are gathering about them, and destiny, in which they wholly confide, teaches them to await the day of trouble and dismemberment. It is to their interest to draw around them the friendly aid and cooperation of the Jewish people throughout the world, by conferring these reasonable and just privileges upon them, and when Christianity exerts its powerful agency, and stretches forth its friendly right hand the right solicited will be cheerfully conferred. When the Jewish people can return to Palestine, and feel that in their persons and property they are as safe from danger as they are under Christian government, they will make their purchases of select positions, and occupy them peaceably and prosperously; confidence will with them take the place of distrust and, by degrees, the population in every part of Syria being greatly increased, will become consolidated, and ready to unfold the standard when political events shall demonstrate to them that the time has arrived.

"Remember, therefore, my countrymen, you whose aid is invoked to assist in the restoration, that we are to return as we went forth; to bring back to Zion the faith we carried away with us. The temple under Solomon, which we built as Jews, we must again erect as the chosen people. You believe that the Messiah has come; you are right in believing so; you have the evidences in the power and dominion, the wealth, the happiness, the glory that surrounds you. He has come for you, but how for us? We are still the peeled, the banished, scattered, and oppressed people; the oil on the surface of the ocean, which mingles not with the heaving billow. For us he is yet to come, and will come. For two thousand years we have been pursued and persecuted, and we are yet here; assemblages of men have formed communities, built cities, established government, rose, prospered, decayed, and fell, and yet we are here. Rome conquered, and there are but few traces now of the once mistress of the world; yet we are still here, like the fabled Phoenix, ever springing from its ashes, or, more beautifully typical, like the bush of Moses, which ever burns, yet never consumes. You believe that Jesus of Nazareth was the Messiah, and you are Christians; were we to believe the same, we should still be Jews.

"With this difference only, what is it that separates the Jew and Gentile? Our law is your law, our profits are your profits, our hope is your hope, our salvation is your salvation, our God is your God. Why should we change? Why surrender that staff of Jacob which has guided our steps through so many difficulties? We can never be separated from our Shepherd; we believe in all that He has promised, and patiently await their fulfillment. Come, therefore, to our aid, and take the lead in this great work of restoration. Let the first movement for the emancipation of the Jewish nation come from this free and liberal nation."

Noah, though hardly in any sphere a radical, was sufficiently independent and unorthodox in a personal manner to be forever rousing his fellow politicians and his coreligionists. The speech on the "Restoration of the Jews" got him at once into hot water. There were many who thought it too free. When his protégé and friend, Lockwood, a Gentile, brought this to Noah's attention, the Major replied, "It will do them good . . . Besides, I can say things to them which no other of our race can. They take it kindly from me."

Noah worried the orthodox especially with his comments upon the Jesus of Christianity.

"I tell you, sir," he would say to Lockwood, "I tell you I admire this Jesus of the Christians. There never was a philosopher like him, and the world has never had another philosophy at all comparable to the system which he taught. In this respect the New Testament unfolds a system of truly wonderful humanizing power . . . Were I traveling in Palestine, and should find his bones, although it would make me immediately rich, I'd never divulge it—the secret should go with me to my grave."

"But why," Lockwood ventured to ask, "wouldn't you divulge it?"

"Because thus to weaken the faith in that system would be in effect to turn back the only tide which has ever been adequate to roll a flood of blessings over the different races of men. It contains in itself such an adaptiveness to the world's wants, it is so unselfish, so indisputably benevolent."[1]

Noah was even accused, by an Anglo-Jewish periodical, in London, of being *anti-Judaic!* To this "most unkindest cut" of the *Voice of Jacob* he retorted with a ringing self-defense.[2]

Noah was not dispirited. Rather, it was for him, he declared, to complain of the *apathy* (his italics) and the want of nationality, that characterized the Jewish people. He, *anti-Judaic?* "It is not so"—he countered. On the contrary, his discourse had been "a complete vindication of Judaism throughout . . .

"It avows that the Messiah of the Jews is yet to come and will come—a broad admission, on which the very foundation of our religion rests. I endeavour in that discourse to convince Christians that in attempting to evangelize the Jews they violate an affirmative precept of their own faith. I endeavour to show its utter failure; I prove by quotations from our prophets, that the Jews are to be restored in their unconverted state; I maintain steadfastly their perpetual belief in the unity and omnipotence of God; I show how peculiarly they are his people; I vindicate the morality of the Jewish character, and appeal to Christians to do them justice, and to temper that justice with mercy. How can this be 'anti-Judaic,' and from one who has always, on all occasions, public and private, proudly avowed himself to be a Jew? But you may say, There were certain portions of that discourse, which relate to the advent of Christianity, which are not conformable to the received opinions of the Jewish people. Now, my reverend friend, how should the Jewish people know anything of Christianity beyond the

[1] See Lockwood, in *Lippincott's Monthly*, vol. 1, pp. 665–670.
[2] See, for Noah's rejoinder, and for the discussion of the speech by the Rev. Dr. Leeser and Noah, the files of Leeser's periodical, *The Occident*, for 1845, pp. 29–35, and pp. 600–606.

certain fact that Christians have long been the religious
enemies of the Jews? The most enlightened of our people
seldom read the New Testament, and the most rigid and
superstitious would shrink with pious horror at the idea of
even touching that book. I have no such apprehensions, no
such prejudices, and I never close the New Testament without being forcibly struck with the superior beauty, simplicity,
and truly divine inspiration of the Bible; and I mean no
disrespect to Christianity when I say, that no unprejudiced
mind can come to any other conclusion. I have studied
Christianity from the New Testament, and therefore profess
to know more of that religion and am better able to explain
its doctrines than Jews who do not read that book at all,
and my own opinions have been made up from study and
reflection, and I feel satisfied that Christians have not com-
prehended the position in which they stand towards the
Jews, nor the obligations imposed upon them by their own
laws, to treat the chosen people with kindness and consideration, and to extend towards them the hand of succour and
of brotherly love. Equally erroneous and unjust have we
been towards Christians, in classing them with idolaters, and
placing them on a footing with the Canaanitic nations. It is
to correct error; it is to produce a more candid union between
Jews and Christians; it is to bind them together by the ties
of charity and good-will, which were the objects of my discourse, and this I maintain can be done without surrendering
a single particle of our ancient and holy faith . . .

"The restoration is to be brought about by human agency,
and can only be accomplished by and with the consent of the
Christian powers, who, from their own active energies, and,
if you please, spirit of conquest, now control, I may say, the
whole world, civilized and barbarian. We can only be peaceably restored by and with their consent, and if so restored,
we shall, beyond doubt, be secure and protected in all our
national rights.

"You appear constantly to consider our position as dangerous; you apprehend the power and untiring influence of

Christians in the work of evangelizing; you seem to look with dread at the progress and the vast pecuniary means at their disposal to achieve such important objects, and imagine that the ground on which the Jews have stood firmly for many centuries, surrounded by all kinds of trouble and calamity, is now crumbling beneath their feet. I do not participate in any such fears. It is natural that Christians who have faith in their own religion, should desire to convert what they consider the 'lost sheep of Israel,' and it may and will happen, that considerations of interest with many and security with the few may produce converts; but there are cardinal points and considerations which in a measure shake their faith, while that of the Jew from natural and philosophical causes, remains firm. For example, many Christians have misgivings about the Trinity; some have their doubts about the spiritual and corporeal resurrection; the contradictions among the evangelists trouble them; Unitarianism, which is not Christianity, is greatly on the increase; Pantheism is apprehended; sects are multiplying; divisions increasing; new doctrines springing up; Romanism is acquiring a spiritual preponderance, and troubles seem gradually encircling the Christian Church. The Jews, being in no such danger, reposing always on the simple rock of their ancient faith, relying on God as their Redeemer, present to the Christian an object of so much interest; of such painful anxiety; they are so ancient, so favoured, so protected—that all sects extend their hands in supplication, and say 'Come to us.' They want the consolation of having God's favourite children to acknowledge the messiahship of Jesus of Nazareth; and although we cannot go to them, although we cannot forsake our ancient Shepherd, we cannot believe in all that they believe, we ought not on that account to treat them unkindly and consider them our perpetual enemies. A great change has come over Christians; the Almighty is at work on them, efficiently, practically— the scales are falling from their eyes—truth begins to dissipate the clouds of darkness which for ages have surrounded them. Not many years ago, few ministers of the gospel

ascended the pulpit without preaching against the Jews;
prejudice was kept alive and fed the flames of persecution:
but now all is changed; all is love, confidence and regard.
The Jews are recognized as God's chosen people, and all his
promises of mercy towards them are to be redeemed; the
'lost sheep of Israel' they have now discovered have never
been lost, and they look at us with eyes overflowing with
tears of affection, as the greatest living miracle that exists
—the true and faithful witnesses of the unity of God and the
truth of the Scriptures. Shall we not profit by this returning
kindness and good-will? They have mistaken the very principles of their own faith in relation to the treatment of the
Jews; shall we drive them back again within the pale of
ancient intolerance? Our own prayers teach us a different
course; the great family of mankind is recognized without
distinction of sect or creed as participating equally in all the
rights, privileges, and immunities of Divine favour and
protection.

"The massacre of Damascus was considered a terrible
affliction—terrible it was no doubt to the sufferers—but I
have always deemed it a most providential dispensation: and
we are too apt in these things to overlook the agency of
divine Providence. It sent a thrill throughout the civilized
world, and the governments of the earth loudly denounced
the cruelties practised towards the Jews, and declared that
they should not again happen. From that moment the
Israelites assumed a rank and a character among the nations
of the earth; they found friends and protectors in Christians;
and would you now counsel us to fall back upon our ancient
prejudices and revive the animosities of centuries? or rather,
keeping pace with the enlightened spirit of the age, forgive
and forget, and seize the hand stretched forth in kindness to
succour us? But then again succeeds your 'ague fit'—'they
want to convert us'—'their kindness is assumed'—'they press
us to surrender our faith.' Take courage—have more confidence, my friend, in the firmness and stability of our religion
—it is not to be shaken. But there is danger I admit—

danger, not from Christians, but from ourselves. Danger from apathy, from indifference—danger from a want of nationality. The Jew who keeps his store open on the Sabbath is still a Jew: he commits a great sin, but pleads necessity. It is his indifference—he has no desire to embrace another religion or to surrender his own faith; but he cares too little for his own religion to induce him to make a sacrifice for it. There are many reasons for this which I have not time at present to notice. The Jews want *nationality*; you cannot rally them on any given point; you cannot inspire them either with faith or enthusiasm. We pray fervently and constantly to be restored to Zion; we believe in the coming of the Redeemer, and pray earnestly for his coming; and yet talk to the mass of our people on the Restoration— on their return to Jerusalem—and they express no confidence in it; few would be willing to go; and the coming of our Redeemer—the advent of our Messiah—seems to give them no trouble, no solicitude at all. They pray for him from habit, and have no faith in what they pray for. What is the cause of all this discrepancy between assertion and belief? The want of nationality, I again repeat: we are a sect, not a nation. The Greeks remained two thousand years in slavery, and yet they arose and redeemed their country. Why should not the Jews do the same? Christians would honour us even if we failed. Nothing therefore in my opinion will save the nation from sinking into oblivion but *agitating this subject of the Restoration*. We should pass the word around the world —'Restoration of the Jews'—'Justice to Israel'—'the Rights and Independence of the Hebrews'—'Restore them to their country'—'Redeem them from captivity.' Christians and Mussulmen should be invoked to aid them in the good cause.

"As to evangelizing, depend upon it the labour is great and the success very limited, and it is not to be feared to the extent you believe. No Jew surrenders his own faith, without satisfying himself that it is inherently false, and no Christian ever asserted or believed that there is any thing false in Judaism: therefore no Jew changes his faith to Chris-

tianity, unless under rare circumstances, except to answer some sinister purpose. It has been said that our religion is Talmudistic and not Biblical. It is directly the reverse: the Talmud is the mere explanation of the Law, and wherever that explanation is in hostility to the Law and the Prophets it should be rejected as anti-Judaic. The Bible is the rock of our salvation. The great secret of consolidating and keeping the Jews together as a nation consists in their inter-marriages; break down that barrier and allow Jews and Christians to marry, and in two or three generations we shall be no longer heard of. Let us be liberal and tolerant to our Christian brethren, and set them a better example than they have hitherto set us. Our sufferings and persecutions have kept us together and have been our protection. Let them if they please use their efforts to convert the Jews; their weapons are not now swords or dungeons as formerly, but mildness and persuasion; and if they fail, let us not add harshness and intolerance to that failure. We want their aid in the great work of Restoration—we cannot succeed without it; it is our duty, if we sincerely believe in that great advent and desire it, to solicit their co-operation—their good feelings—their powerful protection. God is at this moment working upon their minds to favour the Jews, while in many parts of the world He is inclining the Jews to entertain more tolerant views towards the Christians. We in this generation may be impelled to commence the good work, which succeeding generations will accomplish."

At the time of the Restoration discourse Major Noah and his young wife—in 1844 she was but thirty-four years old—were the proud parents of a large family. Of the seven children, but one was a girl. They were, in the order of birth: Manuel Mordecai (the Manny of Noah's solicitous letters), Dec. 23, 1828; Jacob J., Oct. 6, 1830; Robert P. (Abraham), Dec. 4, 1832; Zipporah, sometime between June 26 and

August 27, 1835; Daniel Jackson, Aug. 6, 1837; Henry, Sept. 16, 1839, and Lionel J., Dec. 25, 1843.

The patriotic Major could hardly have foreseen, in the history of his own family, the divergence of faiths that so troubled the thoughts of the Rev. Dr. Leeser, and that may have been rooted in the very apathy and the want of nationality of which, with such eloquence, Noah himself wrote and spoke.[1]

Noah's political loyalty, and, as we have seen, an appreciable degree of his emotional allegiance, remained with the South. His mother lay buried in Charleston, where he had studied law, begun his career as a diplomat, fought his duel, and entered journalism. From this port he had set sail for Tunis. His father lay buried in New York, where Noah had lived out the career born in the languid atmosphere of South Carolina. It is not surprising, then, to discover Noah, even at this date, and after his switch to Whiggery, looking back fondly toward both the Democratic party and the Southern cause.

On October 21, 1846, he wrote from New York a long letter to M. C. Mordecai. In this communication he makes it very clear where his journalistic ambitions and his political sympathies—shall we say, of the moment?—lie.[2] The document is important enough to be reproduced in full.

It will be interesting, as one reads the first part, to remember that, in Noah's early days, during the Charleston period

[1] See Appendix II, "Noah's Wife And Children."

[2] This letter, which I reprint for the first time, I discovered among a batch of Noah correspondence photostated for me in the archives at Washington. Much of the correspondence passed between Duff Green and Noah. The letter in question is not in Noah's hand, but in that of a professional secretary. It is closely written on three sheets of, approximately, legal-size stationery. The signature is undoubtedly that of Noah,—one of the clearest to be had, flourish and all.

of 1811–1812, it was Calhoun who had befriended the ambitious young Jew from Philadelphia. According to obituary notices in the press,[1] Noah had come to the Southern city prepared to train, among other things, for the profession of teaching. It was Calhoun who then had pointed out to him that his career lay in the North.

New York   October 21   1846

"Dear Sir.

"The election in this State and the approaching Session of Congress with the very important results which may grow out of both in reference to the next Presidential campaign have induced me to address you at an earlier period than I contemplated when I had the pleasure of seeing you, in reference to the interests of the South and those of our mutual friend Mr Calhoun in particular. I have for many years been satisfied that the failure of the South in sustaining its rights, its constitutional privileges and the claims of its eminent men has arisen from the simple fact that their war of defence and attack has been confined to their own section of country instead of being waged with zeal and decision in the midst of their opponents and through their own accredited organs.

"The defence of the South should have always been made in the North—and the successful usages and organizations of northern politicians should in a measure have been engrafted on Southern policy. By this mode of sustaining rights, principles and claims, the political belligerents are brought into immediate contact and defence follows closely on attack, explanation follows charges, and the South makes a successful lodgement in the very midst of the enemy. If, therefore, the friends of Mr Calhoun contemplate bringing him forward as a candidate for the next Presidency it is

---

[1] See especially *Atlas*, March 30, 1851, and *Boston Museum*, April 25, 1851.

clearly apparent that his flag should be thrown to the breeze in the North—not in the South; here his friends should be rallied and consolidated, his claims, character and services made known and acknowledged, and his party and his principles organized and sustained. The South on this question should claim a mere concurrence, the fight should be maintained in the North. But if Mr Calhoun should not desire to have his just claims preferred for that station nevertheless the South have great interests at stake which require the support of the North—her constitutional rights should be vigorously defended, and the Tariff question shaped to conform to her principles and uniform convictions, so that Southern influence would prevail to a just extent, and if Mr Calhoun should decline being a candidate his friends would be able to control the Presidential question. The approaching election in this State will in all probability eventuate in favor of the Democratic party. Silas Wright, it is true, has a strong wing of the Democracy opposed to him, but the power of the Whigs when united carrying with them the Abolitionists, Anti masons, and Anti renters is sufficiently alarming to produce union among the Democrats, and there are so many leading men whose offices would be endangered by opposition to regular nominations that Mr Wright may depend on the united vote of the party. There are many Whigs of large posessions who having confidence in Mr Wrights management of the credit and property of the State will vote for him which I think may secure his election by 10,000 majority if not more.

"The success of Mr Wright, however, should not be considered as positively bringing him forward as a candidate for the Presidency as some imagine it will. He is himself without ambition and will not permit his name to be used without a reasonable assurance of success; but it ought not to be disguised that a strong Northern confederacy is at present organizing which may include all parties against the influence and increasing power of the South, and even Democrats so uniformly friendly to the South are now found willing to add strength to the abolition faction and confederate for the final overthrow of Southern influence. Great political sacrifices will be made to accomplish this object; and free States will be invoked by every consideration of interest as well as prejudice to form what they will call a 'holy Alliance' against Southern Slavery and the political claims put forth by the South, and I shall not be surprized to see nearly all north of Mason & Dixon's line including the States of Michigan, Wiskonsin [sic] and Iowa joining the confederacy. Many considerations unite to strengthen this opinion—Fanaticism joined to political ambition, hostility to the present administration strengthened by diss-appointment and neglect may lead to a concert of action calculated to create uneasiness in the South and to the worst feelings between the two great sections of the Union. Apart from any questions on the next Presidency the South is deeply interested in having her rights sustained and her interests defended boldly and justly in the North, and by a confidential organ, which, while it posesses the good will and support of the South may command an influence in the North and check the intrigues and confederacies as well as to overthrow all combinations which may endanger the safety of the Union as well as impair the just rights of the South.

"Having during a long political career been uniformly friendly to the South and familiar with its men and measures, posessing as I hope its confidence and standing well with all the prominent men of the Democratic party in the north I think I could draw around me by discretion, reason, kind feelings, the force of argument and the power of truth and conviction a very large number of friends calculated to make a most favorable impression upon the minds and actions of our leading Democrats.

"Under this conviction I am willing to embark a reasonable Capital of my own in the establishment of a daily paper, but I cannot risk all that will be required for the object. The South must contribute its aid by raising a fund which will be necessary to sustain an establishment conducted with energy and ability. The expense of publishing a daily paper in this city cannot be less than Three hundred Dollars weekly to include every contingency; Commercial, Political and literary. I feel confident from my general success heretofore that I can manage to pay two hundred Dollars myself or in other words that I can make the establishment pay that sum which would leave but One hundred dollars to supply the deficiency. I have a printing office including every material which would be required, consequently that heavy preliminary outlay would be saved.

"If therefore it is desired to have a press devoted to Southern interests in this city and your friends in South Carolina will raise Ten thousand Dollars I will bind myself to carry on the paper until after the Presidential election— with auxiliary aid to that amount, something less than $100. weekly, and I am satisfied that no other person can accomplish it at so small a sacrifice. The amount subscribed can be placed in confidential hands in that State to be drawn for as may be required with the understanding that the paper will be extensively supported in the South, and contributions from the best pens freely afforded. Should this proposition meet the approbation of your friends and the amount required raised I can issue the paper by the meeting of Congress and the sooner the flag is unfurled the better.

"Should your friends prefer placing the press in other hands it will give me pleasure to afford all the facilities in my power in carrying out the really important objects of such an experiment.

I am Dear Sir
Very sincerely Yours

M C Mordecai Esq   M M Noah"

During this interlude of journalistic warfare, conflict on the Rio Grande, and determined alignments for and against slavery, Noah found plenty of time for his life-long interest: education.

It has come to light only recently, for example, that Noah was one of the 168 prominent New Yorkers who answered the call, issued on January 4, 1830,[1] for a meeting to discuss the foundation of a university. From this venture, in which Noah bought his allotment of shares, sprang the New York University.

"The tradition of Jewish association with N.Y.U., begun by Noah", said Joseph H. Proskauer, at the celebration of the centennial, "has been carried on ever since by Jews of the greatest Jewish city in the world."

It is a tradition, indeed, that Noah himself, in 1843 and 1844, was carrying on in New York outside of university limits. To the end of his life, for example, Noah would be sponsoring the establishment of a Hebrew College, where the children of Jews might "obtain a classical education, and at the same time be properly instructed in the Hebrew language; where they can live in conformity to our laws, and acquire a liberal knowledge of the principles of their religion."

As the father of a numerous family, Noah was experiencing trouble with the fuller education of his own brood. Small doubt that his plans for a Hebrew College were suggested not only by his natural interest in communal problems but also by his parental foresight. Indeed, there is a pathetically unconscious prophecy in his words. Speaking of the Christian colleges and boarding schools, he continues, in the prospectus that he wrote for *The Occident*,[2] "The Jewish scholars are compelled to live in daily violation of the Mosaic institutions, to neglect the Sabbath, and attend church on Sunday, in

[1] See *Jewish Daily Bulletin*, April 29, 1931, for an account of Noah's participation, and of the University in general.
[2] Vol. 1, pp. 301-307.

conformity with the regulations of the school. The consequences are that our sons, having finished their education,
return to the bosom of their families, well instructed, it is
true, but retaining only the name of Jews, unacquainted with
the principles of their religion, perfectly indifferent to its
obligations, and probably with prejudices against it, the
result of other and early impressions, and if compelled by the
urgency of business enterprises to go abroad, forgetting in a
short time that they were born of Jewish parents, and marry-
ing in other denominations and communities."[1]

Noah was willing to found the proposed Hebrew College
himself, if no other proper person would come forth to assume
the responsibility. Noah's call, alas, heartily seconded by
editor Leeser of The Occident, passed as unheeded as his
summons to the Utopia on Grand Island.

It was with the same thoughts and fears in mind that
Noah, undaunted by this lack of response, was shortly urging
upon the attention of his coreligionists, in the selfsame
columns of The Occident, support of Dr. Lilienthal's school
on Tompkins Square, New York. Here, announced Noah,
Jewish youth could be trained admirably in languages, deport-
ment, athletics and Hebrew culture. It was, in fact, a miniature college of the kind that he had previsioned. Once again
Noah's concern over his own children appears obliquely,
together with his old suspicion of parental indulgence. It is
a strange forecast, indeed, of our contemporary child psychology. ". . . In such a school the minds of parents are
easy and comfortable in relation to the destiny of their
children. The less they go home the better:—the indulgence
of home destroys the discipline of the school."

[1] Thus Zipporah was sent to a boarding school in Schenectady. See Appendix II,
"Noah's Wife And Children."

Noah appears to have been excessively—even morbidly—preoccupied with the problem of his children. His insistence upon discipline may have been, in part, a protective phase of his love for them. His letters to his wife, sent while he was away on political ventures, echo with his concern for their offspring.[1]

Sometime in 1832 he writes:. . . "When away I am always in the fidgets about my dear Manny, apprehensive that he may be strutting about the streets in this cold weather. My dear Jaky I know will stick close to Miss Stewart's attractive bosom & little Bob won't let go of yours . . . I am never so comfortable as with you & our dear children . . ."

A year or so later: ". . . Tell Judy [his unmarried sister] to go around and see the school that little Loo is going to in Rivington Street. I wish my dear Manny to lose no time, I am apprehensive constantly of some danger by accident or sickness if he runs in the street . . ."

Noah, on some of his frequent trips, would take an elder son along.[2] He was much concerned over Robert. "You cannot imagine", he wrote, sometime about 1841, "how his conduct pains me. I am worried to think what I am to do with him. Keep him in the house. Watch him closely and be careful of everything." Robert, it seems, had jumped out of the cab without saying goodbye to his father, who had thought to thrill him with a ride on the way to the station.

Almost at the same time that Noah was smarting under Greeley's rebuke he was analyzed on the basis of his hand-

[1] I quote from manuscript letters that have come to light recently. They are all in my possession.
[2] I have a letter in Manny's handwriting, sent from Philadelphia on Sunday, May 30, 1841.

writing, for the second time, by Edgar Allan Poe. The first analysis had taken place in the "Autography Papers" of the *Southern Literary Messenger*. This series had run from February to August, 1836. Poe was twenty-six at the time, with a reputation not nearly so great as Noah's. Five years later, Noah was arriving at the end of his active, many-faceted life. Poe, now better informed about his subject, amplified upon his first analysis, not scrupling to plagiarize from himself:

"Judge Noah", he wrote, "has written several plays which took very well in their time, and also several essays and other works, giving evidence of no ordinary learning and penetration on certain topics—chiefly connected with Israelitish history. He is better known, however, from the wit and universal *bonhomie* of his editorial paragraphs. His peculiar traits of character may be traced in his writing, which has about it a free, rolling, and open air. His lines are never straight, and the letters taper too much to please the eye of an artist, and have now and then a twirl, like the tail of a pig, which gives to the whole MS. an indescribably quizzical appearance, and one altogether in consonance with the general notion respecting the quondam Major, and the present Judge, than whom no man has more friends or fewer enemies."

Noah, unfortunately, does not appear in "The Literati of New York City", which Poe contributed to *Godey's Lady's Book* in the summer and autumn of 1846. The gallant Major and the not too Solomonian Judge was not, in any deep sense of the word, a *literatus*; yet, among the many nonentities of whom Poe prattled, a corner might have been found for Noah's eccentricities. The inclusion of his signature in the Poe collection (Poe had a most excellent handwriting himself, and his interest in autography may well have arisen from that fact) testifies to his personal popularity rather than to his literary attainments, and not least to his standing in the editorial offices.

Noah could not long do without a paper at his command. Somebody once said of him that, had he been able, he would have liked to edit every newspaper in New York. He had begun his career as a Figaro,—a voluble townsman, carrying the excitement of gossip and comment as a bee transmits the fructifying pollen from flower to flower. He was ending it as a Falstaff, puffing his way corpulently up and down the editorial stairs, benevolently greeting the younger writers of the day, encouraging their efforts, finding them publishers, and relaxing into reminiscence.

On the failure of *The Union* he founded, in 1843, *Noah's Weekly Messenger*; this was shortly merged with the *Sunday Times* (not to be confused with the ancestor of the *New York Times*) and he edited the merger to the day of his death.

Hudson tells of Noah's proposing, sometime in 1846, just before Bennett was to sail for Europe, that he take editorial charge of *The Herald* while Bennett was abroad. According to this tale the interview between Noah's representative and Bennett did not last very long, and Noah did not edit *The Herald*. Of course, incredible as the story sounds, it may very well have happened. Bennett was one eccentric; Noah, another. Newspaper battles, usually, are but political battles in thin disguise; expedience, rather than noble dedication to a cause, guides their course. On the other hand, Mr. Hudson's history of journalism is frequently unreliable as to fact and as to interpretation. Noah and Bennett had not been on good terms since the days of the split over Jackson and the

United States Bank; Bennett's rancor followed Noah to the grave.

In 1847, as Trowbridge, author of the once widely-read *Cudjo's Cave*, recalled out of an imperfect memory, Noah was still one of the wise men of Gotham.[1] And the kindly ones, too. A power in Tammany until the last, Noah was likewise a benign force in the changing contemporary letters. Once when Trowbridge brought to the littered, dingy office of Noah's *Times* a poem for him to read, Noah was unpoetically frank. Whoever wished to earn money in New York, he insisted, "must write prose and leave poetry alone." It was Noah who gave Trowbridge his first definite encouragement as a writer. Fifty years after, Trowbridge could picture himself as a youth following Noah through the streets of New York, to the charmed precincts of a publisher's office on Ann Street. Every third or fourth person they passed saluted the dean of newspaper row.

His life of activities, however, was fast declining into a series of gestures. To the end, Noah attempted to maintain his leadership, his association with the great ones of the soil. His Americanism was not so chauvinistic that he could not take sides, when his conscience dictated it, against a fellow country-man and in favor of a Britisher. Noah had been among the earliest to recognize the histrionic gifts of Edward Forrest,[2]—to impress them upon his friend, the theatrical manager, Gilfert,—to arrange for puffing Forrest into prominence. Yet, at the time of the disgraceful riots between the

---

[1] See *My Own Story*, by John Townsend Trowbridge, Boston, 1903, pp. 95–101. Noah, according to Trowbridge, had "if I remember rightly, been mayor of New York." The confusion between Major and Mayor, particularly as, in German, the words would be pronounced alike, led to a like error in the German press.

[2] See Montrose J. Moses, *The Fabulous Forrest*, Boston, 1929, p. 68.

274

factions of Forrest and Macready, Noah was one of the forty-eight signatories to the letter addressed to Macready on Wednesday, May 9, 1849, in which the Englishman was urged to fulfill his engagement at the Astor Place Opera House.

On October 31, 1849, we discover Noah, as a member of the board of trustees of the Hebrew Benevolent Society, addressing to Daniel Webster a letter in which the statesman is invited to speak before the Society at their anniversary dinner on the 13th of the next month. Webster, in declining, acknowledged his thanks with one of those tributes to the Jewish people that had been familiar to Noah since 1818, when Madison, Adams and Jefferson had written to the then ambitious grandson of Jonas Phillips in like vein. One need not, in viewing these expressions as a commonplace of semi-political correspondence, always on that account doubt the genuineness of the sentiments expressed. From the text of Noah's letter, incidentally, we learn that the Jewish population of New York City at this time was 13,000.[1]

There is report that some time in 1847 a ball was given to raise funds for the school proposed by Noah four years earlier. A public call issued shortly after attracted twenty-five supporters, from whom Zadoc A. Davis was chosen as President. On July 16, 1848, the Hebrew Education Society was organized with Solomon Solis as President. The school itself was not to open until April 7, 1851, a couple of weeks after its founder had been buried.

Noah, despite failing health, maintained his interests to the very last. His final appearance as a power in Tammany, according to Gustavus Myers,[2] was on April 15, 1850, "when

[1] *AJHS*, vol. XI, 186–188.
[2] Op. cit., pp. 174 ff.

he led, together with former Mayor Mickle, Charles O'Connor, and Francis B. Cutting, the ticket that had been organized as a rival alignment against Grand Sachem Elijah F. Purdy, Isaac V. Fowler, Johan A. Bogert, John J. Manning and others."

A few weeks before his death, indeed, Noah presided at a meeting called by him to inaugurate one of his pet plans: the foundation of a Hebrew Hospital. It was plain that the Major was not well. Yet Noah was contemplating a visit to Jerusalem, there to study the problem of anti-Semitic prejudice.[1] The editor of *The Asmonean*[2] inquired, at the Hospital meeting, how Noah felt; he answered that he was bothered by rheumatism, which he "hoped the genial warmth of summer would dispel."

[1] See *Occident*, vol. ix, pp. 97–103. "A Funeral Panegyric . . ." by A. Wellington Hart.

" 'Tis only a few weeks since," pointed out Mr. Hart in this panegyric, "that a commercial treaty was passed between this government and the Swiss federation. The latter government introduced a clause highly prejudicial to the interests of the Jews, but the vigilant eye of our deceased friend penetrated the stipulations of that treaty—he knew that a large and influential body of merchants were engaged in the trade with Switzerland. He at once called the attention of the executive government to the obnoxious clause which tended to embarrass the Jewish merchants having commercial transactions with their Christian brotherhood, and thus, by his influence, was the objectionable clause obliterated; it savoured of religious bias and persecution, and that alone was sufficient to enlist the Major's influence for its removal." The editor of the *Occident* annotates this section of Hart's panegyric with understandable comment. "Other Israelites likewise discovered the wrong feature in the Swiss treaty, and pointed it out to the government or Senate of the U. S.; but it is not necessary to find fault with our correspondent for his friendship to his deceased cousin."

[2] See issue of March 28, 1851. Peculiarly enough, as at the beginning of Noah's life, so here, after the end, in an obituary notice written by a friend, he is called Mordecai *Manasseh* Noah.

The *Jews' Hospital* was not founded until a year after Noah's death. Its first president was Sampson Simpson. It developed into the great institution that now bears the name it has borne since 1871: *Mount Sinai*.

Summer never came for him. On the second day of Spring, March 22, 1851, he yielded to the second of two paralytic shocks. Two days later, in the afternoon, he was buried in the 21st Street Burial Ground, whither he was followed by mourning throngs. The services were under the direction of the Rev. J. J. Lyons; the funeral oration was delivered by the Rev. Dr. Raphall.

Hours before the time set for the funeral, Broadway was thronged on both sides of the thoroughfare between Houston and Bleecker streets. The home of the Noahs was no less crowded by friends and relations. The very composition of the mourners,—the representation from so many different walks of life,—bore witness to the breadth of Noah's interests and the versatility of his gifts.

"Doctors, authors, musicians, comedians, editors, mechanics, professionals and non-professionals," reported *The Asmonean*, "all classes vieing with each other in eager desire to offer tribute of respect to the mortal remains of Major Noah prior to their departure for their final resting place. Precisely at four o'clock the body was passed to the hearse and the vast procession began to move slowly forward, the hearse accompanied by several carriages, but the mourners and the large body of societies on foot; as the procession detailed its divisions it was visible how numerous was the attendance. Among the societies represented were the Hebrew Benevolent Society of which the deceased had been president; the German H. H. Society, the H. B. Bachelors Association, the Young Men's H. B. A., the Society of Mutual Love, the Noah Lodge of B'Nai Israel, the I. O. B'Nai Berith. The officers lay and clerical, and a large body of members from each of the following Synagogues: Wooster Street, Greene Street, Henry Street, Chrystie Street, Norfolk

Street and Pearl Street. Upon arriving at the burial ground in Twenty-first street, to avoid the pressure and inconvenience from the members whom the reception hall was not a tenth part large enough to contain, it was resolved to perform the Service in the open air and even there it was with great difficulty that space was cleared round the coffin for the circuits during the chanting of the usual hymns . . ."[1]

With Mordecai Manuel Noah a period in the history of American Judaism had come to an end. Noah himself, in his erratic way, had given the impulse to a new one.

His qualities of shrewdness, of political opportunism, of journalistic guerilla-warfare, he shared with the companions of his day. They were part of the need to make a living in a world that was becoming increasingly complex and increasingly hostile.

His finer qualities are attested even by the nature of his failures, which, in almost every case, pointed to success for those who came after. It is, as has been indicated, in the sentiments of his heart rather than in the plans of his head that his importance as a pioneer is to be found. He lived for the spirit rather than for the letter, and thus opened himself time and again to misconstruction and accusation. Idealism and the claims of the practical life contended within his personality for supremacy. He yielded to them both, and the result was a very human compromise that left him outside

---

[1] *The Asmonean*, New York, March 28, 1851, pp. 180–181.

The press, both Gentile and Jewish, was filled with eulogistic comment upon the departed publicist. There is very little, however, in these accounts that has factual or interpretative value for a biographer. There is much loose reporting. This refers to details of his career, which I have tried to clear up in the sections of this book that relate to them.

the circle of heroism, yet at times well within the circle of eccentricity.

His versatility was, by a good measure, curiosity, ambition, the outflow of a tremendous energy of both body and mind. It was brought out, too, by the nature of the era. All nations, in their early history—even as the continents, in their progress toward the higher forms of civilization—produce versatile types. Until specialization sets in, the able men of a country, from the sheer needs with which that country is confronted, take up a multiplicity of tasks. Noah, feeling strongly both his Jewishness and his Americanism, became doubly versatile.

Eccentric though he may have been on occasion, he was neither a zealot nor a fanatic. The Sabbath, in his eyes, was made for man, not man for the Sabbath. His strict interpretation of fatherhood was appreciably a rhetorical one; he was a devoted husband and a fond parent. In his consideration of such central topics as slavery, workmen's problems and woman's place in society he was not in the line of what, today, looks to us like progress. He did not, in such respects as these, transcend the conventional views of his middle-class status. He was not, in the higher sense, a statesman.

When Robert Dale Owen, in 1829, founded the Mechanics' Party—a party for the workingman, demanding people's rights and an educational system "equally open to all", he was assailed even in the Jacksonian press as immoral. The political group whose leader, the President himself, had coined the phrase "fresh from the people", found the ideas of Mr. Owen too fresh from the wrong section of the people. Noah, in the *Courier and Enquirer*, called the ticket of the Mechanics' Party "infidel." In politics, an "infidel" is one who does not believe—in your party . . .

Noah was, indeed, even in possibilities, a pioneer rather than an achiever. He never fulfilled in himself those powers that, at his best, he suggested. And it is for these very contradictions that his character is so interesting. After all, he not only meant well; he did well. He was the sort that initiates with enthusiasm rather than completes with determination. By that same token he made, for his day, an admirable journalist. In all his labors, whether as diplomat, playwright, Zionist, educator, he was the planner rather than the builder.

He was not, however, the merely selfish slave to expediency. Almost everything he engaged in was definitely characterized by a spirit of dedication to his native America and to his ancestral Judaism. Both his Judaism and his Americanism were conceived as twin aspects of Liberty, related to each other by the logic of history and of humanity.

It is, on the whole, as a picturesque personality that Mordecai Manuel Noah survives from the early history of the United States. He is, with the inevitable limitations of the type, a forerunner. His ventures, now clumsy, now half-inspired—always excepting his purely political activities—point unmistakably to a nobler, if more complex, future.

THE END

APPENDIX I

Addenda to Noah's Plays

CASTS OF THE DRAMAS

THE cast of *She Would Be A Soldier*, or *The Plains of Chippewa*, was as follows:

JASPER	Robertson
LENOX	Pritchard
INDIAN CHIEF	Maywood
PENDRAGON	Simpson
JERRY	Barnes
LA ROLE	Spiller
CHRISTINE	Miss Leesugg
ADELA	Miss Johnson

Minor rôles were played by Johnson, Graham, Bancker, Oliff, Nexsen and Mrs. Wheatley.

The cast of *The Wandering Boys*, or *The Castle of Olival*, as presented on March 16, 1820, was as follows:

COUNT DE CROISSY	Mr. Maywood
ROLAND	Mr. Woodhull
HUBERT	Mr. Kilner
LUBIN	Mr. Barnes
PAUL	Mrs. Barnes
JUSTIN	Miss Johnson

BARONESS . . . . Mrs. Baldwin
LOUISE . . . . Miss Dellinger

Mrs. Barnes and Miss Johnson, Odell records, made a great hit as the abused orphan brothers.

The cast of *The Siege of Tripoli* enlisted the following:

YUSEF CARAMALLI . . . . . Mr. Maywood
HASSAN . . . . Mr. Barnes
THE COMMODORE . . . . . Mr. Kilner
HARRY MOUNTFORT . . . . Mr. Simpson
GONZALEZ . . . . Mr. Woodhull
MANNEVILLE . . . . . . Mr. Moreland
PEDRIGO . . . . Mr. Spiller
ROSABEL . . . . Miss Johnson

The cast of *Marion, or The Hero of Lake George:*

MARION, (a Captain of Volunteers
   in the American service) . . Mr. Simpson
COLONEL CONWAY, of the British
   army . . . . Maywood
BEVERLY, Son of Mrs. Fitzhenry . Woodhull
CALEB, A Rich Farmer . . . Pritchard
NICHOLAS, A Peasant . . . . Barnes
LIEUTENANT STANTON, of the
   British army . . . . . Bancker
AID-DE-CAMP . . . . . . Phillips
JAILOR . . . . Nexsen
OFFICER . . . . Wheatley
     Soldiers, Villagers, &c.
MRS. FITZHENRY . . . . . Mrs. Battersby

EMMA	Barnes
CATHERINE	Barrett
BETTY	Miss Jones

The second scene of Act II of *Marion*, records Odell, is "a Parlour. Doors open to the right and left, and in the flat." Caleb's cottage, in the third act, had "stairs, leading to the balcony, with chamber doors." The commentator goes on: "I do not know of anything more interesting or even thrilling to a modern audience than practicable stairs—unless it be a horse. Much use is made of these stairs in Noah's play; there is even a conflict on them, between Marion and Emma, who is disguised as a soldier."

A century later the German producer, Jessner, was to base an entire philosophy of production upon what came to be called *Jessnertreppe*, or Jessner-stairs. It is true that raised planes add to the thrill of theatric excitement.

The cast of *The Grecian Captive:*

TURKS

ALI PACHA	Pritchard
ACHMET	Woodhull
OSMIN	Bancker
NADIR	Nexsen
OFFICER	Wheatley

Mutes, Soldiers, Guards, etc.

GREEKS

KIMINSKI	Maywood
DEMETRIUS YPSILANTI	Simpson
ALEXANDER	Phillips
ROBERTO	Cowell

Burrows, an American officer . Ritchings
Zelia, The Grecian Captive . . Miss Johnson
Female Attendants, Africans, etc.
Scene: Athens

In the dramatis personae of *The Siege of Yorktown* figured George Washington, played by Foot; Captain Olney, acted by Woodhull; Placide played Zekiel and Miss Johnson, Kate.

Noah and Céleste

In 1840, at that time editor of *The Evening Star*, and in his fifty-fifth year, Noah would return to his old, old love, the stage, with a piece written expressly for the French danseuse, Céleste. *Natalie, or The Frontier Maid* was not seen at the Park until May 18; it had been presented to Boston, at the Tremont Theater, on Friday evening, the first of that month, as part of a program that seems in retrospect unconscionably long. Céleste was the rage; the public could not get enough of her. Not only did she act three parts in *Natalie* alone, but she did a new fancy dance, also the trial dance from *La Bayadère* and acted, in the very popular *St. Mary's Eve* (by Bernard) the part of Madeline, the Jacobite's sister. Noah's *Natalie* has been confused, and not unnaturally, with another *Natalie,*—a ballet with the sub-title *La Laitière suisse*. This Swiss milkmaid was frequently danced by Fanny Elssler . . . The main part of the Boston program, provided by Noah, suggests as printed almost a summary of the action. Clearly, Noah persisted to the end in his efforts to acclimate a native drama. The action embraced "two prominent events in the history of the American Revolution." The first act was specially advertised as giving "a view of the

Falls of Montmorenci," and a representation of the storming
of Quebec, "the act terminating with the death of General
Montgomery." Céleste in Noah's piece acted these three
rôles: Natalie, the frontier maid; Neataluk, an Indian Chief;
and Sam Rivers, a bounty boy. The New York cast differed
from the Bostonian. At the Park Theater, Céleste was supported by T. S. Cline as Ruthven, and by Mrs. Thorne as
Janette; in Boston these rôles had been played, respectively,
by Mr. and Mrs. Ayling.[1]

SAMUEL B. JUDAH AND NOAH'S PLAYS

Judah beheld New York as a scene guilt-stained, gain-
greedy, murky with power abused, inviting the retribution
of his prophetic denunciations.[2] As for the theater of the
day, it was

yon house of misery
Where folly reigns sublime, where vice doth pall
At once the sight and senses, where, free
And unguarded, lewdness her riots hold . . .
Thou licensed brothel, in thy charter bold
Vice in thy walls hath sanction . . .

An evil, then, within that greater evil, Gotham. And
Noah, who seems to have stirred Judah to his most impassioned scurrility? Noah was, at the core of this inner evil,
a greater evil still.

. . . still turn thy pains
To letters, nature unknown, and art forgot,
Without a character, a form, a plot,

[1] The cast of *Natalie* is reproduced from the playbill of the Tremont Theater,
Boston, in the Harvard Theater Collection. For *Natalie* in New York, consult
Odell, op. cit., vol. IV, p. 338.
[2] *Gotham And The Gothamites. A Medley.* New York, 1823.

New loads of words thou mayst together lay,
And swear, though damned, it is a play—
Yet I'll disturb thee not; still may you view
In grasp, the gold you eagerly pursue,
Add new crimes the old ones to complete,
For, brainless rogue, there can be no greater cheat
Than thou art already; thou mayst vainly raise,
Fat empiric, new trophies to thy praise;
Go on in folly, till thy rage is spun,
I care not for thee. Now my task is done.

Verse, however, was not enough to relieve the pent-up fury of Judah. He adds a note to his numerous comments upon these impudent iambs. Noah's stuff becomes "insipid garbage, with which he saturates the public yearly, and when rejected by the audience he prints, for the sake of an impertinent preface, which not only exposes his head, but leaves us in doubt of his heart."

APPENDIX II

Noah's Wife and Children

THE FAMILY

THE wife of Noah survived him for some fifteen years, dying in New York on June 7, 1866. Little more than two years later, on August 24, 1868, Judith Noah, the sister of Mordecai, died at the age of 79, unmarried.

With a firm, yet flexible, hand the widow of Noah guided the destinies of her family, which, in its less populous way, carried on the traditions of the noted Phillips household. Of this tradition Mordecai Manuel Noah had been a proud, self-conscious standard-bearer. His patriotic fervor he transmitted to his children.

Daniel had died in his ninth year, on February 24, 1846, as the result of an accident. Not without reason were Noah's letters filled with apprehension for the safety of his sons and his daughter.

Manuel M., his first-born, finally established himself in San Francisco; for twenty years he was the editor in chief of the *Alta Californian*. Jacob J., Robert P., and Lionel J., according to the account of Simon Wolf, published in 1897, were at that time "lawyers and counsellors of the Supreme Court of the United States, the former resident at Washington, and the two latter at New York City." Henry, according to the same authority, "resided in South Carolina, where he held the office of Collector of U. S. Internal Revenue for several years. He was a delegate to the Republican National Convention of 1872, 1876, 1880, and 1884. He served in the War of the Rebellion as an officer of the Thirty-seventh New York Volunteers."

Jacob J., too, had served during the Civil War. He had settled in Minnesota, and had joined the Second Minnesota infantry. After the war, he removed to Tennessee, where he rose to the position of Attorney-General. In Washington, as a member of the "Gridiron Club", and as a prominent journalist, Mason and politician, he was a familiar figure.

Robert P., while still a youth, saw service in the Mexican war. During the war of the Crimea he enlisted in the British forces and served throughout the campaign. From 1857 to 1862 he was, by appointment from President Buchanan, U. S. Naval Agent at Rio de Janeiro. On his return to the United States he went into the law; for a decade, indeed, he was one of the Corporation Attorneys of New York. In 1882 he declined the nomination for a seat in Congress, to which, had he accepted, he would have been elected.

Lionel J., too, studied law in New York under Mr. Henry Morrison. He, like Robert P., steadily refused to hold political office.

As for Zipporah, the only daughter of the Noahs, it is easy to reconstruct, from the correspondence of the family, her vivacious temperament. On November 12, 1856, having turned twenty-one in the previous July, she married Charles Lazarus, a native of Nottingham, England, two years her senior. The name Lazarus was later changed to Lawrence, and in the record of her death, which took place on October 11, 1890, she appears as Zipporah Noah Lawrence.

Synagogal records further report the death of Henry Noah on May 18, 1885, at the Madison Hotel.

Lionel J. Noah, on November 16, 1881, married Lillie H. Levy of Philadelphia; he died on September 23, 1897. His son, Lionel J., was born on October 28, 1884.

"I believe", wrote Robert L. Noah, under date of April 24, 1931, in a letter replying to some inquiries of mine, that "the Phillips family have continued in the original faith, but my own branch and many of the Jackson descendants are of the Christian faith . . .

"Lionel J. Noah is a son of Lionel J. Noah, son of M. M. Noah. Carrie Noah Van Antwerp is a daughter of Jacob J. Noah . . . Harry F. Noah and myself are sons of Robert P. Noah. Catherine McKesson, née Catherine Van Buren Lawrence, is a great granddaughter of M. M. Noah, granddaughter of M. M. Noah's only daughter, Zipporah Noah Lawrence. Bowman N. Baldwin of Washington, D. C., is also a great grand-daughter of M. M. Noah, grand-daughter of his son, Jacob Jackson Noah . . ."

Dr. D. De Sola Pool, Rabbi of the Spanish and Portuguese Synagogue Shearith Israel, wrote to me, on April 15, 1931:

"I have learned that, of Noah's sons, Jacob held office perhaps in the Solicitor General's office in Washington, D. C. He bore a very good name. Robert physically resembled his father very strongly. Like all the other Noah boys, he was very brainy. He was connected with the editorial staff of *Noah's Sunday Times and Messenger*.

"Lionel was also a man of high intelligence, and of good reputation.

"Zipporah, the daughter, had at least two sons,—Walter Lawrence, who was not so long ago treasurer of the now vanished Lyceum Theater in New York, and Percy Lawrence, who lived at the Ansonia Hotel."

A Batch of Letters Addressed to Miss Zipporah Noah, Only Daughter of Mordecai and Rebeccah Noah, While She Was At School in Schenectady

From all the available evidence, Zipporah Noah was a pretty lively little lady, and, like her kind, at times hard to manage. In 1847, Zipporah—the name is Hebrew for little bird, and the family called her Zip for short—was twelve years old. There were no public schools. We find her, then, according to the letters I have, at school in Schenectady, being transformed from a hoyden into an accomplished young lady, at Mrs. Barcly's, and under the tutelage of a Miss Cunningham and a Mrs. O'Brien. Evidently she has been at the school for some time.

And evidently she has been homesick. Maybe, too, she has not been so diligent in her studies as she might be. All this is quite like any other little girl of her own age. I am inclined to think, too, that Zip wanted nice dresses and ribbons from home, and—again like misses of her age—she wrote home either too often or too infrequently. Through the letters from her father and her mother we get a vivid glimpse of this interesting child.

The letters to Zipporah Noah that I have in my possession are dated, respectively, January 13, 1847; October 7, 1847; June 27, 1848; July 13, 1848; July 18, 1848. Two undated letters appear to have been written about the same time. The letter of October 7, 1847, in part, and that of June 27, 1848, were written by Zipporah's mother. All were sent from New York to Schenectady.

Let me quote from these letters. I transcribe them just as they were written, spelling, lack of punctuation, and all. First, the one sent on January 13, 1847. Mr. Noah is glad to learn that his daughter is making good progress, "but, my dear daughter, you should write home only once a week, as too frequent a correspondence will take your attention from your education . . . You should study your French closely also arithmetic & writing. Recollect that we shall not have the pleasure of seeing you at the Passover holidays unless Mrs. O'Brien certifies to your improvement. You must not my dear Zipporah ask for so many things from home . . . I shall with pleasure send you some anchovies . . . I am sorry to hear that the Small Pox is in your place. Pray be careful —go into no strange house & avoid any place where the infection is—You were inoculated about five years ago. Aunt Sophys little girl is named *Eva*—her next she will probably name after you. All your filigree work is neat. We have had no snow . . . Continue to be on good and amiable terms with the young ladies who are at school with you . . . Your fond father . . ."

Nine months later, when Zip is back in Schenectady from her visit home, her mother is trying to console her, and hoping that she is by this time reconciled. "Why have I not received a letter from you? I have had but one since you have been away . . . You must not think of coming home until the spring say for the passover holidays and then only if you are a good girl and attend to your learning but I will come to see you as frequently as I can. When is Miss Cunningham coming to New York. I will send you up something nice when she returns. I have bought you a beautiful blue and white silk dress for the spring if you are good it is plaid very pretty & I have one like it for myself . . . Have you written to Rachel she said you promised her you would write her a letter" . . . After signing "Rebecca E. Noah," mother adds as a postscript, "See that your letters are put into the post office I think there must be some neglect somewhere." Papa Noah then opened the letter to add a few lines to "My dear Sippy." It appears that after Ma had closed it, along came Miss Cunningham with a letter from Zipporah and with gifts from Zip to grandma. So, this time Zip was vindicated!

In the letter of June 27, 1848, Mamma Noah, amidst much family gossip, says, "I send you some hair Ribbons 4 sets and a pair of mitts your aprons I have made . . . I have not put the belt on because I do not know the size . . . You did not mention your Father's name in your letter you must not be so neglectful. Tell Mrs. O'Brien I feel pleased to hear that you are mending and trust you may continue in the same course. When you want shoes I shall feel obliged to Mrs. O'Brien to get them for you. Mrs. O'Brien has no harp how can you learn to play on it. Henry wrote you a letter but I did not send it he shall write another which I hope will be better done and then you shall have it Lionel sends his love says he wants to Frizzle your hair . . . We are all well Thank God and send a great deal of love to you . . . In haste, Your loving mother . . ."

From the letter of July 13, 1848: "Mother sends her love to you and by Miss Cunningham sends you three aprons a (*illegible*) belt and a pound of Candies & Aunt Sophy sends you a box of Guava Jelly—So be careful my dear daughter & dont eat too much at a time particularly as it may injure your teeth & your stomach . . . I am quite pleased and grateful to hear that you are studious and making progress with your education & agree so well with the young ladies your friends I wish you to practise writing so that you may write a neat hand . . ." The letter of five days later is but a brief note with nothing of importance to us.

As for the two undated letters: Zip actually won a medal at school, thus gladdening the hearts—somewhat doubtful hearts, at times—of her parents. "The sooner your education is completed the sooner you will return home . . . I wish you to take great pains with your writing I consider it an elegant accomplishment for a young lady & with your music practise a great deal & I hope to be able to get you a new piano when you come home . . ."

The final letter in my collection was evidently written on Christmas Eve, probably of 1848. Zip has had a cold, whereupon Papa Noah, always ready with solicitous advice on health instructs his little bird to "Take good care of yourself and keep your feet & throat warm and don't run in the snow Had you paid us a visit for the holidays you would have . . . come down and found the river closed when you went up you see what a good thing it is to be contented with our lot Mother has had the influenza but is now better—she has not been out or down stairs since Grandmothers death and has been at work with Mrs . . . in making up mourning. We are all well Henry & Liny are making arrangements to hang up their stockings to night for Christmas Manny is at Uncle Abes at Jamaica . . . It looks as if we are to have sleighing for the holidays—Wrap yourself up warm in this weather should you go out Keep close at your studies & get all the medals you can & particularly practise all your lessons to improve your hand writing . . ."

BIBLIOGRAPHY

A. By Mordecai Manuel Noah

The Fortress Of Sorrento; *a petit historical drama, in two acts;* (anon.) D. Longworth, New York: 1808.

Shakespeare Illustrated; or The Novels and Histories on Which The Plays of Shakespeare Are Founded. Collected and Translated from the Originals, by Mrs. Lenox . . . *With Critical Remarks and Biographical Sketches of the Writers.* [By M.M.N.] In Two Volumes. [Volume II did not appear]. Philadelphia, 1809.

The Wandering Boys; or The Castle of Olival. Richardson and Lord. Boston, 1821. Attributed, in printed form, to the English adapter, John Kerr. Claimed by Noah as an alteration of his Paul and Alexis or The Orphans of the Rhine, Charleston, 1812.

Correspondence And Documents Relative To The Attempt To Negotiate For The Release Of The American Captives At Algiers; *including remarks on our relations with that regency.* Washington City: 1816.

Oration, Delivered By Appointment, Before Tammany Society of Columbian Order, Hibernian provident society, Columbian society, Union society of shipwrights and caulkers, Tailors', House carpenters', and Masons' benevolent societies. *United to celebrate the 41st anniversary of American independence . . .* Printed by J. H. Sherman, 85 Nassau Street. New York, 1817.

Discourse, Delivered At The Consecration of the Synagogue of K. K. Shearith Israel . . . in the city of New York, on Friday the 10th of Nisan, 5578, corresponding with the 17th of April, 1818. C. S. Van Winkle. New York: 1818.

She Would Be A Soldier; or, The Plains of Chippewa; *an historical drama in three acts*. Longworth's dramatic repository, Shakespeare gallery; New York: 1819.

Travels in England, France, Spain, and the Barbary States, in the years 1813–1814 and 1815. Kirk and Mercein. New York: 1819.

Spain and the Barbary States, in the years 1813–1814 and 1815. Kirk and Mercein. New York: 1819.

Essays Of Howard, On Domestic Economy. Birch & Co. New York: 1820.

An Address Delivered Before The General Society of Mechanics and Tradesmen of The City of New York, at the opening of the Mechanic Institution, on November 25, 1821.

Marion; or, The Hero of Lake George: *a drama in three acts, founded on events of the revolutionary war*. E. Murden. New York: 1822.

The Grecian Captive, or The Fall of Athens. *As performed at the New York theatre*. E. M. Murden. New York: 1822.

A Statement of Facts Relating to the Conduct of Henry Eckford, esq., as connected with the National Advocate. J. W. Bell & Co. New York: 1824.

Discourse on the Evidences of the American Indians Being the Descendants of the Lost Tribes of Israel. *Delivered before the Mercantile Library Association* . . . J. Van Norden. New York: 1827.

The Book of Jasher [Sefer Ha-Yashar] *referred to in Joshua and second Samuel*. M. M. Noah & A. S. Gould; New York: 1840. [Translator's name not given. Noah helped to finance the publication].

Discourse on the Restoration of the Jews: *Delivered at the Tabernacle, Oct. 29 and Dec. 9, 1844*. Harper & Brothers, New York: 1845.

Mordecai M. Noah's Discourse on the Restoration of the Jews. *Republished in extract with an introductory note by D. S. Blondheim*; Baltimore, Md. The Lord Baltimore press (1905?)

Gleanings From a Gathered Harvest. C. Wells. New York: 1845.

Same. H. Long & Bro. New York; 1847.

A Letter Addressed to the Southern Delegates of the Baltimore Democratic Convention, on the Claims of the "Barnburners" to be Admitted to Seats in that Convention. New York: 1848.

B. Book References

ADAMS, CHARLES FRANCIS. Memoirs of John Quincy Adams. *Comprising Portions of His Diary from 1795 to 1848.* Philadelphia, 1875.

ALLEN, LEWIS F. Founding of the City of Ararat on Grand Island —by Mordecai M. Noah. Read Before the Society, March 5, 1866. [In Buffalo Historical Society. Publications. Vol. I, Buffalo, 1879]. *An Account of an Attempt Made in 1825 to Establish a City on Grand Island in the Niagara River.*

ALLEN, LEWIS F. The Story of the Tablet of the City of Ararat. [In Buffalo historical society Publications. Buffalo, N. Y.] 1921.

ALLEN, LEWIS F. Early History of Grand Island. The city of Ararat—its corner stone. Mordecai M. Noah. Read before the Buffalo historical society club. Mar. 5, 1866. [*In* Thomas' Buffalo city directory for 1867. Buffalo, 1867. p. 25–37].

ALLIBONE, S. AUSTIN. A Critical Dictionary of English Literature and British and American Authors . . . v. 2. J. B. Lippincott Co. Philadelphia: 1891.

ANTHONY, IRWIN. Decatur. Charles Scribner's Sons. New York. London: 1931. Pp. 252–254.

BARTLETT, ALICE M. EVANS and G. HUNTER. See Evans, Charles W.

BEARD, CHARLES A. and MARY. The Rise of American Civilization. New York, 1930.

BEARDSLEY, LEVI. Reminiscences, New York, 1852. Pp. 156–157.

BENTON, THOMAS HART. Thirty Years In the United States Senate.

BINGNAM, ROBERT W. The Cradle of the Queen City. Buffalo: 1931.

BLUMENTHAL, WALTER HART. In Old America. Random Chapters on The Early Aborigines. *With A Foreword by George Alexander Kohut.* New York, 1931.

BOWERS, CLAUDE G. The Party Battles of the Jackson Period. Boston, 1932.

BROWN, T. ALLSTON. History of the American Stage . . . Biographical Sketches . . . 1733 to 1870; Dick & Fitzgerald. New York. c. 1870.

BROWN, T. ALLSTON. History of the New York Stage, from the First Performance in 1732 to 1901. 4 vols. Dodd, Mead & Co. New York. 1903.

CALHOUN, JOHN C. Letters. American Historical Association. July 14, 1820 [Noah, agent of the Corporation of New York in Relation to Castle Clinton—a fort at the Battery, afterwards Castle Garden].

CLARKE, L. H. Report of the Trial of An Action on the Case, Brought by Sylvanus Miller, esq., Late Surrogate of the City and County of New York, against Mordecai M. Noah, esq., editor of the *National Advocate*, for the Alleged Libel. *Tried at the City-hall, in the city of New York, before the Circuit court held on the first judicial district in the state of New York, by His Honour Samuel R. Betts, on . . . the 12th day of December, 1823.* Printed by J. W. Palmer & Co. New York: 1823.

COAD, ORAL SUMNER. William Dunlap. New York. 1917.

CONGDON, CHARLES T. Reminiscences of a Journalist. James R. Osgood & Co. Boston: 1880.

COWELL, JOE. Thirty Years Passed Among the Players. Harper & Bros. New York: 1844.

DUNLAP, WILLIAM. History of the American Theatre. R. Bentley. London; 1833.

CRAWFORD, MARY CAROLINE. The Romance of the American Theatre.

DURANG, CHARLES. History of the Philadelphia Stage. 1749–1855. *Published serially in the Philadelphia Dispatch.*

EATON, WALTER P. The Actor's Heritage. *Scenes from the Theatre of Yesterday and the Day Before.* Little, Brown & Co. Boston: 1924.

EISENSTEIN, J. D. Ozar Zikronotai (Hebrew) 1929. Pp. 242–246. *Reprint of an article from Bikkure Ha 'Ittim (1827) on the reception of the Ararat idea in Europe.*

ELZAS, BARNETT A. The Jews of South Carolina 1762–1903. Charleston, 1903.

ELZAS. The Old Jewish Cemeteries at Charleston, South Carolina. New York, 1916.

EVANS, CHARLES W. History of St. Paul's Church, Buffalo, N. Y., 1817–1903. Continued from 1889 to 1903 by Alice M. Evans Bartlett and G. Hunter Bartlett.

FITZ-GREENE HALLECK. The Political Works of . . . New York, 1852.

FITZPATRICK. Annual Report of American Historical Association, 1918. "Autobiography of Martin Van Buren".

FORREST, EDWIN. Diary of. *38 double pages of manuscript.* Shaw Drama Collection. Harvard University Widener Library.

FORREST, THE HISTORY OF EDWIN. The Celebrated American Tragedian. Written by an Individual Who Has Known Him From Boyhood. New York: 1837.

FOX, LOUIS H. New York City Newspapers, 1820–1850; *a bibliography.* Chicago, University of Chicago press (1928) 131 p. [Bibliographical society of America. Papers, 1927, v. 21, pts. 1 and 2].

GELBER, DR. M. M. Zur Vorgeschichte des Zionismus. Vienna, 1927. Pp. 62–84. (German).

GODBEY, ALLEN H., Ph.D. The Lost Tribes Theory. Suggestions Toward Rewriting Hebrew History. Durham (North Carolina), 1930.

GOLDSTEIN, ISRAEL. A Century of Judaism in New York. New York, 1930.

GOTTHEIL, RICHARD J. H. Zionism. Philadelphia, 1914. Pp. 38–39.

GUTMANN, HARRY KROLL. Mordecai Manuel Noah, The American Jew. [Prize Essay, Cincinnati: 1931. In manuscript. Consulted through courtesy of the author].

HAMLIN, C. H. The War Myth in United States History. New York, 1927.

HAMMOND, JABEZ D., LL.D. The History of the Political Parties in the State of New York. 4th edition 1846. [pp. 129–130; 235; 333; 334.]

HANSON, WILLIS T., JR. Early life of John Howard Payne. Boston, 1913.

HARRISON, GABRIEL. John Howard Payne. J. B. Lippincott & Co. Philadelphia, 1885.

HARRISON, GABRIEL. Edwin Forrest, the Actor and the Man. Critical and Reminiscent. Brooklyn, 1889.

HASWELL, CHARLES H. Reminiscences of an Octogenarian of the City of New York (1816–1860). Harper & Brothers. New York, 1896.

HEINE, HEINRICH. Letter dated April 23, 1826, to Moses Moser, poking fun at Noah. (See GELBER, op. cit., pp. 288–289.)

HENDRICK, BURTON J. The Jews in America, New York, 1923.

HONE, PHILIP. The Diary of Philip Hone, 1828–1851. Ed., with an introduction, by Allan Nevins. Dodd, Mead & Co. New York, 1927.

HOWELLS, WILLIAM DEAN. Their Wedding Journey. A Novel.

HUDSON, FREDERIC. Journalism in the United States, from 1690 to 1872. Harper & Brothers. New York, 1873.

HUNT, GAILLARD. Editor, The Writings of James Madison. Vol. VIII, 1908.

HUNT, WILLIAM. The American Biographical Sketch book. Nafis & Cornish. New York, 1848.

HORNBLOW, ARTHUR. A History of the Theatre in America: From Its Beginnings to the Present Time. 2 vols. J. B. Lippincott & Co. Philadelphia, 1919.

JUDAH, SAMUEL B. Gotham and the Gothamites. A Medley. New York, 1823.

IRELAND, JOSEPH N. Records of the New York Stage, from 1750 to 1860. 2 vols. T. H. Morrell. New York, 1866.

KALLEN, HORACE M. Zionism And World Politics. New York, 1921. Pp. 41–42.

KERR, JOHN. The Wandering boys: or, The Castle of Olival. Richardson and Lord. Boston, 1821. [See also under Noah's writings, section A of this Bibliography.]

KOHUT, GEORGE ALEXANDER. See BLUMENTHAL, Walter Hart.

LAMB, MRS. MARTHA J. History of the City of New York . . . v. 2. A. S. Barnes & Co. New York, 1880.

LAWSON, JOHN D. Editor, American State Trials, pp. 671–698.

LEBENSON, ANITA LIBMAN. Jewish Pioneers in America 1492–1848. New York, 1931.

LEE, JAMES M. History of American Journalism. New ed., rev. Houghton Mifflin Co. Boston, 1923.

LEGGETT, WILLIAM. Political Writings. Edited by Theodore Sedgwick. 1840.

LEWIS, ALFRED H. Peggy O'Neal, a novel. Philadelphia, 1903.

LOGAN, OLIVE. Before the Footlights and Behind the Scenes. Parmelee & Co. Philadelphia, 1870.

LOSSING, BENSON J. History of New York City . . . George E. Perine. New York, 1884.

LYNCH, DENIS T. An Epoch and a Man; Martin Van Buren And His Times. Horace Liveright. New York, 1929.

MACKENZIE, WILLIAM L. The Lives and Opinions of Benj. Franklin Butler . . . and Jesse Hoyt . . . with anecdotes or biographical sketches of (a number of men) Cook & co. Boston, 1845.

MACKENZIE, WILLIAM. The Life And Times of Martin Van Buren. Boston, 1846.

MACLAY. Naval History. Vol. 2.

MAKOVER, ABRAHAM B. Mordecai M. Noah. His life and Work From the Jewish Viewpoint. Bloch Pub. Co. New York, 1917.

MARGOLIS, MAX L., and MARX, ALEXANDER. History of The Jewish People. Philadelphia, 1927.

MARTINEAU, HARRIET. Society in America. 3 vols. New York, 1837.

MILLER, HUNTER. American Treaties With Foreign Governments. Vol. II. 1931.

MORAIS, HENRY SAMUEL. The Jews of Philadelphia. The Levytype Company. 1894.

MORAIS, HENRY SAMUEL. Eminent Israelites of the Nineteenth Century; a series of biographical sketches. Edward Stern & Co. Philadelphia, 1880.

MOSES, MONTROSE J. The Fabulous Forrest. Boston, 1929.

MOSES, MONTROSE J. Representative Plays by American Dramatists. (For Noah's *She Would Be A Soldier*, or *The Plains of Chippewa*). New York, 1918.

MOWATT, ANNA CORA. Autobiography of an Actress; or, Eighty Years on the Stage. Ticknor, Reed and Fields. Boston, 1854.

MURDOCH, JAMES E. The Stage; or, Recollections of Actors and Acting. Stoddart. Philadelphia, 1880.

MYERS, GUSTAVUS. History of Tammany Hall. New York, 1901.

MUSSER, PAUL H. James Nelson Barker. (With A Reprint of *Tears and Smiles*). Phila., 1929.

NEVINS, ALLAN. The [New York] Evening Post. A Century of Journalism. New York, 1922.

NORTHALL, WILLIAM KNIGHT. Before and Behind the Curtain; or, Fifteen Years' Observations among the Theatres of New York. New York, 1851.

OBERHOLTZER, ELLIS P. The Literary History of Philadelphia. George W. Jacobs & Co. Philadelphia, 1906.

OBERHOLTZER, ELLIS P. Philadelphia, A History of the City and Its People . . . S. J. Clarke pub. co. Philadelphia, 1912. 4v.

O'BRIEN, FRANK M. The Story of The Sun. New York, 1918.

ODELL, GEORGE C. D. Annals of the New York stage. Columbia University Press, New York, 1927–1928.

PARTON, JAMES. The Life of Horace Greeley. Boston, 1889.

PHELPS, H. P. Players of a Century: A Record of the Albany Stage. Albany, 1880.

PHILIPSON, DAVID. Editor, Letters of Rebecca Gratz. Philadelphia, 1929.

POE, EDGAR ALLAN. "Autography". *To be found in any complete edition of his writings.*

POLLOCK, QUEENA. Peggy Eaton. New York, 1932.

POWER, TYRONE. Impressions of America. 1833, 1834, 1835. 2 vols. Bentley. London, 1836.

PRAY. (At first anonymous author of) Memoirs of James Gordon Bennett And His Times. By a Journalist. New York, 1855.

QUINN, ARTHUR HOBSON. A History of the American Drama. From the Beginning to the Civil War. New York, 1923. Pp. 193–194.

RAISIN, REV. MAX. Mordecai Manuel Noah, Zionist, Author and Statesman. Warsaw, 1905. (In Hebrew)

REES, JAMES. The Dramatic Authors of America. Philadelphia, 1845.

REES, JAMES. The Life of Edwin Forrest. With Reminiscences and Personal Recollections. T. B. Peterson & Bros. Philadelphia, c. 1874.

ROSENBACH, HYMAN POLLACK. The Jews in Philadelphia Prior to 1800.

ROYALL, MRS. ANNE. The Black Book; or A Continuation of Travels, in the United States. Three volumes. Washington: Vols. 1 and 2, 1829; Vol. 3, 1829.

ROYALL, MRS. ANNE. Southern Tour, or Second Series of The Black Book. Three volumes. Washington, 1830.

SABIN, JOSEPH. Catalogue of the Library of Edwin Forrest Collins. Philadelphia, 1863.

SACKLER, HARRY. Major Noah. A Play [In Yiddish. Produced by Maurice Schwartz. New York, 1927.] Pub. in 1928, New York.

SCHARF, JOHN T. and THOMPSON WESTCOTT. History of Philadelphia, 1609–1884. v. 2. L. H. Everts. Philadelphia, 1884.

SOKOLSKY, GEORGE. We Jews, New York, 1934. Pp. 254–260.

STOKES, PHELPS. Iconography of Manhattan Island.

THOMAS, E. S. Reminiscences of the Last Sixty-Five Years. Hartford, 1840.

TROWBRIDGE, J. T. My Own Story. Boston, 1903.

WEMYSS, FRANCIS COURTNEY. Chronology of the American Stage from 1752 to 1852. William Taylor & Co. New York, c. 1852.

WEMYSS, FRANCIS COURTNEY. Theatrical Biography; or, The Life of an Actor and Manager. R. Griffin & Co. Glasgow, 1848.

WERNER, M. R. Tammany Hall. Doubleday, Doran & Co. New York, 1928.

WIKOFF, HENRY. The Reminiscences of an Idler. Fords, Howard, & Hurlbert. New York, c. 1850.

WILSON, JAMES GRANT. History of The City of New York. 4 volumes.

WOLF, SIMON. Mordecai Manuel Noah, a biographical sketch. Philadelphia, 1897.

WOLF, SIMON. Selected Addresses and Papers. Cincinnati, 1926. [This contains the biographical sketch of Noah and the essay on the American Jew as patriot, as well as other papers.]

WOLF, SIMON. The American Jew as Patriot, Soldier and Citizen. New York, 1895.

WOOD, WILLIAM B. Personal Recollections of the Stage . . .
During a Period of Forty Years. Henry Carey Baird. Phila-
delphia, 1855.
ZANGWILL, ISRAEL. They That Walk in Darkness. (See tale,
"Noah's Ark"). New York, 1899.

C. PERIODICALS, ENCYCLOPEDIAS, ETC.

A. J. H. S. [The Publications of the American Jewish Historical
Society]. *The General and Special Indexes of this highly
valuable collection should be consulted for specific data.*

Vol. I, pp. 13–24. *Morais, Rev. Sabato.* "Mikve Israel Congregation of Philadelphia".

Vol. II. pp. 45–61. *Phillips, N. Taylor.* For history of David
Mendez Machado.

Vol. II. pp. 107–110. *Friedenwald.* On the letter addressed
by Jonas Phillips to the Federal Convention of 1787.

Vol. II. Pp. 131–137. *Cone, G. Herbert.* "New Matter Relating to Mordecai M. Noah."

Vol. III. Pp. 82–83. On the commercial activities of Jonas
Phillips.

Vol. VI. Pp. 50–54. On the commercial activities of Jonas
Phillips.

Vol. VI. Pp. 123–140. *Phillips, N. Taylor.* "The Congregation Shearith Israel."

Vol. VI. Pp. 115–121. *Kohut, George Alexander.* "A Literary
Autobiography of Mordecai Manuel Noah." (On the letter
addressed by Noah to William Dunlap, for Dunlap's history
of the American theater. See, under *Book References*, Dunlap.)

Vol. VIII. Pp. 84–118. *Kohler, Max J.* "Some Early Zionist
Projects."

Vol. IX. Pp. 186–188. On Daniel Webster and the Jews.

Vol. X. Pp. 65–95. *Hühner, Leon.* "The Jews of Georgia
Colonial Times".

Vol. X. Pp. 119–128. *Jacobs, Joseph.* "The Damascus Affair of 1840 and the Jews of America."

Vol. XIX. *Oppenheim, Samuel.* "The Jews and Masonry in the United States Before 1810."

Vol. XX. Pp. 11–30. *Kohler, Max J.* "Unpublished Correspondence Between Thomas Jefferson and Some American Jews."

Vol. XX. Pp. 147–149. For text of letter from Eduard Gans to Noah (January 1, 1822) inquiring about the colonization of Jews in America.

Vol. XXI. *The Lyons Collection.* The Index of this volume should be specially consulted. See also Vol. XXVII.

Vol. XXI. Pp. 172–174. For data on Naphtali Phillips.

Vol. XXII. Pp. 71–100. *Friedenberg, Albert M.* "The Correspondence of the Jews with President Martin Van Buren."

Vol. XXVI. Pp. 173–200. *Hühner, Leon.* "Jews in the War of 1812."

Vol. XXVII. Pp. 55–57. Record of Noah's attendance at the School of K. K. Shearith Israel.

Vol. XXX. *Rosenbach, A. S. W.* "An American Jewish Bibliography."

Allgemeine Zeitung des Judenthums. 1898. Pp. 101–103. "Ein Judenstaat-Gründer", by *Dr. M. Kayserling.*

American Historical Review. *Levermore, Charles R.* "The Rise of Metropolitan Journalism. 1800–1840." [Issue of April, 1901. Vol. VI].

American Jewish Year Book, 1902. *Wolf, Simon.* "A Sketch of the History of The Jews in the United States".

American Literature. Vol. I, May, 1929. *Spiller, Robert E.* "Fenimore Cooper, Critic of His Times".

Appletons' Cyclopaedia of American biography . . . V. 4. Noah, Mordecai Manuel. The Press association Compilers, inc. New York, 1915.

Argus, Albany. Issue of February 1, 1823. Letter of Noah that led Silvanus Miller to believe himself libeled.

Asmonean, The. Issue of March 28, 1851. Article by editor on "Mordecai Manasseh Noah".

Atlas, The. Issue of March 30, 1851. Obituary of M. M. Noah.

Bikkure Ha 'Ittim. *Ben Jonah, Judah.* A sarcastic summary of Noah's proclamation. Pp. 45–49. (Hebrew)

Boston Museum, The. Issue of April 25, 1851. Obituary of M. M. Noah.

Buffalo Historical Society. Vol. I. *Folk, Rev. S.* "A History of the Israelites in Buffalo". 1879. Vol. XXV. "The Book of the Museum", 1921.

Charleston Times. Issues of April 16, 1812; May 9, 1812; June 2, 1812; June 4, 1812; June 13, 1812; June 23, 1812. [See p. 57 of text]. Comprising the "Muly Malak" letters of Noah.

Columbian, The. Issue of November 18, 1817. p. 2. "Intercepted Letter".

Commercial Advertiser, New York. Issue of May 20, 1823. Report of a trial in which Noah figured as lawyer for the plaintiff.

Cyclopaedia of American Biography. New York, 1888.

Cyclopaedia of American Literature. Duyckinck, Evert A., and George L. Charles Scribner, New York, 1856.

Dictionary of American Biography. New York, 1934. Vol. XIII. pp. 534–535. Noah, Mordecai Manuel. By H. W. S.

Encyclopedia Americana. American corporation. Noah, Mordecai Manuel. New York, 1927.

Evening Post, New York. Issue of January 29, 1824. Noah, on a plan to bore the earth for pure water. Issue of January 17, 1821: for Noah's controversy with Miller. Issue of May 16, 1830: for Noah's controversy with Coleman.

First Session of the Twenty-Second Congress, The. Vol. IV, reports 460–463. Washington, 1831.

Gazette, New Hampshire. Issue of January 16, 1821. On Noah's idea of the town of Newport, R. I., as a spot for a Jewish colony.

Hashiloah. Vol. XIII, 1904. nos. 3 to 6 inclusive. Raisin's work [see RAISIN, MAX] on Noah was originally published in these pages.

International Monthly Magazine of Literature, Science and Art, May, 1841. Obituary of Mordecai M. Noah.

Jewish Daily Bulletin. Issue of April 29, 1931. "Recall Role of Jews in N. Y. U. History As University Marks Its Hundredth Anniversary".

Jewish Encyclopaedia. Vol. II: "Ararat."

Jewish Encyclopedia. New York, 1916. *Kohler, Max J:* Article on "Ararat". Vol. I. *Raisin, Max:* Article on "Mordecai Manuel Noah." Vol. IX.

Lamb's Geographical Dictionary of the United States, v. 6. Noah, Mordecai Manuel. Federal Book Co. Boston, 1903.

Lippincott's Magazine. Vol. 1; 1868. pp. 665–670. *Lockwood, Samuel.* "Major M. M. Noah".

Lyons, Jacques J. The Lyons Collection . . . Publications of the American Jewish historical Society, Vols. XXI and XXVII. [See under A.J.H.S.]

Maccabean, The. "The First American Zionist", by *Abraham Lipsky*, Ph.D. (On Noah as forerunner).

Menoral Journal, The. Vol. XIII, pp. 51–62. "Major Noah," by *Herbert Solow.*

Menorah Journal, The. Vol. XXIV, pp. 276–293. "Mr. Noah, American," by *Isaac Goldberg.* [With six letters of Noah].

National Cyclopaedia of American Biography . . . v. 9. Noah, Mordecai Manuel. James T. White & Co. New York, 1907.

New York Herald. Issue of August 11, 1895. M. M. Noah's tomb photographed and described.

New York Historical Society. Letter from Noah to Governor Seward, dated February 22, 1841. [In manuscript.]

Nile's Register. Issue of January 21, 1825, pp. 350–351. For copy of letter to Noah from Grand Rabbi of Cologna, and for reply from Noah.

Occident, The. *Edited by Dr. Isaac Leeser.* (The files of this magazine, especially during the years 1843, 1844 and 1845, are interesting for side-lights upon Noah's activities in the communal life of the New York Jews. They are valuable, indeed, for the general background of the period.)

    Vol. I. Pp. 301–307. On Noah's project for a Hebrew College.

    Vol. II. Pp. 249–251.

Vol. II. Pp. 347–349. Letter from Noah on the use of Lard Oil.
Vol. VII. Pp. 563–564. Controversy over Noah's contention
   that in Tunis he had been "representing a Christian nation."
   Discussion between Editor Leeser and Noah on Joel Barlow.
Vol. IX. Pp. 97–103. *Hart. A. Wellington*, "A Funeral Pane-
   gyric" to M. M. Noah.
[Year 1845] Pp. 29–35; pp. 600–606.
Recorder, City Hall (New York) 13;3. 27.
Reformer And Jewish Times, The. Issue of November 15, 1878.
   Noah, Robert P. Article on M. M. Noah.
The Times And Messenger. Issue of April 6, 1851.
Twentieth Century Biographical Dictionary of Notable Americans
   . . . V. 8. Noah, Mordecai Manuel. The Biographical Society.
   Boston, 1904.
Union, New York. Issue of July 20, 1 42. Article by Noah, "My
   First Duel".
Welt, Die. January 31, 1902. For resumé (in German) of European
   journalistic comment upon Noah's Ararat plan. By *Dr. Hein-
   rich Loewe.*
Young Israel. February 1933, p. 5. *Goldberg, Isaac.* "Miss
   Zipporah Noah at School In Schenectady".

In addition to these selected references to periodicals, the current
issues of contemporary organs, such as the *National Advocate, The
Courier and Enquirer, The Sun, The Evening Star,* and so on,
should be consulted. I may add that unless the reader has in
mind the checking up of a specific item there will be very little use
in such consultation.—I. G.

INDEX

INDEX

INDEX

INDEX

Marion, **15**
Marshall, 28
Marsollier, 69
Marx, A., 247
Mathews, 165, **167**
Maxwell, 152
McIntyre, 205
McKegan, 12
McKesson, Catherine, 289
Mendola, 202, 208
Meyers, 158–9, 218, 227, 275
Mickle, 276
Miller, H., 118
Miller, Silvanus, 155, 163, 179
Minis, **5**
Mohammed, 104
de Molina, Tirso, 89
Monroe, 45, 80, 91, 112, 113, 119, 122–126, 136–139, 142, 148
Montefiore, 247
Monte Sano, 6
Montgomery, 139
Moore, 9
Mordecai, 264, 268
Morris, G. P., 236
Morris, R., 14, 20
Morris, Governor, **71**
Morss, 233
Morton, 152
Moser, 211
Moses, J., 7, 10
Moses, M., 167, 274
Mowatt, 218
Munk, 247
Murden, 183
Mustapha, 122
Myers, 10

Napoleon, 47, 57, 73
Nathan, 12
Nelson, 144

Nevins, 238
Nissen, 102, 120–1
Noah, Daniel Jackson, **287**
Noah, Harry F., 289
Noah, Henry, 288
Noah, Jacob Jackson, 263, 287–9
Noah, Judith, 16, 154, 271, 287.
Noah, Lionel J., 264, 287–9
Noah, Lionel J. [son of above], 289
Noah, Manuel Mordecai [father of Mordecai Manuel Noah], **14**, 129, 154
Noah, Mordecai Manuel, ancestry, 1–8; in Philadelphia, 9–22; amateur theatricals, 22–34; as playwright, 34–36; 67–70; 164–188; 246; see also Appendix, "Addenda to Noah's Plays;" on Shakespeare, 36–41; in Charleston, 42–73; "Muly Malak" letters, 50–57; as Consul to Tunis, 74 ff.; in London, 85–88; in Spain, 88–95; in France, 95–96; in Tunis, 98–125; journalism, 131–146; 216–219; 224–227; 231–238; 242–245; 265–268; 272–276; Zionism, 146–152; 189–215; 238–242; 254–263, 247–248; politics, 155–164 (shrievalty of New York); domestic life, 219–224; 228–230; (see also Appendix, "Noah's Wife and Children"); as Judge, 248–250; on slavery, 251–254; on education, 269–271; death, 276–280.
Noah, Manuel Mordecai [son of above], 263, 271, 287
Noah, Rachel, 156
Noah, Rebecca Esther, 222, 224, 228, 291
Noah, Robert L., 289
Noah, Robert P., (Abraham), 250, 263, 271, 287–9

INDEX

INDEX

315

INDEX

★

Text set in Caslon Old Style Type by the Press of the Jewish
Publication Society. This book has been printed
on Monoplane Antique, and bound by
the Haddon Craftsmen,
Incorporated.

★

was a notice of Noah's recall because, wrote the Secretary of State: "At the time of your appointment, as Consul at Tunis, it was not known that the Religion which you profess would form any obstacle to the exercise of your consular functions. Recent information, however, on which entire reliance may be placed, proves that it would produce a very unfavourable effect. In consequence of which, the President has deemed it expedient to revoke your commission." This was a mortal wound for Noah, who was absolutely surprised that religion should enter into the question. It seems likely, however, that he went beyond his instructions although he was finally exonerated with reservations, and he published a defense of his activities as consul.

On his return to America he plunged right into New York City politics and his uncle gave him a position as editor of "The National Advocate," official organ of Tammany Hall. He not only became Tammany's spokeman but also was one of the earliest advocates of Pan-Americanism. By 1820 he had become one of the two virtual leaders of Tammany, the strongest political group in New York. In a few years, however, he was forced out of his editorship because of political intrigue in which he probably played a part. He immediately organized his own newspaper and again tried his hand at play writing. "As a leading editor, a prominent politician, a paunchy orator, a figure much in the public eye and ear, with a number of books to his credit, not to speak of a couple of plays, Noah was bound to take a leading role in the theatrical life of the day."

One play after another now appeared and most of them were well received. "Noah compares not at all ill with the playwrights of his day," suggests Goldberg. "That, to be sure, is a negative compliment. Dramatic taste was still at a low ebb, and even when fine words were used they referred to mediocre performance. Crudity was the rule in dramaturgic conception and in production, nor is it unlikely that if we were to witness the acting of his time we should be less pleased than were our ancestors with the strutting, declamatory methods of the oil and gaslight epoch. . . . Noah is an ancestor of all such as, in our theatre, wave stoutly the American flag."

While his pen was busy Noah, nevertheless, found time to work for a haven for the persecuted Jews of Europe. He might properly be called the first real Zionist. Certainly he deserves a place as a worthy pioneer in the history of Jewish self-determination. He tried, unsuccessfully, to found a Jewish Utopia on Grand Island in the Niagara River. From this failure of Noah's promised land, he turned to the political world again and uncovered scandals in New York. After the election of Jackson to the Presidency he was rewarded with the surveyorship of the Port of New York but in a few years he broke with the Jacksonian Democrats. In 1841 he turned to the Whigs and for a short time served on the New York bench. Meanwhile the political turnabouts on the editorial page of his newspaper caused considerable comment and many persons wondered if Noah accepted bribes for his shifts.

In the last decade of his life Noah became a proponent of ritualistic reform in the synagogue, and of Jewish educational institutions.

AMERICAN JEWISH PIONEER

The Story of Major Noah as Told by Isaac Goldberg
Issued by the Jewish Publication Society

Reviewed by NATHAN G. GOODMAN, Ph.D.

[Written for the Philadelphia Jewish Exponent and reprinted from the Issue of April 2, 1937]

NOT many Jews came to colonial America in quest of economic and religious freedom. Of the few who were settled here in the early years of the Republic, several took an active and creditable part in public affairs. Mordecai Manuel Noah, who was born in Philadelphia in 1785, was an engaging and dynamic if not always a lovable and attractive figure in the political, theatrical, journalistic, and religious life of the nation for almost a half century before his death in 1851. His restlessness and his ceaseless lust for power have at times been mistaken for brilliance. Nevertheless, the story of his ups and downs as told by Isaac Goldberg establishes the man as a journalist and dramatist of the first rank in his day. His experiences as a diplomat, orator, philanthropist, and

Major Noah: American-Jewish Pioneer. By Isaac Goldberg. Illustrated. 316 pp. Philadelphia: The Jewish Publication Society of America. $2.75.

the proponent of Utopian projects, furnish excellent opportunities for interesting as well as exciting biographical diversions. For here was a man who never fell into a rut because he was constantly in search of new goals after which to reach. He jumped from one job to another and from one set of friends to another. There are phases of his life which still remain curious and unexplained, and it is this mystery which gives the story of a checkered career a special flavor, inviting and appealing.

Noah's father was a merchant from Germany, and his mother was the daughter of Jonas Phillips, local merchant. Noah tried to trace his ancestry back to the Nunez family of Portuguese Inquisition fame. Unfortunately, his mother died when the boy was six years of age and at the same time his father disappeared. The boy now went to live with his maternal grandfather, who was the source of that patriotism for Israel and for America which was to be the dual motif of Noah's career. It appears that